Leadership for Season Change

Public Christians
in
A Secular Age

NEIL JOHNSON

Published in Australia 2022.

Author: Neil Johnson

Email: njohnson@vision.org.au

Podcast content: www.vision.org.au/20twenty-podcasts

ISBN   978-0-6452646-0-9 (Paperback)
        978-0-6452646-1-6 (Hardcover)
        978-0-6452646-2-3 (E-book)

Cover Design and Layout by Steven Worby | www.wotnotmedia.com

Cover Photograph by Ehrman Photographic | www.shutterstock.com

Printed in Australia.

Dedication

I dedicate these thoughts to my wife Charmaine, and to our family, including Allison and her husband Brent. To Sheridan and her husband Zech. To our daughter Holly and her husband Johnny. And to our youngest daughter Charity. May grace, peace and courage be yours as you 'find your voice' in a fruitful place of service in the Kingdom of God.

Endorsements

'...this book explains the traditional meaning of the word 'secular' and how this has now "morphed from a benign framework for managing plurality, to its own formation of religious alternative". In this context, this book contains the sobering warning that the broader Church is 'at risk' of succumbing to the deleterious influences of a "disempowering secularisation'.

Prof Augusto Zimmermann – Legal Philosopher

'There are plenty of books discussing the emergence of the secular age and how so many are succumbing to it. But few are discussing how we can resist such a threat, especially Christian organisations, businesses and ministries. In this helpful book Neil Johnson incisively and carefully informs us how this can be done. A unique and significant volume.'

Bill Muehlenberg – Culture Watch

God has blessed his church with thinkers and doers. Neil Johnson is both. With a deep appreciation for Australia's Christian heritage, an acute awareness of the rising tide of doubt and disbelief, and a lifetime of acclaimed experience in Christian media, Neil offers priceless insights for everyone seeking to be public Christians in this secular age.

Kurt Mahlburg – The Canberra Declaration

'This does represent a very significant shift from the focus of Kingdom Business teaching. It is looking at every area of your business from a more wholistic kingdom approach and could well become the seminal work that we are needing in this area.'

Wes Leake – Business Blessings

'People who are interested in thinking seriously and deeply about the critical importance and profound influence of Christian media will find it is well worth it.'

Elizabeth Kendal – Religious Liberty Analyst

I'm the fill-in guy when Neil needs a break. And what big shoes they are to fill! This book contains a very important message for our times. I believe God has raised up Neil to be a voice in our nation in these crucial times, and this book will be used to inspire many with it's message!

Ps. Matt Prater – History Makers

About the Author

Neil Johnson's media career spans four decades in broadcast/journalism running parallel to his vocation as a Christian minister of the Gospel.

He's been the host of the long running morning talk-radio program 20Twenty on Vision Christian Radio since 2010. Vision is heard in more than 770 cities and towns around Australia. Listeners are introduced to deeper Christian discussion about life, culture, science, ethics and politics in an interview format rarely heard on Australian radio.

His earlier media career spanning four decades began in commercial radio, but as Christian ministry aspirations deepened, he began exploring ministry and media leadership roles in Christian Radio, serving as Program Director (96.5 Family), and later General Manager (Rhema/Life FM/Juice 107.3 FM Gold Coast). These operations became the seedbed for deeper thinking about leadership dimensions for 21st century Christians.

He is passionate about Christian media, Christian education, and the importance in both city and country expressions of the 'local church'.

He's travelled internationally to report on the deep issues facing the 'persecuted church' in the Middle East (2014) at the height of the Syrian Isis/civil war refugee crisis, and the aftermath of revolutions in Egypt.[1] Neil also conducted intensive broadcast training for Christian and mainstream broadcasters in Papua New Guinea (2015).

He holds a M.Min (Leadership) degree from Christian Heritage College (Australia) and has an affinity for exploring deeper Christian realities in contrast to those that are rampant in our 'Secular Age'.

---

1 A field trip as a guest of Open Doors.

Acknowledgements

Special thanks to my long-time friend, and academic mentor Dr Sam Hey (Christian Heritage College – Citipointe College of Ministries) the author of 'Megachurches', for his unwavering encouragement in shaping an academic leadership ethos and recognising the value of building deeper foundations for Christian media. Thanks for posing multi-disciplinary questions of relevance to scripture, tradition, reason and lived experience.

To Dr Stephen Beaumont (Christian Heritage College – Brisbane Australia), for nurturing an enlarged capacity for 'critical thinking' with an unwavering expectation for evidence-based research. And for your personal demonstration and commitment to practical Theology.

To Phil Edwards (CEO Vision Christian Media and Chair of CMAA) for your open door, and your trust and enthusiasm for the delivery of often controversial radio content, and for leadership in the nurture of practical expression around the purpose and practices of Christian media.

Thanks to Craig 'Elmo' Johnstone (Content Manager Vision Christian Media) for helping to facilitate elements of my research into beliefs and practices of those 'gate-keepers' of program content on Christian radio.

To Dianne Popoola, thankyou for your eye in proof-reading.

And special thanks to my wife Charmaine, who has never wavered through my many years of Christian ministry, my aspirations to enhanced higher learning, and the sacrifices necessary in the process of completing this book project.

Table of Contents

Foreword

I am delighted to write the Foreword to Neil Johnson's *'Public Christians in a Secular Age: Leadership for Season Change.'* My delight stems from the fact that I have a sincere admiration for its author. Neil Johnson is the voice for a well-known talk-radio program called 20Twenty, on Australia's Vision Christian Radio. He has a distinguished career in journalism, evangelical ministry, and academic pursuits.

'Public Christians in a Secular Age' explains how the emergence of Christian Radio in the 1990's enhanced the opportunity for the emergence of a new expression of Christian ministry, in a landscape where Christian expression on mainstream media had previously been in decline.

Australia, according to this book, has outstanding Christian radio expressions not only in capital cities but also in regional centres and remote outback communities. This book then contains a survey carried out in 2018, which sought to ascertain the views and attitudes of Christian Content Managers in key Australian radio markets. It is common in Christian media, according to its author, "to acknowledge the person of Christ as being central to their ethos".

An important goal of this book is to identify elements that fuel human flourishing from a biblical perspective, and to recommend how best they may be publicised. A couple of testable assumptions are identified, which nurture a reorientation for 'spirituality' in the broader culture. In later chapters, readers are invited by its author to explore the application of the concept of 'transcendence' in day-to-day organisational structures, including business, media, church, politics, and families.

The Old Testament is mentioned in this book as providing an illustration of the contrast between 'immanence' and 'transcendence' in the formation of civil government. God's intention, its author reminds us, was to be the sole 'King' of the people of Israel. However, the people noticed that all the other nations had their own human kings and demanded one for themselves.

The consequences of displacing God as King did not come without the sober warning through the prophet Samuel, of what the people of Israel should expect by choosing to emulate the nations around them and appoint their own king (1 Sam 8:11-18). Ultimately, writes the author, "the people's trust in God was 'eclipsed' by the desire to trust in one who would make them slaves".

An important focus of this book is on the dynamic role of Christians serving in public leadership roles, coupled with the emergence of a strong Christian media in all of its forms which may contribute to the spiritual formation of public Christian leaders. Accordingly, this book explains the traditional meaning of the word 'secular' and how this has now "morphed from a benign framework for managing plurality, to its own formation of religious alternative".

In this context, this book contains the sobering warning that the broader Church is 'at risk' of succumbing to the deleterious influences of a "disempowering secularisation". In our society, secularism is often elevated to a concerted effort to banish any element of religious influence from the public sphere. As this book explains, one of the problems for public Christians today is in the relentless hardening of a national ethos increasingly susceptible what may be an Australian brand of the pervasive "secularisation thesis", which includes the minimisation of the historical importance of Christianity in this nation.

While the role of Christianity in Australia's history is irrefutable, it is also irrefutable that this nation has considerably departed from its Christian origins.[1] When the first census was taken in 1911, 96 per cent of all Australians self-identified as Christian. By 2016, this figure had fallen to 52 per cent and nearly a third of Australians (30 per cent) reported to have no religion at all.[2] To make it worse, Michael Quinlan, Law Dean at the University of Notre Dame Australia, comments that

> *Many [Australians] associate Christians with negative stereotypes such as being judgemental, opinionated, hypocritical, intolerant,*

1 See: Augusto Zimmermann, Christian Foundations of the Common Law – Volume III: Australia, Brisbane/Qld 2018

2 Australian Bureau of Statistics, 2016 Census: Religion, 27 June 2017, https://www.abs.gov.au/AUSSTATS/abs@.nsf/mediareleasesbyReleaseDate/7E65A144540551D7CA258148000E2B85

insensitive, rude, greedy, with outdated beliefs that they seek to impose on others. Some consider that even discussing the traditional Christian – particularly the Catholic – position on, for example, sexual morality, confession, abortion, euthanasia or marriage – is hateful, bigoted and offensive and merely an excuse for protecting child abusers, covering up child sexual assault, sexism, homophobia, transphobia and discrimination akin to racism, apartheid and slavery.[3]

The forces of secularism have decided to wage a war on anything that appears as inconsistent with their "articles of faith". As a result, a hardened form of secularism is developed and there is an increasing demand that biblical reasons should be completely excluded from debate in the public square.[4] We are witnessing an aggressive form of secularism, which views Christian values and beliefs with great intolerance and dismissiveness.[5]

Ironically, the very existence of our liberal-democratic traditions are built upon principles derived from Christianity. These principles were wrought into the texture of Western societies by Christianity, not only as a school of thought but as a way of life and feeling: as a worldview, in short. Accordingly, it is not safe to assume that the liberal-democratic ethos can persist while the faith and doctrine that gave birth are being deliberately abandoned. As noted by Jeffrie G. Murphy, the Regent's Professor of Law, Philosophy and Religious Studies at Arizona State University:

"The rich moral doctrine of the sacredness, the preciousness, the dignity of persons cannot in fact be utterly detached from the theological context in which it arose and of which it for so long formed an essential part. Values come to us trailing their historical past; and when we attempt to cut all links to that past we risk cutting

---

3 Michael Quinlan, "An Unholy Patchwork Quilt: The Inadequacy of Protections of Freedom of Religious in Australia", [in:] Iain T. Benson, M. Quinlan, and A. K. Thompson (eds.), Religious Freedom in Australia – A New Terra Nullius?, Sydney/NSW 2019, p. 45.

4 A. Keith Thompson, "Should Public Reason Developed Under U.S. Establishment Clause Jurisprudence Apply to Australia?" The University of Notre Dame Australia Law Review 2015, Vol. 17, p. 109.

5 Alex Deagon, "A Christian Framework for Religious Diversity in Political Discourse", Brisbane/Qld 2019, p.152.

the life lines on which those values essentially depend. I think that this happens in the case of Kant's attempt – and no doubt any other attempt – to retain all Christian moral values within a totally secular framework. Thus 'All men are created equal and are endowed by their Creator with certain unalienable rights' may be a sentence we must accept in an all or nothing fashion – not one where we can simply carve out what we like and junk the rest".[6]

This important book reminds us how, from the beginning in the Garden of Eden, the very first temptation (Genesis 3:5) is for Eve to have her eyes opened to become 'like God'. As such, the very first step on the journey towards prevailing secularism started with that first "desire to replace the wisdom of God with the wisdom of men". So it is no wonder that rebellious feminists often perform counter-readings of the Bible in order to conceptualise Lucifer as a liberator of womankind. As this satanic narrative goes, Eve's ingestion of the forbidden fruit places her in a heroic act of rebellion against the "patriarchal tyranny" of God and Adam. Accordingly, the evil one is diabolically portrayed as the liberator of women in the struggle against God and his Son.

This book reminds us that in our fallen condition we tend to resist moral coherence and to require the arbitrary rule by "charismatic leaders". Whereas the acknowledgement of a transcendental order makes us acknowledge a "higher ruler beyond humanity", thus enabling any nation or community to flourish and to prosper according to God's natural order, a break from the protection of biblical ethical standards inevitably "opens the society to the likely danger of subservience for the entire populace, to the 'dark side' of charismatic elitist leadership".

Through charismatic leadership, wrote the late German sociologist Max Weber, power is not legitimised via transcendental source of authority but instead by means of devotion to the "exceptional sanctity, heroism, or exemplary character of an individual person, and of the normative patterns

---

6 Jeffrie G. Murphy, 'Afterword: Constitutionalism, Moral Skepticism, and Religious Belief'. From: Alan S. Greenwood (ed.), 'Constitutionalism: The Philosophical Dimension'. New York: Greenwood Press, 1988, p 249.

or order revealed or ordained by him".[7] This leads to 'charismatic leadership' being socially accepted as a more powerful form of political legitimisation rather than the rule of law. According to Sir Ivor Jennings KBE QC FBA, an English lawyer who served as the Vice-Chancellor of the University of Cambridge,

> *If it is believed that the individual finds his greatest happiness, or best develops his soul, in a strong and powerful State, and that government implies... the unity of the people behind a wise and beneficent leader, the rule of law is a pernicious doctrine.*[8]

The response to COVID-19 by the authorities prompted some Australians to blindly worship at the altar of the almighty State. They expect government to be the ultimate provider for all things. Arguably, this is the inevitable consequence of a society's lack of faith in the God of the Bible, coupled with its unshakable faith in their political masters. Call it a form of idolatry if you wish. As a result, Australia has effectively become a nation of slave-like people with elected politicians acting more as masters, without providing the servant leadership that a free people expect of their leaders.

This book is not "religious" but a book about a personal relationship with Jesus Christ. Its author seems to be motivated by love more than by a sense of right and wrong, justice and injustice. Jesus Christ himself commanded his disciples to be the 'Salt and Light' of the world. However, Jesus also admonished us that if salt loses its saltiness it is worthless (Luke 14:34). This is the 'Great Commission' by which all followers of Christ are called to serve God in every sphere of their lives, including the areas of law and politics.

To conclude, 'Public Christians in a Secular Age' reveals Neil Johnson's passion and commitment to Christian media and education, coupled with a concern about the growth of an intolerant form of radical secularism in Australia, which is evident is so many parts of the public and private sectors. Accordingly, it is important to recognise in this book his ability to pose some very important questions concerning not only the ultimate goals and practices of Christian media, but also related to the broader matters

7 Max Weber, Theory of Social and Economic Organization (New York: Praeger, 1983) 215.
8 Sir Ivor Jennings, The Law and the Constitution (London: University of London Press, 1959) 46.

of scriptural hermeneutics, our Judeo-Christian tradition, and Australia's society in general. In sum, this is an important book and I hope you enjoy the read as much as I did!

Perth, 21st March 2022.

Professor Augusto Zimmermann PhD, LLM cum laude, LLB, DipEd, CIArb

Professor and Head of Law, Sheridan Institute of Higher Education
Professor of Law (Adj.), The University of Notre Dame Australia
President, Western Australian Legal Theory Association (WALTA)
Editor-in-Chief, The Western Australian Jurist
Law Reform Commissioner, WA (2012-2017)

Introduction

Imagine you're in a court of law, standing accused, facing trial before a Judge and jury. A court official approaches you to 'swear an oath' before you are compelled to give evidence. A book bearing the title 'Holy Bible' is thrust in your direction and you nervously reach out to hold it while you are asked to repeat these words, '*I swear by Almighty God that the evidence I shall give will be the truth, the whole truth and nothing but the truth."*

Today for many who make that promise 'swearing' on the Bible, there remains a profound hangover from what feels like a bygone era. Our western traditions demand that when appearing in court, facing justice means telling the 'truth' was not just as an obligation before an earthly court, but more importantly, to an even higher authority. The promise is intended to be made to the almighty God, the 'Divine Judge' who presides over ultimate justice.

Acknowledging the presence of a 'transcendent' God is an assurance that 'false witness' lies are clearly visible to the One who knows intimately, our human heart. It is He who has set the supreme standard against the concept of telling lies or 'bearing false witness'.

But not everyone today has a healthy fear of the Divine Judge. Why would the unbeliever wilfully heed the compulsion to tell '*the truth, the whole truth and nothing but the truth*'? How does the alternative in the form of an 'affirmation' affect the heart of the accused where reference to God is deleted, and truth-telling is based on a 'solemn and sincere declaration'? Is there enough substance in the pre-supposed 'goodness' of humanity to ensure the truth is told, and justice is done?

When we have doubts that the 'transcendent' God hears and holds to account our 'false' testimony, we know that we have weakened our system of justice and fallen into the murky waters of the 'secular'. Broadly today truth-telling and integrity are no longer measured by the Divine standard of the transcendent God, but 'un-truths' have been elevated to become an equally acceptable defence. Divine measure is no longer considered ultimate. Times are changing, and so are definitions of once held absolutes. Numerous dimensions of our complex culture are morphing to the new 'secular' normal where the consequences are disturbing.

Perhaps definitions in a secularised world look different from nation to nation. My focus in the chapters ahead is on my nation of Australia and broadly embracing similar challenges across Western nations, as historic foundations are under the revisionist blowtorch.

A secularising contamination has been sweeping through Western nations accompanied by radical revisionism and prideful intimidation to silence poorly defended religious foundations. Historians Stuart Piggin, and Robert D. Linder venture a contemporary definition of the secularised Australia, in their outstanding volume, '*Attending to the National Soul, Evangelical Christians in Australian History*' (2020):

> '*...the retreat of religious concerns in the public square, the reduction of religion's power to shape the national culture or consciousness, and the decline in religious belief and practice. Secularism is an ideology, the belief that religious influence on society is usually weak and unimportant and always detrimental.*'[1]

While Professors Piggin and Linder argue that Australia has been significantly shaped by Christian values, they suggest a deeper dimension worthy of our concern. They argue that even Christian Australia manifests 'secular-values', unaware or ignoring the fact that many of those values first-of-all, required a Christian culture for their conception and maturation. The irony they say, is that Australians are more Christian than they know, and Australian Christians are more secular than they know.

In the chapters ahead we'll explore an accelerating Aussie secularism, and we'll highlight the dynamic realities that fuel 'seasons of change'.

We'll acknowledge the Christian foundations that permeated 'colonial culture' that began with the arrival of the First Fleet, bringing both the displacement of first people's culture, and the seeds that have grown into a modern nation glowing with Divine 'transcendence.'

In contrast we'll discuss what it is to live under a growing 'anti-spirituality' that denies that Divine influence and wants to airbrush the religious contribution from the history books and from the national psyche. We may discover a concerning reality, that this accelerating 'anti-spirituality' makes humanity the measure of all things, is subtly dampening the fires of Australia's embedded Christian spirituality with an alternative that logically leads only to likely tensions between homogenous groups sharing common identity, and the prospect for the rise of authoritarian rule.

Enchantment, Disenchantment and Re-enchantment

From evidence of a widespread Western world 'disenchantment' expressed as a denial of the 'transcendent', we will explore pathways to a new reinvigorated Judeo-Christian, 're-enchantment' that alerts, equips and empowers a people, to be resistant to the 'anti-spirituality' of the secular. Consequently, we'll identify some testable assumptions, and uncover new evidence to spark and nurture a reorientation for 'spirituality' in the broader culture as expressed in the 'incarnate' Christ and demonstrated in the vigorous and vital growth of the church from biblical times to the present.

These concepts of 'enchantment', 'disenchantment' and 're-enchantment' can be imagined in a metaphorical sense as though they are portraying our presence in a 'magical world' like an 'enchanted' kingdom.

These are spiritual and meaningful ways for Christian and non-Christian alike, to appreciate the Divine dimensions at work in our present day. 'Magic' filled words create an impression loaded with meaning from a 'storybook' expression of powers that are beyond human capacity. In a world inhabited by God, what seems impossible for man, is not at all impossible for God.

We will ponder the possibilities, and the practical consequences of those elements that have emerged in contrast to the biblical notion of God 'at work' in the world, where honouring Him leads to a flourishing of humanity, and where dishonour has the opposite effect. Rejecting God as is demonstrated in the national formation of the people of God from the Old Testament brings dysfunction and deterioration under consequences outworked in the 'sinful' human condition.

The wider pursuit of an increasingly secularised people, living in a secular 'bubble', self-isolated in the snare of entertaining secularised media creates its own 'secular eco-system'. Starvation of the biblical 'transcendence' narrative builds an alternative pursuit of meaning rapidly shifting away from the perceived 'virtues of belief' found in the goodness centred character of the transcendent Creator.

The alternative that is promoted as being intelligent, scientific and sophisticated is not quite as it seems. It's seductive, luring followers towards a lesser, 'deflated singular-dimensional' model. The new 'Secular' is like a shrivelled balloon, that has lost its air, and deflated to a flat, wrinkly, spiritually lifeless existence without the hope that springs from the presence of the transcendent God.

To use another metaphor popularised by one of this century's most significant thinkers, Canadian philosopher Charles Taylor, the secular resembles captivity within an 'Immanent Frame'.[2] The Frame, like a 'picture frame', has a rigid surround that blocks all but a few 'rays' of transcendence that beam through portals like faint glimmers of light. We are all, both Christian and non-Christian alike, trapped within this darkened 'frame', without exposure to the rays of light that are at full strength beyond the borders of the frame. To use another analogy, we've all experienced a cloudy day, where beams of sunlight pierce the clouds like spotlights on the darkened landscape.

Under the emerging secular cloud, the light of transcendence has become dim. Distortion is rife, and 'meaning' is hazy for those exposed solely to the invasive and all consuming 'public media sphere'. Without exposure to the Divine light, meaning is restricted to the pursuits of human centred 'meaning-making' around issues like money, power, pleasure, and celebrity. We might consider this alternative thinking as a pursuit described as misdirected meaning-making or 'mis-enchantment'. [3]

If trends in the prominence of 'Divine transcendence' continue to incrementally diminish, we might expect to encounter more of the society wide 'spiritual stagnation' that Western nations are increasingly finding to be the 'new normal'. The new way of thinking and feeling is an entrenchment of what philosopher James K.A Smith[4] calls alternative 'secular liturgies' that capture our hearts by capturing our imaginations Ultimately we become re-oriented to 'love something different' from the pursuit of the living God and his kingdom.

What appears normal across the whole media landscape promoting a version of 'human flourishing' based on money, power, pleasure and celebrity, should provoke an alternate response from Christian leaders who can see through the deception. There is a contrasting alternative that we expect to hear from Christian leaders with a public voice. But what if those Christian leaders in Church, politics, business, or indeed our families remain silent? What happens when communication of deeper issues is being stifled? What happens when prevailing thought for a new generation assumes that what the Church has to say is 'powerless' and 'out-dated'?

For the Public Christian the increase of the 'secular' creates a challenge as we recognise the need to contrast our secular age with the timeless elements of the 'sacred'. These sacred elements are based in a biblical 'image' of God and his dealings with humanity where belief and obedience fuel a demonstrable form of 'human flourishing'. This is evidenced in communities and cultures, as they have formed in relational connection to the Divine with a prevailing sense of the 'transcendent'.

One of the goals of this book is to identify key elements that fuel biblical human flourishing and to recommend how best, they may be publicised. Nothing of substance will change until the 'horse is before the cart', and we can confidently identify God's purpose and plan as distinct from the variety of secularised alternatives.

The original intent for this book was for Christian media professionals and entrepreneurs, to help define what makes Christian media 'Christian', not just another secularised pursuit. The end product is much broader addressing how we function in every organisational setting being led by Christians who want to be good stewards of their enterprise. Every leader may find that Christian media is a good case study that goes beyond mere theory.

In later chapters we'll explore the application of the concepts of 'transcendence' in more practical day-to-day organisational structures that we all find ourselves to be part of, either in business, media, church, politics or families. And we'll address the very important question as to whether-or-not, the broader Church is itself 'at risk' of becoming secular. In practice, when our public Christianity neglects the influence of 'transcendence' we risk becoming just another secular expression, disguised with cleverly applied make-up', like the old expression of putting lipstick on a pig to improve its appearance. Imagine for a moment, a world where public Christians are reduced from being a dynamic expression of a Kingdom centred expression like what we see in the book of Acts, to being carriers of a 'deflated' rationalised, lifeless expression of the Gospel. Our prayer may be that we might be carriers of the same Christian Gospel that historically 'turned the world upside-down.' [5]

In the chapters ahead, we address a new ignorance, and empower the challenge for serious influence of a new generation, where the trend of secular hostility towards faith continues to rise in opposition to the timeless Gospel message.

Endnotes

1   Piggin S., Linder R.D, 2020, Attending to the National Soul, Evangelical Christians in Australian History 1914-2014, p.15.

2   Taylor C. 2007 A Secular Age, Belknap Press of Harvard University Press, Cambridge, Massachusetts, USA and London, England. p 539.

3   Segal M.T. 2013 Reflections on Latour, Tarnas, and the Misenchantment of the World, Footnotes 2 Plato, p.1. https://footnotes2plato.com/2013/03/10/reflections-on-latour-tarnas-and-the-misenchantment-of-the-world/ [Accessed 28 July 2018)

4   Smith J.K.A. 2009 How (Not) To Be Secular Reading Charles Taylor, Eerdmans, Michigan, USA. p.88

5   Acts 17:6 'But when they did not find them, they dragged Jason and some brethren to the rulers of the city, crying out, "These who have turned the world upside down have come here too.' (NKJV)

Chapter 1:
The Loss of
Transcendence

For this is what the high and exalted One says—he who lives forever,
whose name is holy: "I live in a high and holy place, but also with the one
who is contrite and lowly in spirit, to revive the spirit of the lowly
and to revive the heart of the contrite.

Isaiah 57:15

Disenchantment: Winter and Spring

'Always Winter and never Christmas; think of that!' These are the words of
C.S. Lewis, penned in his 1950 classic children's adventure fantasy 'The
Lion, the Witch and the Wardrobe'.[1] Mr Tumnus the Faun uses this 'winter
and Christmas' imagery to describe to Lucy the way the land of Narnia
has fallen under the control of the White Witch who has *'all Narnia under
her thumb'.*[2] At first pass these are the fantasy words of a creative writer
skilfully forming the imaginary for a 'magical world', setting the scene for
an action-packed children's fantasy adventure with strange and mythical
creatures under a 'wintery' spell caught in a land where everything looks
'Christmassy' but the joy of Christmas never comes, and the beauty of
'springtime' is a distant hollow memory.

Lewis's children's story is famous for its captivating allegory casting an
insightful, and spiritually mature light on modern realities. He uses
simple images, that on one level create a magical world as a storyteller, but
in an alternative dimension taking the reader into a sophisticated depth
of appreciation for the battle of 'light against darkness'. It's the struggle of

'good against evil' with wisdom and insight for an anticipated deepening modern battle of 'faith against unbelief'. It's also the contrast between the 'shiver of winter', and the glow of the warm spring sunshine.

Icy winter, and warm springtime were not far from the thinking of C.S. Lewis who is renowned as one of the 20th Century's leading theological thinkers. For Lewis changing belief was like a seasonal transition. In describing his personal conversion from atheism to Christianity he wrote:

> *'I felt as if I were a man of snow at long last beginning to melt. The melting was starting in my back--drip--drip and presently trickle-trickle'. (1955-XIV)*

His personal journey to faith in the transcendent God, was that of a 'slow thaw'. For Lewis, this is personal, with imagery that may be the experience of many of his readers, 'frozen' and captive without the hope that comes with the possibility of 'springtime'.

In relation to the way we might form an approach to modern social phenomena like a deepening secularisation, it may be valuable to reflect on Lewis's allegory of a 'freezing landscape' and 'wintry effects' upon a once flourishing landscape. The subsequent application of the 'winter-spring' metaphor applies to his own journey of faith discovery. And the application extends to the wintry effects on a whole community, or indeed an entire civilization as was the case in his Narnia chronicles. Of interest to our modern story, is the concept of how a 'counter-phenomenon' brings the new arrival of springtime with its warmth and fresh new flourishing flora and fauna.

Later in Lewis's classic story we are inspired that even the mention of the name of 'Aslan the Lion' brings a *'strange feeling – like the first signs of spring, like good news...'.*

> *'Wrong will be right, when Aslan comes in sight,*
> *At the sound of his roar, sorrows will be no more,*
> *When he bares his teeth, winter meets its death,*

And when he shakes his mane, we shall have spring again.[3]

As Aslan the Lion in Lewis's famous allegory embodies the presence of Jesus, perhaps this too, has a modern Western equivalent in a transition of seasons with the pending possibility of 're-enchantment'. We may ask ourselves, what effect might there be with the roar of Aslan in today's world? And if he shakes his mane today, will springtime displace the current wintry pessimism?

We may appreciate the application more deeply as we introduce evidence of 'disenchantment' and the consequent effects of the emergence of a modern wintry pessimism wherever there is a diminished presence of an applied Divine 'transcendence'.

Disenchantment – The Godless Nature

The metaphoric descriptive of 'Disenchantment' which characterises the 'loss of transcendence' came to prominence in a 1917 lecture by German Sociologist Max Weber describing the loss of meanings, magical expectations, connections to animism, and spiritual explanations that had from medieval times characterised the traditional world. American historian Michael Saler[4] in his historiography of Modernity and Enchantment notes Weber may have drawn the phrase from poet, historian and philosopher Friedrich Schiller in a late 19th Century poem *'Die Götter Greichenlands'.*[5] In the 19th century the word 'disenchantment' (die entgötterte Natur! - the Godless Nature) was synonymous with the concept of 'pessimism'. Weber sought to encapsulate a long-standing critique that started with early Romantics in the 18th Century and continued through the 19th and into the 20th Century. Romanticism as a philosophical movement reacted against scientific rationalization of nature in the Enlightenment. The emphasis of the critique was on the Enlightenment promotion of 'reason and science' as replacement for other ways of interpreting the world.

Weber had sought to master all things by 'calculation' in arguing that there were no 'mysterious incalculable forces that come into play'. For him this was 'instrumental rationality' that meant that the world is 'disenchanted'.

As this discourse continued to become popular among Western intellectuals in the 20th Century, the concept of defining religion 'amongst the superstitions' empowered individuals to explain away those wonders and marvels of the enchanted world. They were relegated to an outdated popular culture to be replaced by a new 'mass culture' that explained them in terms of natural laws.' Those who sought to keep ideas of 'enchantment' alive were tagged by their critics as 'reactionary anti-modernists' engaged in a futile struggle to recapture a lost world.[6]

Weber's 'Iron Cage' – Sensualists without Heart

Weber[7] viewed rationalization as a process taking place in manifold dimensions of human life, each with its own logic, different values and ends. One point of view may well be irrational from another. South Korean political theorist Sung Ho Kim[8] concludes that for Weber the loss of freedom and agency that comes from formal rationalization reduces individuals to being like a 'cog in a machine' or being trapped in an 'iron cage'. This 'iron cage' metaphor is just one of the 'pessimistic dimensions' of the modernity born in rationalization. Philosopher Lawrence Scaff[9] interprets Weber's 'iron cage' metaphor as being concerned with only the material world, emerging from the idea of 'objectification of material culture' and 'inexorable power'. Charles Taylor[10] has a different take on the metaphoric restriction. He describes Weber's 'iron cage' as a 'time-frame' or a constructed environment where we live according to uniform secular time. This lower, confined construction of time is contrasted with that perception of being 'not restricted' by hands on a clockface. The 'cage' makes all 'higher time' harder to conceive. At its apex, or the peak of rationalization Weber saw 'moderns' suddenly finding themselves living in the same kind of world as the ancients did, one not yet disenchanted of its 'gods and demons'.

Alternative Ways of Transforming Society

Unilinear disenchantment was not Max Weber's only descriptive. It may also be worthy of note that the context of Weber's 'iron cage' metaphor was ventured in his critique of the excesses in the rise of 19th century capitalism. He argued that disenchantment had ushered-in the monotheistic religions in the West and was preparing the ground for a new unified system of meaning. He saw the new meaning culminating in the Puritan ethic of 'vocation' based on modern science.

Here was a 'new' way of transforming the 'self'. An integrated personality mastering the world with tireless energy as a new unity. The 'Protestant Ethic Thesis' became part of a genealogical account of modern times, leading to the perception of a 'civil society'. However, Weber saw the grounds of this new mastery of 'modern science' as deeply problematic suggesting it is a 'nihilistic enterprise' constantly asking to be made obsolete *ad infinitum*, on an endless road of relentless deconstruction.

So, for both pursuits, either religious or scientific the result is irretrievable. The value judgements of science stand in antagonism to religious values. What is tasteful to one, may be tasteless to the other. Kim[11] notes that Weber viewed the two contradictory images as a single problem contributing to an 'inertia of modern individuals who fail to take principled action' and creating *'sensualists without heart'* and *'specialists without spirit'*, an illustration of the 'disempowerment of the modern self'.

It is conceivable that the missing values of 'heart' and 'spirit' are best described as values that come from a different dimension. The true value of 'transcendence' to our 21st Century world trapped within an 'immanent frame' may be the factor that releases 'Heart' and 'Spirit' as the 'missing ingredients' to Weber's 'problem'. These may be a significant part of the explanations sought in the study of the contrast between disenchantment and re-enchantment.

Taylor's Immanent Frame - Imprisoning Captives

What is it that holds the prisoner captive within the cage, or within the frame? Is it the shackles on the ankles of a slave, or the bars on the cell block windows? Could it also be the effect of isolation from civilization for one who is an 'exiled' individual cut off from society? Or, could it include the psychological restrictions of the ideological authoritarian government?

For Charles Taylor[12] the idea of an 'Immanent Frame' revolves around the construction of a 'social space' that constitutes a contrast between a 'natural' order and a 'supernatural' one. For Taylor, it's the contrast between an 'immanent' world and a 'transcendent' one. His use of the 'frame' as a metaphor similar to Weber's 'iron cage' may be an intentional way of softening the imagery used by Weber. Storey[13] argues that Taylor wants to 'rattle' Weber's cage with a different account of what it is that 'imprisons captives'.

In the modern world captives are not bound by iron bars, but by a 'social imaginary'. Taylor describes the natural order as being dominated by 'clock readings' with secular time as a resource that dare not be wasted and where one thing happens consecutively after another.

The contrast to 'secular time' is 'higher time' where the affairs of 'eternity' become the primary focus. As an example: 'prefiguring-fulfilling' occurs where the events of the past coincide with the events of the present. In the biblical narrative, Old Testament events often hold deep meaning in relation to the New Testament like connection between Abraham's obedient action preparing to sacrifice his son Isaac, and the provision of a substitutionary sacrifice in the crucifixion of Christ. They are linked because of a 'Divine Plan'. In this notion of 'transcendence', there is a simultaneity of 'Sacrifice and Crucifixion'. Taylor argues that 'time is a moving image of eternity', and that rising to eternity is 'rising to participate in God's instant', something we only have access to when we participate in God's life. To live in the 'transcendent' is to have access to the ideas and thoughts of the Creator, past, present, and indeed the future.

When 'higher time' is outside of 'secular time' the alpha and omega (beginning and end) is already known by God. Participation in the Divine nature pushes the door ajar and lets a glimmer of eternal light shine on the immanence of the presence and eternal purposes of God in human affairs.

It could be argued that many Christians become aware of this 'higher time' when they encounter God in times of worship, meditation, prayer, and the testimonies of others who describe their encounters with the Divine. Stories of the miraculous, and indeed of soundly explored biblical prophetic fulfilments[14] in our present day, affirm the biblical narrative, that drips with the miraculous. The words of Jesus, '...*whoever believes in me will do the works I have been doing, and they will do even greater things than these, because I am going to the Father*' (John 14:12) affirms the presence, power and activity of God today. Christians recognise that the source of miracles, healings, and fulfilled prophecy demonstrates a 'just as He promised' moment. We are affirmed in our faith because of the enabling power of the Holy Spirit to affirm his purposes for humanity.

On a practical level for present day leaders within the Christian church, there is an important question. Is the concept of re-enchantment solely a work of the Holy Spirit' in the way Evangelicals imagine the concepts of 'spiritual awakening' and 'Christian revival'? Is God's purpose only about stories of the miraculous, or is it the onward march of 'Christian Soldiers' in a battle to advance the Kingdom of God in all spheres of life? What we ask about our role in the stewardship of our church, business, our community, nation, or the world, is how the followers of Christ today position themselves in preparation for a biblical Christian 're-enchantment'.

I believe that re-enchantment is a 'co-missional' responsibility. In other words, it is a work of God, that He does through his followers. It's a responsibility of Christian leadership as a function of discipleship. Even if we argue that it 'may be one or the other', our wrestling with the problem will likely result in the answer being 'both'.

Christians humbly address the question of what 'role' leaders have as stewards to pursue a re-imagined course of action. Our challenge is to arrest what we may perceive to be a society-wide decline in the plausibility of Christian faith and practice. Our practical response is to 'strategise' ways of addressing the rising power of the 'secular' that tries to quench the fires of Christian faith.

'Modernity Wrestling with Enchantment' —A Missing Dimension

Our modernity wants to exchange the 'Revelation of God' with natural explanations. Understanding elements of the relationship between 'enchantment' and 'modernity' enlarges our appreciation of the influence of 'transcendence'. It is important to identify the elements of the debate that have sought to squeeze modern imaginaries into the flatter 'singular-dimensional' rationalism described in the metaphoric 'immanent frame'. Remember this 'frame' is like a picture frame, blocking the incursion of the extra dimension of the transcendence of God. The frame inhibits the light of God, incarcerating those within and restricting their 'imaginary' to human reason alone.

Michael Saler[15] reminds us that 'modernity' is hard to define, but forms his definition as a mix of 'political, social, intellectual, economic, technological, and psychological factors', that arose in Western culture through the 16th-19th centuries. Modernity has come to be synonymous with the emergent difference between cultural spheres like 'East and West', and is marked by 'the dominance of secularism, nationalism, capitalism, industrialism, urbanism, consumerism and scientism'. The common line peddled by 'cultural pessimists' is the emphasis that modernity is 'disenchanted'. It is reactionary against enchanted religion. The reason why this cultural pessimism is 'bad' is not only that it leads to 'flatter deflated imagination'. It's because pessimism is opposite to the satisfying elements of 'meaning and purpose', and of 'wonder and surprise', fuelled by enchantment that starts with the concept of transcendence. And this powerful transcendence comes from the biblical creator - God.

Heuristic labels for these approaches may be inadequate, but Michael

Saler[16] outlines three approaches forming a contextual historic setting in which the fires of enchantment are under the 'water-hoses' of rationalism, and yet are not easily extinguishable. A heuristic is like a 'rule of thumb' that here can help us understand the extent of the influence of what the immanent frame does to 'transcendence' diminishing our understanding of the biblical reality. The first is 'the Binary', the second 'the Dialectical' and the third which relates most closely to our present day, is what Saler calls the 'Antinomial'.

1. The Binary

In the first of these, Enchantment is defined as 'superstition'. Two streams of 'early modern' practice emerged. As Daston[17] reflects on the emerging challenges of the Enlightenment he notes, the issue of religious leaders arguing to distinguish between 'genuine miracles' and a 'demonic counterfeit'. Meanwhile, Judges presiding over witchcraft trials sought to distinguish between 'natural oddities' and 'sorcery'. Michael Saler[18] calls these two streams the 'Binary' approach. It is an 'either/or' model that emerged out of the scientific revolution of the 17th century, and the Enlightenment of the 18th century.

Enchantment ideas of 'wonders and marvels' were defined by elites as 'superstitions' of organised religion. It included alternative spiritual phenomena like astrology, witchcraft, ghosts, fairies, divination, magical healing, and ancient prophecies. These were relegated to 'the ghettos of popular culture', ahead of the successor driving a new 'mass culture' in the late nineteenth and twentieth centuries. In our Christian context the momentum continued as elites sought to replace the concept of 'revelation' with explanations confined to uniform natural laws.

These views continue to inform the debate today, where a body of thought that became known as 'Traditionalism' from the late 19th and early 20th centuries developed a reputation as 'anti-modernist'. So, the first rule of thumb that the secularist argues, is that transcendent Christian faith is aligned with ancient 'superstition'.

We may be able to glean encouragement that there is biblical wisdom to apply to the modern social imaginary. Jesus was himself accused of being just another proponent of 'power' aligned to the realm of superstition when accused of driving out demons by the power of Beelzebul":

> *14 Jesus was driving out a demon that was mute. When the demon left, the man who had been mute spoke, and the crowd was amazed. 15 But some of them said, "By Beelzebul, the prince of demons, he is driving out demons." 16 Others tested him by asking for a sign from heaven.*
>
> *17 Jesus knew their thoughts and said to them: "Any kingdom divided against itself will be ruined, and a house divided against itself will fall. 18 If Satan is divided against himself, how can his kingdom stand? I say this because you claim that I drive out demons by Beelzebul. 19 Now if I drive out demons by Beelzebul, by whom do your followers drive them out? So then, they will be your judges. 20 But if I drive out demons by the finger of God, then the kingdom of God has come upon you.*
>
> *21 "When a strong man, fully armed, guards his own house, his possessions are safe. 22 But when someone stronger attacks and overpowers him, he takes away the armor in which the man trusted and divides up his plunder.*
>
> *23 "Whoever is not with me is against me, and whoever does not gather with me scatters." (Luke 11:14-23 NIV)*

Today, as Christian leaders, being aware that we are often seen as coming from an outdated traditionalism, we enjoy and promote the abundance of evidence for genuine miracles, stories of provision, the evidence for creation or indeed modern prophetic fulfilment, not because they are an end in themselves, or that they are an element of Christian entertainment or fascination, but because just as it was in the first century ministry of Jesus, the presence of miracles are today evidence of *'the finger of God'* (Luke 11:20 [NIV]) and that the Kingdom of God *'has come upon'* the people. As we might imagine, the potential in all forms of Christian media in the proliferation of miracles grounded in evidence, becomes an important element in countering the concept of being grouped with other 'superstitions'.

To reject or resist discussion or the reporting of miracles is capitulation to the secular argument that all such stories are nonsense and in the realm of superstition. To report miracles and wonders without evidence, or attribution giving glory to God, as though biblical expectation is purely coincidental, is also a capitulation to the secular stronghold of disenchantment. A solution: Perhaps our goal as cultural leaders, and public Christians is to do all we can to multiply awareness of 'wonders' as commonplace in the realm of the God of the Bible.

2.   The Dialectical

The second 'rule of thumb' that describes the modern view of enchantment, is known as the 'Dialectical' approach. It's also described as an either/or approach and as a little more inclusive suggesting that modernity is 'enchanted' in a negative sense. The 'Dialectical' approach casts 'modernity' itself as inherently 'irrational' and as dangerously oppressive and inhumane. It's a construct that contains the same 'mythical' elements as the very magical superstitions that it sought to overcome, and along with the new developments, some dangerous risks. Alexander[19] laments the lack of engagement of social theory on the 'evils' of modernity. He argues that modernity brings about 'good' and 'evil' simultaneously where dark and light are 'fused at the hip'. Aspirations in a community of self-regulating and independent people are only one part of the equation, with the other 'dark' side there is a 'fearful' need to keep 'irrational, dependent and despotic forces at bay'.

Max Weber[20] acknowledged that there were dangers that came from modernity including the 'impoverishment of human experience' that accompanied rationalism, and the risk that emerges where masses become subservient to leaders who possess a 'charismatic' authority. Modernity is 'exposed' as a dangerously oppressive and inhumane condition, hypocritical in its delivery of the promised pursuit of 'reason, progress, and freedom.' This 'dialectical' view of Modernity is just as 'enchanted' as under the 'binary' view, but in a very negative sense as giving rise to 'self-interested ideologies, false consciousness and bad faith.' Michael Saler[21] notes that the dialectical approach is prevalent in the writings of Karl Marx and Friedrich Nietzsche. He suggests that Weber straddled the 'binary' and the 'dialectic' and warned that the 'repressive cultural forces of modernity along with advances of science and technology could eventually lead to humanity's self-destruction' where individuality is abolished, human nature distorted, and autonomy repressed. The charismatic authority seizes power and takes the place of the magician, leading by delusion.

3.   The Antinomial

The third view that gives us context for understanding 'modernity and enchantment' is called 'The Antinomial' approach. This approach is considered more 'true to the lived experience' combining a 'both/and' logic for the relationship between modernity and enchantment. Michael Saler's argument here is that there are competing conceptions or models of modernity or what he calls 'alternative modernities.' There are 'fruitful tensions' between the seemingly irreconcilable forces, contradictions and oppositions called 'antinomies' where the complexities of modernity become 'messy.'

These are forms of 'Modern Enchantment' that have become compatible with the tenets of modernity. 'Modern Enchantments' often depend on 'Modern Disenchantment', enchanting and disenchanting simultaneously. It's the tension that comes when 'disenchanted reason' exists alongside an 'enchanted imagination.' The 'antinomial' approach is the impression that modernity is enchanted in a disenchanted way. A study of developments in early 20th century Germany[22] aligned the rise of the 'occult' alongside modern psychology. A mass culture had a yearning for modern wonders, be they illusion or so called 'natural sciences' like mesmerism. Showmen and magicians like P.T Barnham, and Jean Robert-Houdin (Europe) were cleverly able to manipulate the emerging mass media to promote debates about the authenticity of their exhibits, exploiting the curiosity of the masses, and keeping consumers of their entertaining spectaculars 'perpetually excited but never fully satisfied.'[23] Alternative modernities whether authentic in magical power or clever illusion tended to blur the difference between art and reality, shaping the perceptions of media consumers with a form of scepticism, that served to harden a resistance to manipulation by those seeking to shape culture, either by truth or deception.

With the rise of mass media came the emergence of a more widely accessible fiction writing, including the prominence of 'science fiction'. Appealing to both reason and the imagination, new challenges emerged to challenge the concepts of 'binary' and 'dialectical' views of modernity. As a consequence they reinforced the 'messy' complexities of what it is to be modern.

For the Christian leader today, these three positions summarised are a useful tool for navigating a 'Kingdom' oriented future. The modern assault on transcendence wants to replace 'revelation' with 'natural explanation' including the inherent dangers that accompany such an action. Charles Taylor[24] describes the process of disenchantment in the form of a series of 'subtraction stories' where myths are dispelled by reason, and religion is supplanted by science.

I believe what is overlooked by those quick to accept the 'defeat' emerging from the subtraction stories, is the logical ramification where the 'subtraction of God' leaves only human constructs of reality and governance. Subservience of the masses to an emerging 'rationalist elite' is a potential outcome if power that enables freedom is seized by 'charismatic elites' leading to expressions of ideological forms of authoritarian and repressive leadership.

Endnotes

1   Taylor C. 2007 p.20

2   Smith J.K.A 2009 p.143

3   In Stuart Piggin and Bob Linder's 'The Foundation of Public Prosperity: Evangelical Christians in Australian History 1740-1914', 2018, their insights extend well before the colonisation of Australia (1788) to include the transforming influence of the Great Awakening upon identities and decisions that led to the arrival of the First Fleet, and early foundations.

4   Secular comes from 'Saeculum', a century or age. Taylor (2007 p.54)

5   Tidball D. 1987 p.71

6   Tidball D. 1987 A World Without Windows: Living as a Christian in a Secular World, Scripture Union, London. P.69

Chapter 2:
The New Secularism

'... what is seen is temporary,
but what is unseen is eternal.'

2 Cor 4:18 NIV

Exchanging 'revelation' for 'reason' leads to many new problems, as a militant form of secularism moves to take hold of power. The common definition of the word 'secular' appears to have morphed from a benign framework for managing plurality, to its own popular formation of 'religious alternative'. It has become the 'catch-cry' of the militant atheist and the ideological opponents of freedom of religious expression. The pace with which the definition in common language has changed, has rendered historic definitions redundant. The 'new secularism' argues that in an age of knowledge and technology, religion will suffer fatal decline, and a new enlightened secular age will emerge based on 'exclusive humanism'. What is promised is a new form of utopia free from the constraints of religion. This is the secular goal for human flourishing. I'm asking whether the classical form of the 'Secularization Thesis' may not yet be redundant, and is very much a subversive undercurrent, alive in our Australian context, even though in a universal application, the thesis has long been proven false.

The narrative of the new definitive 'exclusive humanism' that says, 'I don't believe in God' can be contrasted and countered, when public Christians are equipped to articulate the effects of a secular age, and form a new 'resistant strain', 'counter culture', or as Taylor suggests a 'stronger magic'. It may be the empowerment, or a new enhanced sense of identity, that all forms of public Christianity have been searching for where Christian media becomes the vehicle for a transcendent, revelational, 'culture engaging' framework that presents a 'higher good'.[1] The expression takes us beyond the implausible human perfection aspired to by exclusive humanism, and places Christianity in a necessary contrast, firstly as 'saints' in a world of 'sinners', but secondly as ones who are before God as merely 'sinners saved by grace'.

For public Christians the challenge will be to present a faith that goes beyond the bounds of the 'natural' into a dimension for living without the restrictions imposed by the 'immanent frame'. In an age where two extremes may be identified as 'transcendent religion' and 'exclusive humanist denial', public Christians do well to understand the historic, theological and sociological elements that will enable an effective navigation through 'deception and confusion' with the grace to address the resulting pessimism and despair that follows secularism.

Grandeur of God vs Secular Pessimism

The new modern prevalence of a 'materialistic flattened naturalism'[2] is a contrast to the 'grandeur of God' who is present in a worshipping people. A 'disenchanted mechanistic worldview' threatens to further weaken the long-established ethos in Australia including the Judeo-Christian foundational culture which we can identify as being present since before the beginning of colonization[3] and with sporadic periods of strength and nation forming influence. The gradual emergence of new 'alternative meaning' paradigms appears to have caught Christian leaders off-guard in the later 20th Century, leaving a bruised and lack-lustre 'cultural Christianity' under-equipped and doubtful, succumbing to the influences of a disempowering secularization.

The problem intensifies, where the notion of a separated 'sacred' from the 'secular' becomes increasingly blurred, and the 'defined sacred' itself is seductively enticed by the disenchantment fruits of the secular, subtly placing Christians at risk of being overwhelmed. Because of the timeless nature of the authority of the Judeo-Christian Bible as Divinely inspired, along with the personal and corporate empowerment of the Holy Spirit for the Christian believer, the potential for arresting decline, along with the possibility of renewal, and a 'new reformation' breathes oxygen on the glowing embers of biblical Christianity. Expectation grows of a new imagination of Divinely sanctioned human flourishing as part of a holistic Gospel presentation.

21st Century Australians appear to have become vulnerable at best, to a new captivity to the 'secular'[4] as Charles Taylor definitively characterises secularization as the notion of people becoming embedded in 'ordinary time', in contrast to those who live for the affairs of 'eternity', or the parallel distinction of the 'temporal' contrasted to the 'spiritual'.

Australian Secularisation

The problem for public Christians today is in the relentless hardening of a national ethos increasingly accepting what may be an 'Australian brand' of the pervasive 'secularization thesis'. It includes the minimization of the historic record from the 18th Century 'Great Awakening' as a forerunner of formation of Australian values since colonization. This cultural revisionism is simply a 'secularized' re-interpretation of Australian Christian history, with the purpose of redefining the past with the current 'disenchanted' philosophical present. Revisionism has effectively become another battlefront that marginalises the Christian Church and its message, emasculating the motivations for Evangelical Christian leaders to 'contend' in the marketplace of influence in national values. The urgency of the reorientation required is based on the concept that 'Transcendence' in national discourse is quickly becoming a lost reality.

As we will discover in the following chapters, the contrast between the sacred and the secular attributes of modern society are distinctive. As Derek Tidball[5] reflects the secular world is not only a 'boring' world, but a 'bad' world. It is a world tainted by pessimism. In our Australian context, our future may depend on public Christians being able to discern what is of true value, and what produces 'boring and bad'.

Forbidden Fruit Looks Delicious

From the beginning in the Garden of Eden, the very first temptation (Genesis 3:5) is for Eve to have her eyes opened to become 'like God'. We might argue that the very first step on the journey in secularism starts with the desire to replace the wisdom of God with the wisdom of men. The 'forbidden fruit' was pleasing to the eye and desirable for gaining 'wisdom and knowledge'.

The earliest development of technology has its own story of separation between the sacred and the developing secular. Mankind not only makes tools for building cities, he also makes weapons for war, another foundation for a 'separation alternative' that becomes a 'live' issue when those opponents argue for the placement of faith in humanity, rather than God. Time and again, the people were drawn to place faith in human leaders perhaps summed up in the narrative, '*Some trust in chariots and some in horses, but we trust in the name of the Lord our God.*' (Psalm 20:7 [NIV])

Possessions and Power

The desire for land and possessions can be a Divinely appointed desire, if humanity is to have 'dominion' over all the earth. The transcendence of God is intimated in the reflection of Psalm 115:16, '*The highest heavens belong to the Lord, but the earth he has given to mankind*'. Where the land is a 'gift' from God, so possession of it seems legitimate. The challenge comes not only in the 'possession of', but the 'responsibility for' the land. Management of the land is achieved in the context of recognition that it ultimately remains the property of God. A neglect of this contextual positioning of the land can only lead to the result of arrogant self-interest and destructive exploitation.

Covetous arrogance is another pessimistic fruit of secularism, as an expressed desire to take that which is in our possession and displace God who is the giver of the land as a 'gift'. When humanity exclusively rules the resource, the outcome is that the resource begins to rule humanity. Even the environment has the potential to take on the role of a deity as reflected in the words of the Apostle Paul, *'they exchanged the truth of God for a lie, and worshipped and served created things rather than the Creator...'* (Romans 1:25).

In the Old Testament, one of the clearest illustrations of contrast between the transcendent and the immanent, or the sacred and the secular, is in the formation of governance and economics. The intention of God was to be the 'King' of the people of Israel. His humanly appointed agents of government would be subject to the rule of God's revealed 'Law', setting the people of God apart from other nations. But the people saw that other nations had their own 'kings' responsible for their security and protection. The consequences of displacing God as King and appointing a human 'king' did not come without warning. Through the Prophet Samuel, God warned the people what to expect if they chose to emulate the nations around them and appoint their own 'king'. He said:

> *'This is what the king who will reign over you will claim as his rights: He will take your sons and make them serve with his chariots and horses, and they will run in front of his chariots. He will take your daughters to be perfumers and cooks and bakers. He will take the best of your fields and vineyards and olive groves and give them to his attendants. He will take a tenth of your grain and of your vintage and give it to his officials and attendants. Your male and female servants and the best of your cattle and donkeys he will take for his own use. He will take a tenth of your flocks, and you yourselves will become his slaves. When that day comes, you will cry out for relief from the king you have chosen, but the LORD will not answer you in that day.'* (1 Samuel 8:11-18)

Ultimately the people's trust in God, was 'eclipsed' by the desire to trust in one who would make them slaves.

An Autopsy on Secularism

Secularism equals 'pessimism'. The writer of Ecclesiastes sums up this pessimism in what is described by Tidball as an 'autopsy on secularism.'[6] A life lived 'under the sun' is one that is lived on a horizontal level alone. It is a level that is separated from the oversight, or even the existence of God. There is no meaning or pleasure to be found, and the verdict of the writer in this timeless book of wisdom, is:

> *"'Meaningless! Meaningless!" says the Teacher. "Utterly meaningless! Everything is meaningless"'.*

These are not flippant words delivered in a moment of emotional distress, but the product of a life-long pursuit of meaning and significance with reflection on the pursuit of wisdom, pleasure, work, power, and money. In applying himself to the pursuit of wisdom and knowledge, madness and folly, the final conclusion is that a life lived in a horizontal dimension alone is merely a '*Chasing of the wind*' (Ecclesiastes 1:16,17).

However, a mere glimpse of the transcendent, shines a glimmer of light into the pervasive darkness of the pessimism of the secular. The Teacher recognises that it is God who has '*set eternity in the human heart*' (Ecclesiastes 3:11). This creates a picture of contextual positioning of 'creatureliness' in contrast to the 'majestic holiness' of the Creator who becomes the source of the possibility of satisfaction, hope, and of justice. For a conclusion of the matter of meaning, the Teacher reflects, '*Fear God and keep his commandments, for this is the duty of all mankind*'. (Ecclesiastes 12:13)

We find ourselves surrounded by modern alternatives that stand in contrast to the profound wisdom of the writer of Ecclesiastes. Other views of the world are presented as the 'real world' in which we live. However, the so-called modern world may not be much different to the ancient world, where the themes we may grapple with today, have already been the subject of much meaningful reflection. I have long, been in awe of the depth of pessimism described in the passages of Ecclesiastes. I now realise more deeply that this wisdom speaks profoundly into today's developing ideas of living in a secular world trapped within the metaphoric 'immanent frame'.

Public Christians Negotiate Change

In the 21st Century, the culture of Western Civilization continues to undergo rapid and diverse change. For contemporary Christian leaders the growth of knowledge and technology as predicted in the 'Secularization Thesis' requires thoughtful reflection and correlation to the effects on religious belief and practice in our communities and in the nation. This is not just a relational proximity between those shaped by Christianity and those who are characterised as 'exclusive humanist', but also within the spectrum of religious dimension that we might define in contrast with earlier periods of Christian vitality, including exemplary New Testament models.

A functional presence of 'transcendence' based on scriptural models has the effect of fuelling polemic tensions between some factions of Christianity. This is not new, but appears to be deeply embedded in differences raised between the likes of Catholics and Protestants that dates to the 16th century Reformation.

It is argued primarily by Catholic theologians and philosophers including Charles Taylor and Brad Gregory that the ructions that emerged from the challenge to Catholic authority by the Reformers, along with the emergence of ad hoc religious fervour, and scripture in the hands of ordinary believers who were untrained theologians, weakened the fabric of establishment religious authority in the 16th century. For these modern thinkers, the Protestant Reformation gave rise to the possibility of what we see as this modern form of 'secularism'.

It appears that this may mean that in addressing the challenges of the Secularization Thesis, this is not just an apologetic battle, with humanist ideas alone as the enemy, but also an internal polemic rift that may need to be humbly and sensitively explored. In a secular age, in the broadest dimension all Christian denominations engage in the battle on the same side. For many Christian leaders from the variety of denominational persuasions, established paradigms that held true in earlier contexts have been under pressure to adapt to developments that threaten 'all Christian belief' and discipleship aspirations. A movement away from concepts of 'transcendent reality' may be the fuel that fires what may be akin to a philosophic 'arms race' where dimensions including apologetic defences and demonstration of 'the authentic Christian life' have become crucial elements in emerging challenges of rising secularism. In other words, how we behave matters, and the public image of why we behave the way we do also matters.

It behoves us to make our own critical analysis, with the view that the rise of the 'exclusive humanist' secular society creates an environment of deepening disenchantment of the populace, and a marginalising of religion in the marketplace. For the co-missional leader, a framework for understanding the change, along with the navigational tools to engage in the contest of ideas from the 'watercooler' to the 'parliamentary chamber' will equip us with substance in the pursuit and practice of public Christian leadership.

A primary focus of this analysis is on the dynamic role of Christians serving in public leadership roles and the emergence of stronger Christian media in all of its forms, to connect the theoretical possibilities, with the practical professional and spiritual formation of public Christian leaders.

Endnotes

1   Lewis C.S. 1950 The Lion, The Witch and the Wardrobe, A Story for Children, Macmillan, Project Gutenberg Canada, ebook #1152 Samizdat, http://www.samizdat.qc.ca/arts/lit/PDFs/LionWitchWardrobe_CSL.pdf [Accessed 25th Oct 2018]

2   Ibid p.8

3   Ibid p.41

4   Saler M. 2006 Modernity and Enchantment: A Historiographic Review, American Historical Review, USA. http://chnm.gmu.edu/courses/omalley/393/saler.pdf p.695

5   Poem in German Language – 21st Stanza https://www.uni-due.de/lyriktheorie/texte/1788_schiller.html

6   Ibid. Saler (2006 p.696)

7   Ibid. Saler (2006 p.696)

8   Kim, Sung Ho, 2017 'Max Weber', The Stanford Encyclopedia of Philosophy (Winter 2017 Edition), Edward N. Zalta (ed.), https://plato.stanford.edu/archives/win2017/entries/weber [Accessed 11th Aug 2018]

9   Scaff L.A. 1991 Fleeing The Iron Cage: Culture, Politics, and Modernity in the Thought of Max Weber, University of California Press, USA p.88

10   Ibid p.59

11   Kim, Sung Ho, 2017 'Max Weber', The Stanford Encyclopedia of Philosophy (Winter 2017 Edition), Edward N. Zalta (ed.), https://plato.stanford.edu/archives/win2017/entries/weber 4.2

12   Ibid. p.542

13   Storey D. 2009 Breaking the Spell of the Immanent Frame: Charles Taylor's A Secular Age. Published in Rethinking Secularization: Philosophy and the Prophecy of a Secular Age (pp.177-209). www.academia.edu/1816674/ [Accessed 25th Oct 2018] p.3

14   We might include the re-formation of the nation of Israel (1948) as an obvious fulfilled biblical prophecy.

15   Saler M. 2006 Modernity and Enchantment: A Historiographic Review, American Historical Review, USA. http://chnm.gmu.edu/courses/omalley/393/saler.pdf [Accessed 24th Jun 2018]

16   Ibid 2006 pp.695-700

17   Daston L. 2001 The Nature of Nature in Early Modern Europe, p.8 https://pdfs.semanticscholar.org/5d19/a5414d061949fb60c3acf5f2662d14cd7d86.pdf

18   Ibid p. 695

19   Alexander J.C 2007 On the Interpretation of the Civil Sphere: Understanding and Contention on Contemporary Social Science, The Sociological Quarterly 48 (2007) p.643.

20   Saler (2006 p.698)

21   Saler (2006 p.700)

22   Treitel study – cited by Saler

23   Cook J.W, The Arts of Deception p. 16 - cited by Saler.

24   2007 p.22

Chapter 3:
The Value of
Transcendence

I pray that the eyes of your heart may be enlightened in order that you
may know the hope to which he has called you, the riches of his glorious
inheritance in his holy people, and his incomparably great power for us
who believe.

Ephesians 1:18-19

Transcendence and Human Flourishing

The Western concepts of 'human flourishing' are demonstrably grounded
in a biblical Judeo-Christian ethos as typified by the peaks and valleys of
pre-Christ, and post ascension biblical history. Attention to the biblical
narrative, gleaning profound concepts for human flourishing creates
a standard by which comparison can be made. In more recent history
alternative images of 'human flourishing' are contrasted with nations
founded on Western ideals including both Greco-Roman and Judeo-
Christian notions.

Australian historian Stuart Piggin, and his co-writer American historian
Robert D. Linder appear to have been very intentional about the title
of their history account of 'Evangelical Christians in Australian History
1740-1914'. Their carefully chosen title 'The Fountain of Public Prosperity'
tells the story of the effects of the spiritual characteristics that marked

the shaping of early settlers and the processes implemented in a young nation that became a springboard for economic development and social formation. Piggin and Linder[1] masterfully highlight the vitality of Christianity and the effects on the institutions founded by evangelicals including practices of governance, the legal system, banking, libraries, the press, the pulpit, and charities that shaped the formation of what has become the Australian nation. Piggin describes an evangelical sense of transcendence as 'other-worldliness' which gave a perspective on the new frontier enabling a shaping of a society living simultaneously in both worlds. He suggests these evangelicals were equipped by their faith to make the best of each world, valuing the 'transcendent' elements of their meaning system.

Historically, we can identify the rise of alternatives which have limited reference to the powerful Judeo-Christian transcendence. In other systems, authoritarian dictatorships emerge, with seemingly 'good intentions', promising their own brand of human flourishing, but ultimately end up delivering repression and in many cases hostility and oppression to opponents and dissenting minorities. Rubin[2] assesses modern dictatorship models that emerged in the developing world as sharing common characteristics. He describes the likes of Nasser (Egypt), Castro (Cuba), Khomeini (Iran), Quaddafi (Libya), Peron (Argentina) and Nyerere (Tanzania) as leaders who pretended to care for the masses who were 'ignored in the past'. It's argued that these leaders melded the inventions of Marxism and fascism with their own national history and conditions to gain a new kind of 'legitimacy'. They became populist as a 'people's tribune', nationalist as 'defender against imperialism', revolutionary as destroyers of an 'old order', and socialist mobilizing and 'managing a national economy'.

In coming to power these leaders were viewed as having brought national salvation and self-respect, improving living standards, education, and opportunities for personal advancement. In the dictator's early days of rule, promises are delivered, the old systems collapse swiftly and completely, the power of the earlier regime evaporates, and the new dominant mood is 'apocalyptic' in the glow of a leader who turns an old hierarchy upside-down. Detractors or opponents who are exiled, imprisoned or executed are dealt with under acceptance by the masses who previously suffered under earlier rule. The leader is considered the architect of a 'miracle'.

Over the course of time, for these nations, cynicism grows, some suffer new repressions, a new 'torturable' class emerges including officers or intellectuals who may challenge the dictator. Authoritarian rulers, or dictatorships are above the law, and unlike democratically elected leaders who accept a peaceful transition of power following defeat, authoritarian elites pursue a course of political survival that may also be their only option in physical survival.

The modern dictator has tools at their discretion for maintaining rule. The main attribute is the ability to communicate directly to the masses, bypassing intermediaries like newspapers and the legislature. In Nazi Germany it was called the 'Fuhrer Principle'. Under the Italian fascists a creed emerged, 'Mussolini is always right'. Under Stalin in the Soviet Union there arose Stalin's 'cult of personality', in China, Chairman Mao's *Little Red Book* was called the 'mass line'. In North Korea, Kim Il Sung developed a form of cult leadership called *juche*. The thoughts and ideologies of the charismatic dictator are often characterised as the 'third way' and made to seem attractive by the concentrated power of 'political propaganda' using modern public relations techniques. Lasting popularity rests solely on reputation generated by a leader's propaganda machine extolling honesty, patriotism, and faithfulness to the people. These leaders assume their own form of 'transcendent' rule in the absence of the type of rule we observe in Western nations where the concept of Divine 'transcendence' has been the historic foundational ethos for governance, law, human rights, business, education, and the welfare of the vulnerable.

Much more can be developed around these dimensions of 'flourishing' and the transcendence that has shaped Western societies differently to non-western cultures. In the 2010's, a significant debate emerged around the validity of teaching Western Cultural formation in Australia's 'sandstone' universities. Opponents of even the presence of a course promoting Western civilization were being criticised, because the success of the West appears 'elitist' to non-western cultures that see themselves as disadvantaged minorities. I suspect this is partly because of pressure placed on freedom of thought, the academy, and political communication, suppressing the glimmers of light that shine through the 'immanent' frame that is in denial of the virtues of Divine transcendence and the effect on the West.

A definitive discussion of secularism cannot ignore the insightful scholarship of historian Tom Holland who masterfully demonstrates that even the concept of 'secularism' is a product of Christianity. The historic contrast between the sacred and the profane, and the distinction between the pure and the corrupt are Christian formations. saecularia and religio[3] highlight the opposing dimensions of earthly appetites and commitment to Christ. Jesus introduced the distinction in his response to a question designed to entrap Him when He is asked whether it was permitted to pay taxes to pagan Rome in Matthew Chapter 22.

> [17] Tell us then, what is your opinion? Is it right to pay the imperial tax[a] to Caesar or not?" [18] But Jesus, knowing their evil intent, said, "You hypocrites, why are you trying to trap me? [19] Show me the coin used for paying the tax." They brought him a denarius, [20] and he asked them, "Whose image is this? And whose inscription?" [21] "Caesar's," they replied. Then he said to them, "So give back to Caesar what is Caesar's, and to God what is God's." (Matt 22:17-21 NIV)

The distinction between two positions is compelling. Later, the historic concept of 'secular' saeculum is introduced by St Augustine (354-430) who imagined a 'city of God' unshackled by worldly cares. In dramatic form the seeds of these ideas grew to new maturity in the formation contrasting saeculum with religio in the reforms introduced by Pope Gregory VII (1073-85). Gregory required consecration across the Christian world in anticipation of a re-ordering of the entire world in obedience to a conception of purity. So deep were his reforms that even a Caesar would be required to humble himself before a pope. Gregory argued that if the customs of rulers cannot be conformed to 'truth' they should be abolished. Gregory called his teachings 'new counsels' making a model for reformation giving the Latin West a taste of revolution.[4]

We tend to take for granted that secular 'laws' in the West also obligate our rulers as much as the common citizen. We have the formation of Christianity under God to thank for the concept of equality under the Law. Both the 'rich and powerful' and the 'poor and weak' were delivered entitlements that we've come to know as 'human-rights'. Even though early formations of Roman civil and canon law were secular, the content of Christian creeds, doctrines and morality debated in church councils created the compounding effect of refining a concept or 'truth'. Mangalwadi argues it took the blood of martyrs to win the liberty of the rule of law[5], shedding their blood in a war for tolerance and liberty.

Transcendence and Secularization

As the argument continues to deepen, in the chapters ahead I expect to form views around the 'utility' (usefulness) of the variety of communications and 'values shaping' forms of mass media, and 'new media' that have an influential effect on the spirituality, religiosity and values formation of people in the 21st century. Christian media is certainly a useful tool in expressing the Judeo-Christian concept of Divine 'transcendence', and forms part of a broader societal influence of 'transcendence' emanating from the emergence of an 'exclusive humanism'. It should be noted with caution that while philosophers like Charles Taylor may have developed a metaphoric image of an 'Immanent Frame', conclusions that there is a permanent or enduring blockage to the 'transcendent' should be resisted. Some important concepts demand deeper definition as we explore the relationship we have today with 'transcendence'.

An Exploration of Definitions – Secularism

Traditional and historic definitions of a 'secular' society don't subtract the expression of spirituality, but modern definitions do. Bouma[6] notes that under the traditional view 'secular' societies are not irreligious, anti-religious, or lacking in spirituality, and that in modern 21st Century Australia spirituality is not itself in decline, but rather the 'spirituality' has seeped out of monopolistic control of formal organisations like churches.

To reiterate earlier comments, it appears that in the 2010's and into 2020's the common definition of the word 'secular' has 'morphed' from a benign framework for the management of plurality, to its own popular formation of 'religious alternative'. Authoritative definitions of the word 'Secular' show some alignment with tradition: Oxford[7] - *'Not connected with religious or spiritual matters'*. Or, Merriam Webster[8] - *a. of or relating to the worldly or temporal – secular concerns b. not overtly or specifically religious – secular music. c. not ecclesiastical or clerical – secular courts – secular landowners.* However, a popular French definition has taken the concept deeper discouraging religious involvement in Government affairs redefining the principle of 'separation of Church and State'.

France's separation of Church and State in 1905 was in response to problems posed by Islam. Barbier[9] notes that people interpret the word 'secular' as they see fit, according to their situation and their needs. The mass of studies devoted to it tend not to clarify a definition, but rather obscure it. It has become a 'fluid, flexible notion' but broadly is defined as either 'secularism-as-separation', or 'secularism-as-neutrality'.

In Australia's modernity, where the 'Power-centric' definition is applied, anti-Christian ideologically driven sectors have adopted the word as part of their agenda. It has become the 'catch-cry' of the militant atheist and the ideological opponents of 'freedom of religious expression'. The pace with which the definition in common language use has changed, has rendered historic definitions redundant. The 'new secularism' reinforces elements of the 'failed' Secularization Thesis that portrayed a dismal fate for religion where in an age of knowledge and technology, religion will suffer fatal decline, and a new enlightened secular age based on 'exclusive humanism' will create a new form of utopia. It might appear that the historic motivations of the French Government's definitions in resistance of the 'religious excesses' of Islam, contributed to the mid-20th century rise of the 'Secularization Thesis' with consequences emanating from state policy that downplays the proliferation of all concepts expressing 'transcendence'.

Is the 'Secularization Thesis' Valid?

Social scientists are rightly sceptical about the validity of a 'universal' application of the 'Secularization Thesis'. Many including Peter L. Berger who once championed the concept now distance themselves from the validity of the idea, since too many inconsistencies have emerged to allow the theory to be universally applied. Berger[10] unequivocally argues 'the assumption that we live in a secularized world is false'. He[11] argues that globally, most nations are 'as religious as they ever have been'. He identifies resurgences in the major world religion traditions like Hinduism, Buddhism and Judaism, everything except 'Secularization'. Contrary to the Secularization Thesis, Berger identifies two 'big explosions' of religious passion in the world. One is the upsurge of Islam, and the other is the 'meteoric rise of Pentecostalism.'[12] He questions the idea that Modernity is the cause of secularization, asking how you might explain the religiosity, both socially and politically in the United States where religion is vibrant, like most of the rest of the world. Stark[13] contextualises the massive global growth of Christianity by arguing Christianity is becoming more globalised than is 'democracy, capitalism or modernity'. It's not just growth but a 'revolution' in Latin America, venturing that it is not just protestantization but 'Christianisation'. In Africa as many as half of all sub-Saharan people are now Christians. And these huge growth patterns are likely to soon be dwarfed by the growth of Christianity in China.

Europe, however, is identified as the 'big exception' to vibrant religiosity, with Western Europe having become 'very heavily secularized' compared to other parts of the world. Significantly for our considerations in this discussion, Berger[14] considers that Australia is another one of 'the exceptions' inferring that we are not as far along with Europe, but in Australia, along with Quebec in Canada secularization is occurring. In terms of the sociology of religion in Europe there is no single reason for secularization, but he identifies the most important reason as the terms of the relationship between church and state.

Until the 19th century 'Church and State' were closely connected, in contrast to the separation that existed in the US. Modernity is not 'the cause' of secularization, however in certain cases Berger admits that 'it may be.' Davie[15] argues that in Europe, as 'the big exception', three formative themes have shifted and evolved over time including the presence of Judeo-Christian monotheism, Greek rationalism, and Roman organisation. A close-knit history, and the importance of future unity form a context for what has become an 'unchurched' population, rather than a 'secular' population.

At the turn of the 20th century there was not an identified abdication of religious belief, but an abandonment of 'many deep-seated religious inclinations.' Davie[16] builds upon a popular connection for secularization in Europe dating back to the Reformation, where the rise of 'individualism' that threatened the communal basis of religious belief and behaviour, and 'rationality' that removed many of the purposes of religion and made many beliefs implausible. The two combined resulting effects of the Reformation in 'rationality' and 'individualism' changed the nature of religion in the modern world.

As Europe's political life became more sophisticated, religion diminished in the public sphere. Davie[17] notes that Europe's religious life became something of a 'prototype' of global religiosity along with the now failed assumption that all other nations would follow suit and the modern world would automatically secularize. This is what makes Europe the 'big exception', because this has not been the story of the rest of the world, especially in glaring contrast to American society with its vibrant religiosity along with its well-developed modernity. Davie[18] concludes that Europe's churches today function on a form of 'vicarious memory' delegating to 'Church' some elements people can't do themselves like articulating meaning at times of national crisis or celebration. Further reflection beyond this study would explore similarities in the Australian context, perhaps clarifying evidence for Berger's suggestion that Australia may also be 'one of the exceptions', and that secularization is happening.

Patterns of Secularization

Pollack[19] suggests that trying to 'define the indefinable' and produce 'causal statements' based on religious experience and 'measuring feelings' is considered a 'deadly sin' in the European sociology of religion. Part of the 'indefinable nature' is the fact of inability for categories to be applied universally, and the need to rely on specifics in historic contexts. Pollack suggests that support for the Secularization Thesis has become unpopular within 'fashionable strands' of sociology and is considered 'outdated and obsolete'. However, his rare support of the validity of the Secularization Thesis comes not as one who sees the sophisticated theoretical argumentation, but as one who is persuaded by the overwhelming empirical evidence provided in favour of the Secularization Theory.

The work of Norris and Inglehart[20] (2004) entitled 'Sacred and Secular' including their time series of church attendance or 'belief in God' over an unprecedented timespan dating back to 1947 with data from over 80 countries has produced statistical analysis that strikingly demonstrates the applicability of the major assumptions of the Secularization theory. Norris and Inglehart have been able to argue that the comparison of many decades of data gives a more reliable indication of patterns, that show the significant causes underlying the behaviours and attitudes like the 'erosion of religious beliefs' that have undermined churchgoing habits and practices. Furthermore, they predict[21] that globally, the expanding gap between the sacred and the secular societies will have consequences for world politics, making the role of religion 'increasingly salient on the global agenda'.

One of the great challenges for modern political policymakers, philosophers, theologians, and the 'gate-keepers' of Christian media content is to deal systematically with the reality of transcendent phenomena, and the legitimacy of people's experiences. Corr[22] argues reflective analysis does not 'discover or disclose' transcendent reality' in people's experience, but what comes to light are 'signals of transcendence' that are part of the common human experience.

While a naturalistic interpretation of transcendent experience is always possible, a complete denial of transcendence is a denial of the richness of human experience. Within Churches where traditional religious beliefs may have become empty of meaning we risk being swamped by a plurality of worldviews. This modern phenomenon made possible by great leaps forward in the digital information age, brings us 'full circle' back to basic questions of 'truth' including basic signals of transcendence as a personal re-discovery of the 'finger of God' in supernatural phenomena.

The Modern Social Imaginary— A Sense of Legitimacy

The expanding gap between sacred and secular, is not only an individual issue, but extends to the shaping of prevailing culture. Charles Taylor[23] uses the term 'social imaginary' to embody something deeper, broader, and even more complex than the typical explanations of intellectual schemes used to describe 'social reality'. Understanding 'social imaginary' is to appreciate social reality in a 'disengaged mode'. It's the contrast between 'thinking' and 'imagining', reflecting on social existence, fitting together with others, relationality, and deeper notions that underlie the expectations. This concept for Taylor goes against the grain of intellectual theory in the minds of the elite and tries to identify what 'ordinary people' imagine about their social surroundings as expressed in images, stories and legends. The concept of 'social imaginary' is capturing the way our senses draw on our whole world. It's a collective sense-giving for large groups of people, rather than grappling only with theory, which may be the possession of a small minority. For large groups, and whole societies it is the 'common understanding that makes possible common practices and a widely shared sense of legitimacy.'

Modernity and Transcendence— Shifting Structures

As change extends across whole societies, there are those who will be winners, and others who will be losers. Michael Saler[24] argues that 'Modernity' is one of the most ambiguous words in the historian's lexicon. A broad outline signifies a mixture of political, social, intellectual, economic, technological, and psychological factors, which permeated the West from the sixteenth to the nineteenth centuries. It's the rise of the autonomous and rational subjects, the rise of liberal and democratic states, the emergence of psychologism, and the dominance of secularism, nationalism, capitalism, industrialism, urbanism, consumerism, and scientism.

The main characteristic of modernity that is consistent with these developments is the concept of 'disenchantment.' Mark Elvin[25] argues that formulating 'modernity' only in terms rationalizing economics, politics or religion falls short. His definition is not based on chronology but enables combinations of 'modern' and 'non-modern' elements. 'Modernity' is a complex of realized concerns with 'power.' Modernity is 'the *power* to change the structure of systems.'[26] Power over human beings, states, groups or individuals. Power over nature in a practical way in terms of economic production. And power over nature, in the form of capacity for expressed understanding. 'Power' is thought of as a 'capacity to direct energy.'[27] And with a changing social imaginary comes the dangers and opportunities that accompany a shift in 'power' structure.

Enchantment to Disenchantment – 500 Years

Charles Taylor approaches his idea of a 'Secular Age' with the contrast of a view of life in a medieval society[28], with a modern context that has become possible as a product of 'intellectual multiplication.' In describing what the new secular imaginary looks like, he establishes background dating 500 years to the time of the 16th Century Protestant Reformation. He identifies features of that historic upheaval to include three dimensions that functioned as obstacles to 'unbelief' leading him to suggest that in the 16th century it was impossible 'not' to believe in God because of:

1. The natural world they lived in, which had its place in the cosmos they imagined testified to divine purpose and action. The natural order including storms, droughts, floods, plagues and years of exceptional fertility and flourishing were considered 'acts of God'.
2. The existence of society in terms of 'a Kingdom'. In practice societies, parishes, boroughs, or guilds could not be conceived as being something grounded in human action. Something higher was necessary.
3. And thirdly, people lived in an 'Enchanted' world, not with the modern connotations on 'light and fairies', but in the Pagan world, where the outlook of European peasants would have been that the Christian God was the ultimate guarantee that 'good' would triumph, or at least hold the forces of darkness at bay.

Over the past 500 years, the difference between then and now, is that these three features of 'enchantment' have vanished. For Taylor this is the status of what happens when there is a recession of the cosmos before a universe to be understood in mechanistic terms.[29]
He identifies the period 'post-Reformation' as being the end of paganism and polytheism. This 'disenchantment' describes an end to the idea of a cosmos of 'spirits respondent to humans'.

Transcendence and Judeo-Christian Culture Formation

Judeo-Christian perspectives on 'transcendence', the 'cultural mandate' and the application of 'power' emanate from Genesis and are acutely important for our understanding of human communication and the 'utility' of modern media. Essentially, the character of 'communication' emerges at the beginning as Adam is tasked with the naming of God's creatures. Quentin Schultze[30] notes that this initial task is a basic symbol of the mandate of God to Adam and is given as a foundation of 'culture stewardship'. The responsible use of 'symbols' in communication would be for the care and protection of the creation.

With humanity as a communicative species, human relationships would become possible and people groups would be able to act collectively through words, and images. The emerging meaningful frames of reference become 'culture'. The word 'communication' comes from the same Latin root as 'communion', 'community', and the politically charged concept of 'communism'. [31]

'Communication' is the currency of modern mass media. It is the process we use to make common actions, meanings and creating the 'artefacts' of organisations, communities and whole societies. The 'artefacts' are the essential components of what is visible in an organisation as Edgar Schein[32] notes, these include the language, products and technology, and all of the architecture of the physical environment. But communication in respect to modernity has what Schultze describes as a 'two-edged sword'.

1. On the first 'edge' mass media contributes to worldwide modernisation where the modern culture is fast becoming global.
2. On the other side of the sword, the alternative 'edge' is that modernity itself is interpreted through a 'cultural lens' that emanates from the media. The downside risk to a 'flourishing' society is the permeation of 'false-consciousness' or a misperception of reality, be that through advertising, economic considerations, politics or religion.

When humanity fails to exercise ethical 'communication' according to a Genesis model of 'God first', the risk is sustained alienation from God and His ways. The consequences may be illustrated in the history of Israel as the people of God. We might contrast the developments through the Old Testament where flourishing occurs under contextual relational communication with God as an active acknowledgement of the Divine transcendence. This flourishing demonstrated in the times of the

Children of Israel was because of Divine blessing according to obedience to the 'law' of God given to Moses.

The alternative embodied moral and cultural 'decline', and replaced the upswing of flourishing because of ignorance or rebellion as a choice to identify with the governance ethos of surrounding Pagan nations.

The 'cultural mandate' has a vision beyond the immediate plan of God for the redemption of His people, first Israel and then the Church. Key to the outcomes of the cultural mandate and salvation is the substantial physical and spiritual result illustrated in the demonstrable aspects of how nations flourish.

Pennington[33] describes aspects of 'Human flourishing' as a meta-theme for all humanity where a desire to live in peace, security, love, health and happiness are common to all not just as cultural values, but as motivation for those who have belief in religion, and for those who hold a position of rejection of religion. Human flourishing is a strong biblical theme culminating in promises of abundant and eternal life. The Hebrew word 'shalom' takes us beyond the defined greeting of 'peace', to a state or relationship reflecting a more significant depth of Divine 'peace'. 'Shalom' refers to completeness, maturity, and well-being relationally, economically and in health.

God's redemption of His chosen people, and the New Testament Church is described as 'Shalom', because the result is human flourishing. Pennington notes this includes not only a sense of tranquillity in the removal of enmity between God and humanity, but also of reconciliation and personal tranquillity between people and with creation. He suggests that one of the singularly most important passages in scripture for a 'whole of Bible theology' is in the scripture in Isaiah 52:7 *'How beautiful on the mountains are the feet of those who bring good news, who proclaim peace, and who bring good tidings, who proclaim salvation, who say to Zion, "Your God reigns!"'* It's much more than just a nice sentiment, when we understand the power of the good news is accompanied by 'shalom'.

In the Old Testament God is 'King', who establishes his reign on the earth through His people. The implication is that 'flourishing' is a core component of Bible teaching on salvation and redemption. Spirituality and godliness are only part of the Divine project, where physical, economic, psychological and relational flourishing are consequential outcomes of the cultural mandate, and reliant on humanity's hold on 'transcendence'.

In the Sermon on the Mount (Matt 5-7) the 'wise' believer builds his house on the rock and weathers the storm. The believer stands with dignity in contrast to the 'fool' who builds his house on the sand and is overwhelmed when the storm comes. God centred human flourishing is part of the 'discipleship mission' of the Church, informed by the reality of the coming Kingdom, centred on Jesus and empowered by the Holy Spirit.

Without this anchoring, the pursuit of human flourishing is driven by human reason, misdirected in relation to the purposes of God, not biblical, and therefore without reference to Divine transcendence. The rise and fall of human flourishing may teeter on the status of a nation's application of transcendent realities, otherwise it is purely a secular pursuit, and carries the risk of deterioration and human misery under authoritarian humanist rule.

Further Old Testament considerations beyond the mandate to steward creation, include the concept of man being created to have 'fellowship' with God through praise, worship and obedience (Isaiah 43:21 and Gen. 2:15). Kim[34] notes 'walking with God' as in the life of Enoch (Gen. 5:24; Heb 11:5) and Noah (Gen 6:9) implies 'relationship' that pleases God where the transcendence of God accompanies His immanent appearance to man.

Abraham is called a 'Friend of God' (2 Chron 20:7; Isaiah 41:8; Jam 2:23) intimating capacity to have fellowship with the Creator. The immanent relationship intensifies when God moves to establish a 'Father-son relationship' with His people (Exod 4:22; 2 Sam 7:14; Jer 3:19; Hos 11:1). This relational immanence of 'sonship' continues into the New Testament where Jesus indicates that believers have a right to call God

'Father' (John 1:12).

In the Old and New Testaments, the presence of the Holy Spirit is evidence of the continued immanence of God as a presence in the life of believers. Kim[35] notes the 'Spirit of God was hovering on the waters' (Gen: 1:2) and later He's described as an eagle hovering over 'it's young' as God's people (Deut. 32:11). This same 'Spirit of God' with believers in the Old Testament gives empowerment to defeat the enemies of Israel as in the case of Gideon (Jud 6:34) and Saul (1 Sam 11:6). In the New Testament on the day of Pentecost the promised Spirit of God is shown to dwell among believers permanently and is evidence of God's immanence among believers.

The importance of influencing culture is elevated to highest levels in the outcomes and consequences of acknowledging the 'transcendent' God. As communication is the '*process of creating, developing and maintaining culture*'[36] the content of media is an overlooked pre-requisite that must arrest our attention, since right now, secularised media is far from God and in many cases is anti-Christian.

Endnotes

1   Piggin S., Linder R.D. 2018 The Fount of Public Prosperity: Evangelical Christians in Australian History 1740-1914, Monash University Press, Clayton, Australia. P.15,17.

2   Rubin B. 1987 Modern Dictators: Third World Coup Makers, Strongmen, and Populist Tyrants, Gloria Centre Global Research in International Affairs, McGraw-Hill, New York, USA, p.8.

3   Holland T. 2020 Dominion: The Making of the Western Mind, Abacus, London, UK. P.211

4   Ibid. p. 215

5   Mangalwadi V. 2019 This Book Changed Everything Vol.1 The Bible's Amazing Impact on Our World, Sought After Media, Pasadena USA. P.87.

6   Bouma G. 2009 Australian Soul: Religion and Spirituality in the Twenty-first Century. Cambridge University Press, Melbourne, Australia. P.5.

7   Oxford Dictionary - https://en.oxforddictionaries.com/definition/secular [Accessed 2nd Sept 2018]

8   Meriam Webster Dictionary - https://www.merriam-webster.com/dictionary/secular [Accessed 2nd Sept 2018}

9   Barbier M. 2005 Towards a Definition of French Secularism, (Translated by Elliot G.), https://www.diplomatie.gouv.fr/IMG/pdf/0205-Barbier-GB-2.pdf p.1

10 Berger P.L. 1999 The Desecularization of the World, Resurgent Religion and World Politics, Eerdmans, Michigan, USA. P.2

11 Berger P. 2011 – Youtube Dr Peter Berger on Religion & Modernity, Faith Angle Forum on Religion, Politics and Public Life. https://www.youtube.com/watch?v=bv3aLp27sO4 [Accessed 29th Sept 2018)

12 Ibid. 2011 - Youtube

13 Stark R. 2005 The Victory of Reason, How Christianity Led to Freedom, Capitalism, and Western Success, Random House, New York, USA. P.234

14 Ibid. 2011 - Youtube

15 Davie G. 1999 Europe, The Exception That Proves the Rule, Chapter 5. The Desecularization of the World, Resurgent Religion and World Politics, Edited by Peter L Berger, Eerdmans, Michigan, USA. P.66

16 Ibid p.74

17 Ibid p.76

18 Ibid p.82

19 Pollack D. 2006 Reviewed Work: Sacred and Secular: Religion and Politics Worldwide by Pippa Norris, Ronald Inglehart. Reviewed by Detlef Pollack, European Journal of Sociology Archives Européennes de Sociologie / Europäisches Archiv für Soziologie Vol. 47, No. 3 (2006), pp. 417-420. [Accessed 30th August 2018]

20 Norris P., Inglehart R. 2004 Sacred and Secular: Religion and Politics Worldwide, Cambridge Studies in Social Theory, Religion and Politics, Cambridge University Press. P.35

21 Ibid p.241

22 Corr C.A. Peter Berger's Angels and Philosophy of Religion, University of Chicago Press, The Journal of Religion Oct 1972, Volume 52, Issue 4. p.435

23 Ibid p.171

24 Ibid p.294

25 Elvin M. 1986 A Working Definition of 'Modernity', Past & Present, No 113 (Nov.1986) pp.209-213, Oxford University Press on behalf of the Past and Present Society. P.210

26 Ibid p.211

27 Ibid p.211 Examples: (1) 18th century thermodynamic revolution discovered how to turn heat (undirected energy) into usable work (directed energy). (2) And, military power or internal administrative control increases output per person of goods and services.

28 Ibid p.25

29   Ibid p.357

30   Schultze Q.J. 1993 Media and Modernity, Transformation, Vol 10, No. 4 The Bible, Truth and Modernity (October 1993) pp. 27-29, Sage Publications.   p.27

31   Ibid p.27

32   Schein E.H 2017 Organizational Culture and Leadership, 5th Edition, Wiley & Sons, New Jersey, USA. P.17

33   Pennington J.T. 2015 A Biblical Theology of Human Flourishing, Institute for Faith, Work & Economics

34   Kim, S.M. 2009, Transcendence of God, A Comparative Study of the Old Testament and the Qur'an, PhD Thesis, University of Pretoria, South Africa. p.217,218.

35   Ibid p.236

36   Ibid p.27

Chapter 4:
Secular Transcendence –
'Fools Gold'

"As the heavens are higher than the earth,
so are my ways higher than your ways
and my thoughts than your thoughts."

Isaiah 55:9

A Secular Jesus—
Judeo-Christian vs New Paganism

Christians today see the Bible as 'the source' of God's wisdom and
revelation. It is the primary place we immerse ourselves, to appreciate
the contrasting dimensions and consequences of 'belief vs unbelief',
and the way the world functions differently when viewed through
a 'transcendence' lens. Belief is the key to unlocking the riches of
transcendence and understanding the vulnerabilities that come when the
sense of that transcendence is waning or lost.

How does a Secular Age differ from an age of Paganism where the worship
of other 'gods' results in futile thinking? When Judeo-Christian moors
are abandoned with the goal of building a secular philosophic 'Tower
of Babel', we may need to question whether the same consequences
of confusion and chaos are likely? Alistair McGrath[1] in addressing
the conflicts between Atheism and Christianity notes that among the

eventualities of opposing God is the tendency to 'transcendentalize alternatives' including things like 'liberty' and 'equality'. He calls them quasi-divine authorities which none are permitted to challenge, noting the example of the French Revolution when traditional notions of God were relegated to obsolescence and replaced by a new form of 'transcendentalized human values'. If the dreams of Atheists were to 'all come true' McGrath[2] argues that the divisions within humanity would not end as the utopians might believe, but that the emerging communities would 'self-define', and begin to identify those who are 'in' as friends and those who are 'out' as enemies.

A Secular Image of Jesus

Research appears to show that Australians relate more closely to a 'secularised image of Jesus' rather than the image of Jesus we read about in scripture. Findings of 2016 research into Faith and Belief in Australia[3] indicate that faith and belief are changing with the number of Australians not identifying with a religion or spiritual belief, rising to almost one in three not identifying with a religion. As the pendulum swings away from predominance of the historic Judeo-Christian moors, attitudes to biblically founded morality and acceptance of Divine 'transcendence' appear to be changing. Of interest, are the findings of research into 'repellents' and 'belief blockers' identified in Australian research. They may be aligned to disenchantment changes in perception, that we may be able to correlate to the emerging political and media reporting landscape as they relate to concepts of 'transcendence'.

As political policy takes on a religiously dismissive fervour, and media reporting applying the blowtorch to long held Christian morality, the public attraction to Christian faith and belief has become strained. Social researcher Mark McCrindle in his research[4] notes that some of the commonly accepted expressions of Christian faith have become 'repellents' to Christianity in the Australian community.

Results show 'Hearing from public figures and celebrities who are examples of Christian faith' (75%) are no longer as acceptable and embraced by the wider community. Also, less acceptable to the community palette are 'Miraculous stories of people being healed or supernatural occurrences' (65%), and 'Philosophical discussion and debating ideas' (34%). The intensifying pressure in these categories appears to correlate to the idea that Australians are deepening a resistance to concepts of 'transcendence' reflected by public Christian leadership figures, and that testimonies of a transcendent spirituality such as 'answered prayer' or stories of the miraculous are less welcome. The research found that the biggest 'belief blockers' that inhibit Australians from engaging with Christianity resulted in direct opposition to long-held biblically founded moral and faith issues.

The biggest 'belief blocker' was the Church's stance on homosexuality (47% block completely, or significantly). Secondly, 'How could a loving God allow people to go to hell?' (43%). And thirdly, supernatural elements, like 'miracles, angels, demons, and resurrection.' McCrindle[5] suggests that these responses may be because of negative influences on perceptions about Christians including publicity from the fallout from institutional child sexual abuse, or church leaders involved in scandals. Religious 'wars' rated second to abuse issues, and thirdly 'hypocrisy' fuelling the perception of 'judgementalism.' But, it's not only the negatives that reinforce evidence of growing disenchantment, but also the apparent misunderstanding of the person of Christ, as portrayed by the Church.

The attribute of Jesus that Australians most positively connect with is His 'love.' This 'love' connection strikes a chord across regular church attenders (73%), those who identify with Christianity but never go to church (62%), non-Christians who are warm to Christianity (56%) and, also for those who are non-Christian who are cold to Christianity (21%). Of interest in these responses, is the absence of attributes that reflect Jesus 'transcendence.' The most popular 'other' words people use to relate to Jesus include the second choice after 'love', the word 'hope', and the third is 'care.'[6]

Gen Z positively connects with Jesus' 'wisdom' (38%) and 'strength' (36%). The older generations connect with 'truth' (Builders 46%, Baby Boomers 39%, and Gen X 30%)[7]. It appears that Australians did not warm to connecting Jesus with concepts of 'salvation, grace, or miracles.' For further reflection we might note that there are a growing number of Australians who most closely relate to a 'secular Jesus' or the Jesus of history who has little to do with the present day.

Denial of Divine Transcendence— The Apostle's Warning

In the famous interview between Jesus and Pontius Pilate (John 18:28 – 19:16) ahead of his sentence to crucifixion, Jesus makes a statement of his purpose, '*The reason I was born and came into the world is to testify to the truth. Everyone on the side of truth listens to me.*' As we have been building on foundations in the early chapters, the concept of absolute truth is only possible with recognition of higher 'transcendence.' But Pilate hearing the exhortation to recognise the presence of Divine transcendent reality retorts with words that echo the 'immanence' of our own modern age. His question '*What is truth?*' (vs.38) is infused with a denial of his own God, since Pilate himself was a Jew (vs 35).

Soon after seeing no way to deny the angry mob's calls for crucifixion, Pilate threatens a now silent Jesus with his own superior power and position, saying '*Don't you realise I have power either to free you or to crucify you?*' Indian philosopher Vishal Mangalwadi[8] contends that when we believe that 'truth' is unknowable, 'we rob it of any authority.' What remains is 'brute force, exclusively wielded by those who claim power.' Mangalwadi argues that these consequences extend today, to nations that refuse 'truth', who stand already condemned to life under the rulership of 'sinful men.'

The Apostle Paul in his epistle to the Romans appears to reflect this line of thinking with an emphatic expression based on his first century observation of what happens to good people, and even God's people, when their knowledge of God becomes hardened. He reflects that the 'loss of Divine transcendence' leaves a moral and spiritual void, and the object of devotion and desire becomes misdirected. I've highlighted words in this prominent passage from Romans 1:21-28 (NIV) that illustrates disenchantment and the 'consequences' of denial of Divine transcendence as observed in the first century:

> *21 For although they knew God, they neither glorified him as God nor gave thanks to him, but their **thinking became futile** and their foolish **hearts were darkened**. 22 Although they claimed to be wise, they became fools 23 and **exchanged the glory of the immortal God** for images made to look like a mortal human being and birds and animals and reptiles.*

> *24 Therefore God gave them over in the sinful desires of their hearts to sexual impurity for the degrading of their bodies with one another. 25 **They exchanged the truth about God for a lie, and worshiped and served created things rather than the Creator**—who is forever praised. Amen.*

> *26 Because of this, **God gave them over to shameful lusts**. Even their women exchanged natural sexual relations for unnatural ones. 27 In the same way the **men also abandoned natural relations with women** and were inflamed with lust for one another. Men committed shameful acts with other men, and **received in themselves the due penalty for their error**.*

> *28 Furthermore, just as **they did not think it worthwhile to retain the knowledge of God**, so God gave them over to a **depraved mind**, so that they do what ought not to be done.* (Romans 1:21-28 NIV)

This first century observation is an authoritative inspired biblical insight into the practical consequences, of what happens when imbalance develops, and humanist materialism usurps the transcendent supernatural social imaginary. The alternatives to the worship of the immortal transcendent God, whether they be actual idols made of 'wood or stone,' or newly developed 'quasi-divine authorities' appear to have the same outcomes, and one might speculate as the Apostle Paul warns, the same consequences.

Biblical and Theological issues—
Transcendence and Immanence

The Divine 'transcendence' of God is not 'hidden' Neither is it a subjective philosophical concept. Transcendence is a prominent foundation from the very first verse in Genesis 1:1 - *'In the beginning God created the heavens and the earth'*. Without any ambiguity, God is described as 'creator' and therefore as sovereign ruler. This transcendence does not inhibit God from entering His creation, nor does it stifle His communication with creation.

The fuller picture of God's presence includes His 'immanence'. It's the way we describe his presence 'within' the created universe, as the Psalmist writes *'Where shall I go from your Spirit? Or where shall I flee from your presence?'* (Psalm 139:7)

The historic theological understanding of the biblical God as 'Trinity' is the only model of both 'transcendence' and 'immanence' in perfect harmony. As Willsey[9] notes, each of the persons of the Trinity is at the same time 'transcendent' to each of the others, and simultaneously sharing the same essence 'co-equally and co-extensively'. This perichoresis deepens our understanding of the interpenetration of persons of the Trinity sharing the Divine essence. Each of the persons of the Godhead is involved in the existence and actions of the 'other two', and yet remaining in 'distinct individualization of the essence'. God is transcendent to the creation, not 'one with it', as is the error of pantheism. Functionally, God is immanent in a relational capacity with creation, everywhere present and active. In this secular age, the concept of an 'Immanent Frame' illustrates the minimising of the connection between Divine Transcendence and Divine Immanence and is left with a 'humanist immanence' without or in denial of the Divine transcendence.

While the 'Immanence of God' affirms His personal closeness to creation, the 'Transcendence of God' affirms His status as 'independent' of creation. St Anselm's 11th century reflection on Divine transcendence[10] connects the 'eternity' of God, with 'created things' that have not yet experienced their part in eternity which is yet to come. God is before all and transcends all. Nothing exists without Him. Created things can be conceived to have an end, but God 'by no means.' For St Anselm cogent reasoning asserts God to be powerful and 'all-powerful', above every substance, without end or beginning, for if God did have an end, or beginning, he would not be from true 'eternity'. [11]

The Apostle Paul described a simple definition of this 'closeness' to the philosophers at the Areopagus on Mars Hill saying God is '...not far from any one of us, for in him we live and move and have our being.' (Acts 17:27-28). Immanence has various dimensions. Not even the term 'wisdom', embodies the full revelation of God whose elevation is far above all things, transcendent with a peculiar natural character. On the 'closer' end of the spectrum, Millard Erickson describes 'immanence' as the 'activity of God within' nature, human nature, and history.[12]

These concepts of the 'immanence of God' were not veiled in biblical times. At the very beginning in Genesis 2:7 we read that God 'breathed' into man and he became a living being. These thoughts are reiterated in the book of Job with several references to Job who says, 'the breath of God is in my nostrils' (Job 27:3) and, 'The Spirit of God has made me; the breath of the Almighty gives me life.' (Job 33:4).

Within nature even the birds of the air, and the flowers of the field are ascribed by Jesus as being under the direct control of God (Matt 6:26-29). To speak of God as being 'transcendent' alone, de-emphasises His capacity for being personal. An imbalance of understanding of transcendence and immanence has consequences. Erickson[13] warns of 'immanence' in an extreme form resembling the concept of 'pantheism' or the idea that God and nature are equal. In pantheism, nature minus God equals nothing, but God minus nature also equals nothing. According to the ideas of pantheism God does not exist without the creation of the natural order. For Christians it's important to recognise that while God is both transcendent and immanent, he has an 'independent status' to nature.

Historically there have been excesses and imbalances in appreciation of the nature of God's relation to the whole of creation. As Hammond[14] notes both Transcendence and Immanence are descriptive of God's 'omnipresence'. Those imbalanced views that have led to error have included:

1. An over-emphasis on God's inscrutable mystery leading to 'Agnosticism'.
2. Over-emphasis on God's transcendence leads to 'Deism'.
3. Stressing His immanence results in 'Pantheism'.
4. Stressing 'personality' – Theism.

Christianity has blended the alternatives in harmony where each one in balance gives an impression of God, who is immanent in the world, yet distinct from it. He is the self-existent one who inhabits eternity, as Paul writes '*one God and Father of all, who is over all and through all and in all*.' (Eph 4:6)

Secular Transcendence – A Critique

To appreciate the God who is both 'transcendent' and 'immanent' gives us a context in which we might understand the imbalances developing in individuals, and broadly in nations. 'Secular Transcendence' appears to be a contradiction or an oxymoron. Anti-Christian, atheist arguments describe the concept whereby individuals or collective groups experience a perceived 'spirituality' defined more closely to reaching 'higher level' feelings of happiness, forgiveness and aspirations for the welfare of humanity. These are the descriptors used by positive psychologist Jonathan Haidt[15] who argues that most people consider themselves to be 'spiritual' in some way. He contends that forms of 'secular transcendence' go beyond the alternative pursuits of meditation techniques, psychedelic drug taking, or forms of eastern exercise or dance. He uses a simple metaphor referenced to William James describing a person as being like a 'house with many rooms.' Inside the house, a door appears 'out of nowhere' and opens to a staircase. On climbing the staircase people appear to experience an altered state of consciousness. Haidt[16] argues that religious groups have been helping people climb the staircase and experience higher level 'feelings' replacing the state of their 'self'.

Haidt also suggests that self-transcendence is found in nature, and at 'rave parties', and significantly, through the corporate experiences of communities and nations in the pursuit of nationalistic ideals like 'going to war' where the experience of soldiers in battle, or the common aspiration of a people brought together through conflict have a 'common cause' that creates 'special' moments. He argues that for the soldier in the heat of battle, the promise of immortality may make easier, feelings of self-sacrifice. The 'self' melts away and it feels good and uplifting.

Haidt[17] references Durkheim's description of humanity as having two levels – 'homo-duplex'. The first is the level of the 'profane' as ordinary or common, and contrasted with the second level - 'sacred'. For people who consider themselves 'religious' Durkheim believed that the function of religion was to unite people into a group, or moral community. A trigger he calls a 'phase change' can take people beyond individual goals. Anything that unites people can take on an air of sacredness that a team will fight to defend. He illustrates his point by acknowledging what 'collective joy' must have been experienced by the British at the announcement of the end of WWII, or the 'collective anger' of the Egyptians in the Tahrir Square protests, or the 'collective grief' of Americans following the 9-11 terror attacks on New York.

Haidt is asking the question, 'Is the staircase a feature of evolutionary design? Or is it a 'bug' like a mistake in the system?' His observation is that the challenge of modern life is to 'find a staircase'. He says all people are searching for their staircase in a world where modern secular society is built to satisfy our lower profane selves.

Positive Psychologists like Jonathan Haidt are described as the psychological community's 'optimists'. However, his critics argue[18] that Haidt is promoting Positive Psychology's new emotion called 'elation' with champions like Barack Obama and Oprah Winfrey. We might expect something different, in how this same message from Haidt, delivered to a different cultural mix other than a Western affluent audience, or at a different time than the present, would be received, where the positive attributes of self-sacrifice and compassion were not as readily recognisable as they are in a nation founded upon Judeo-Christian virtues.

Haidt denies 'Divine Transcendence'. He anticipates that people 'climbing the stairs' will naturally seek the manifestation of humanity's higher or better nature. This, of course is a contradiction to the modern secular idea that passions are neither good, nor bad. Other emotions like 'fear' and 'evil' are also prevalent, but the secular case denies the presence of a 'master intellect' to rule the emotions. Haidt's flaw is the same as any modern godless argument. He relies on the goodness of what appears in Western thinking which is easily connected to the continuing residual presence of historic Christian permeation in present day western society.

The inherent weakness in the pursuit of 'secular transcendence' is simply put, that those things measured as morally good, or morally evil are only 'relative', since these concepts in a disenchanted world are only evaluated by human reason. For the Christian believer, concepts of a 'revealed' Divine presence including the permeation of His presence (biblical commandments) as an image of the character of a transcendent moral God, are substantially affirmed in the revelation of the incarnate Christ as the perfect 'image' of God in both 'transcendence' and 'immanence'.

Christians see the aspiration to 'goodness' as being enabled by the transcendent empowering of God the Holy Spirit, affirming a process of sanctifying conformity to the revealed image of Christ. This New

78

Testament historic descriptive affirms the presence of 'external' influence upon individuals in communities being rescued from a 'fallen' state and restored by relational connection and reconciliation to God who is 'transcendent'. The danger of relying on an emotion like 'elation' on Haidt's internal 'staircase' is 'mistaking this secular transcendent emotion for a prima-facie good'.[19]

On the explanation of religion as a rationally driven formation of 'community', Haidt[20] however, makes a very astute insight, as one that contradicts his own argument. He speculates on a practical consequence that is presented as something resembling a 'cost-benefit analysis'. He observes that, 'The very ritual practices that the New-Atheists dismiss as costly, inefficient, and irrational turn out to be the solution to one of the hardest problems humans face: co-operation without kinship'.

Haidt recognises that it is 'sacredness' that is the binding agent bringing people together. Selfish and contentious people will refuse to voluntarily cohere, and without coherence nothing will be affected. This assumption can't be easily dismissed and is demonstrably part of the constitution of humanity significantly defined in a biblical sense. Haidt denies divine transcendence, but recognises the corporate and societal benefits of co-operation without kinship. What unites the people from generation to generation across cultural bounds? The answer is – a 'transcendent' God.

Belief in the Divine, transcendent God of the Israelites enabled the formation of a 'people for Himself' as promised to Abraham, delivered under Moses, and extended to the Gentile world through Christ. The New Testament result of this formation expands to the 'ends of the earth' through the Church which only coinheres as a 'body' in the process of co-operation and co-mission.

In a 'fallen' state people resist moral coherence and require enforced rule by 'charismatic elites'. But with 'transcendent' otherness, acknowledged as a 'higher ruler beyond humanity' the enabling of a nation to form and flourish became a distinctive for the Children of

Israel, and a distinctive in the formation of the 'new humanity' formed in Jesus Christ.

Haidt's illustration of ascending the 'inner staircase' is a humanist rationalist way of describing a phenomenon that some experience, without the permission or nurture of positive psychology. We may speculate that on exposure to both the cognitive reasoning, and the experiential presence of God there is an 'innate' apprehension of the 'sacred' in contrast to the 'secular' indicating the longings of human spirituality.

The so-called 'secular transcendence' can certainly be contrived, shaped and manipulated, but it appears more closely aligned, and perhaps too generously, to the metaphor of 'watching a 3-D movie on a flat-screen TV.' Wearing special 3D glasses may produce an illusion, or the appearance of an artificial third dimension, but it remains only a shadow of the reality of Divine transcendence.

The Christian experience of 'believing' opens the heart, mind and spirit of the individual to new horizons, and new dimensions, with a 'depth of field' that comes by illumination understood in theological terms as God revealing reality, or like the restoration of sight to the blind.

In John 9:1-41 Jesus heals the man born blind after putting mud on his eyes. In the ensuing debate over this man's blindness and the fact of his being able to see again comes the deeper message to Jesus' hearers, and to all humanity. In vs 40 some of the Pharisees ask Jesus '*What? Are we blind too?*' The point of the narrative is that we were 'ALL' born blind. Even though we can see our immanent surroundings, it is 'belief' that opens the eyes to the presence and active purpose of God. Revelation triggered by 'belief' opens the eyes to the immediate 'depth of field' which is only accessible when looking 'outside the immanent frame' or beyond the limitations of the 'flat screen' that holds humanity captive.

Secular transcendence is a reasoned attempt to hold a spiritual philosophy, but without a formal adherence to a religious foundation.

The 'Spiritual' section of your local bookstore is packed with self-help titles and the pursuit of happiness. It's a form of psychologism conforming to a scientific worldview seeking a form of 'truth' that does not come from a 'higher power'.

The emergence of mindfulness meditation and a secularised form of yoga are the Eastern equivalence to a secular transcendence, and may best be described as religiously 'humanist' attempts to rise above the material world and manage behaviours by focusing thoughts and feelings. Indian philosopher Vishal Mangalwadi describes the Buddhist origins of these eastern techniques as 'sophisticated philosophies, psychology, rituals and psycho-technologies, to try to escape life and its sufferings'.[21] They are 'pessimistic' because Buddhism sees 'suffering' as the essence of life. In our present day these humanist forms of 'secular transcendence' which are evident in a variety formats, including expressions of 'online spirituality' with websites, forums and messaging systems, and 'techno spirituality' in keeping with the Secularization Theses are not so much compatible with, but competing against a true Divine 'transcendence enabled' spirituality.

Images of Divine Transcendence

The biblical narrative is saturated with unambiguous concepts of Divine 'transcendence'. Adam's closeness to God indicates that there was a far closer connection prior to the fall. Kim[22] describes the relationship as less of a transcendental gap, reflecting man's purpose as co-worker. Later, Abraham is described as the 'friend of God' in a relationship initiated by God bringing the possibility of immanent relationship with the Divine[23]. The presence of God's voice heard by Moses at the 'burning bush' is an illustration of both immanence and transcendence indicating a reaction with proper reverence in the removal of sandals and the formation of boundaries as Moses is limited in his advance towards the holy fire.

The nature of fallen humanity prevents man from coming into the full presence of the Holy God as was the case in the 'burning bush'

Theophany on Mr Sinai (Exodus 19) where Moses had the experience of the 'intimate outward appearance of God with the limitation of not being able to see God directly'.

Later, the pillar of cloud guiding the Children of Israel in the wilderness was as much practical manifestation as spiritual presence. On one level, the cloud provided shade and rain in the desert, and on another level, the cloud showed revelation of the transcendent God and the manifestation of his immanent presence. The immanent 'Shekinah'[24] presence of God with believers in the Old Testament empowers them to defeat their enemies, as evidenced through the presence of the Tabernacle and the Ark of the Covenant as the place of God's dwelling with His people. The Ark of the Covenant is the symbol of God's immanence with His people, although both unapproachable and 'not touchable', reflecting His transcendence. [25]

Kim notes the effect of this transcendence on 'leaders' and prophets who were considered the mouthpiece of God. Before Moses' death on Mt Nebo, God promised a successor, with the implication that another prophet like Moses will continue the intimacy of relationship with God[26]. Moses had been the physical reflection of the transcendent God to the people, and reciprocally a representative of the people to God. As the new prophet and leader Joshua was to succeed Moses, God's promise to Moses for his successor is that He will put '*words in his mouth*' (Deut 18:18 [NIV]).

Just as the Old Testament Shekinah (presence of God) was realised under Moses, later, this same presence continues in the 'new exodus' under the ultimate prophet, the incarnate Jesus. He would be the one to speak God's word to the people. And as Jesus promised, the 'Paraclete' (comforter) Holy Spirit would be the continuing transcendent-immanent presence of God after Jesus' ascension.[27]

What has Humanity to Lose?

Those famous words of St Anselm ring true in our contemplation of the transcendence of God:

'The believer does not seek to understand, that he may believe, but he believes that he may understand: for unless he believed he would not understand.' [28]

Profound questions arise that illustrate the gulf in understanding.

'Lord, if thou art not here, where shall I seek thee, being absent? But if thou are everywhere, why do I not see thee present?' [29]

We are led to the stark realization of loss, asking 'What has departed, and what remains?' In losing the blessedness we are left with misery for which we were not made. St Anselm describes humanity in our fallen sinful condition as wretches, driven out, hurled, and consigned to ruin. We are cast into exile from the vision of God, into blindness, and from the 'joy of immortality into the bitterness and horror of death.'[30] For Anselm this life is a *'miserable exchange of how great a good, for how great an evil!'* with heavy loss and heavy grief. Our sins that separate from God are infinite and immeasurable by offence, and therefore what is demanded is infinite satisfaction. The defining response from the Creator was through the arrangement of an infinite and immeasurable satisfaction, by recourse to substitution leading to the necessity of the incarnation where God became 'flesh', Christ died a substitutionary death and acquired an infinite recompense which falls to humanity, as 'pardoned, forgiven and saved.'[31] For the seeking soul that finds Him, nothing better can be conceived. He is 'life' itself, light, wisdom, goodness, eternal blessedness, and blessed eternity[32].

So, what are we to make of the different flavours of 'secular transcendence'? Whether it be in the form of mindfulness as spirituality without religion, or music that brings a transcendence experience especially when combined with expressions of dance, secular expressions are everywhere. Secular transcendence is commercialised in westernised forms of yoga, and martial arts. Drug use often begins with desire for a higher experience. Sex is for many, a pursuit of a transcendent state. Athletes pursue an optimal performance being 'in the zone'. Armies are motivated by nationalistic ideals. Cults create their own concepts of transcendence often led by people who are considered 'mystics'. And even the pursuit of wisdom is about enhancing 'insight', in the search for reality.

The Christian experience of 'Salvation Assurance' takes us above the natural state, as a realization of the power of God to preserve us from separation. The Apostle Paul describes the comfort of the transcendent, in contrast to the pessimism of the secular:

> 'For I am convinced that neither death, nor life, nor angels, nor principalities, nor things present, nor things to come, nor powers, nor height, nor depth, nor any other created thing, will be able to separate us from the love of God, which is in Christ Jesus our Lord. (Romans 8:38-39)

There can be no adequate human way of replacing the profoundly simple consequence of 'belief' that opens the embrace of God, and switches on the 'light' to illumine Divine reality and contextualise our place in His purposes.

Endnotes

1   McGrath A.E. & McGrath J.C. 2007 The Dawkins Delusion? Atheist Fundamentalism and the Denial of the Divine, IVP Books, Illinois, USA. p.81

2   Ibid. p.81

3   McCrindle M. 2017 Faith and Belief in Australia, McCrindle Research, Baulkam Hills, Australia www.mccrindle.com.au

4   Ibid p.26

5   Ibid. p.32

6   Ibid. p.45

7   Ibid. p.45,46.

8   Mangalwadi V. 2011 The Book That Made Your World, How the Bible Created the Soul of Western Civilization, Thomas Nelson, Nashville, USA. p.392

9   Willsey, J.K., 2003 Recovering Transcendence and Immanence, NARBC Pastors Conference. P.1

10   Anselm St. 1926/2017 The Works of St Anselm, Proslogium; Monologium; An Appendix in Behalf of the Fool by Gaunilon and Cur Deus Homo, Translation by Sydney Norton Deane (2017), Global Grey Books. P.55

11   Ibid. p.101

12   Erickson M.J. 1987 Christian Theology, Unabridged, one-volume edition, Baker Book House, Michigan, USA. p.302

13   Ibid p.303

14   Hammond, T.C. 1968 In Understanding Be Men, A Handbook of Christian Doctrine (edited and revised by David F Wright), Inter-Varsity Press, Leicester, England. P.45

15   Haidt 2012 Religion, evolution, and the Ecstasy of Self-transcendence' https://www.youtube.com/watch?v=2MYsx6WArKY [Accessed 20th Sept 2018]

16   Ibid – Youtube 2012.

17   Ibid – Youtube 2012.

18   Everyday Thomist https://everydaythomist.wordpress.com/tag/haidt/ [Accessed 20th Sept 2018]

19   Ibid.

20   Haidt J. 2012 The Righteous Mind, Why Good People are Divided by Politics and Religion, Penguin, Random House, New York, USA. p.299

21   Mangalwadi V. 2011 The Book That Made Your World, How the Bible Created the Soul of Western Civilization, Thomas Nelson, Nashville, USA. p.11

22   Kim, S.M. 2009, Transcendence of God, A Comparative Study of the Old Testament and the Qur'an, PhD Thesis, University of Pretoria, South Africa. p.204

23   Ibid p.207

24   The word Shekinah (   ) is a Talmudic term meaning "presence of God".

25   Ibid p.177

26   Ibid p.249

27   Ibid p.76

28   Anselm St. 1926/2017 The Works of St Anselm, Proslogium; Monologium; An Appendix in Behalf of the Fool by Gaunilon and Cur Deus Homo, Translation by Sydney Norton Deane (2017), Global Grey Books. P.30

29   Ibid p.30

30   Ibid p.31

31   Ibid p.7

32   Ibid p.47

Chapter 5: Transcendence in Australia

'You are from below; I am from above.
You are of this world;
I am not of this world.'

John 8:23

Having laid a foundation of definition and reflection on the philosophic and theological foundations of modernity, and the consequences of a loss of 'transcendence', let's turn our focus to historic parallels in Australia. There are many factors, but I want to focus more specifically on changes in Christian spirituality that may be evidenced in their correlation to the rise of mass media in the 20th Century. This will be one of the contributions to the to the waning dimension of church attendance and affiliation.

In the big-picture reflection Charles Taylor identifies a historic process of disenchantment that he calls a 'Great Dis-embedding'.[1] The former primacy of God is reconceived as primacy of individuals, or a new entrenched 'self-understanding' of social existence. In earlier times, under prevailing plausibility of God's transcendent reality, communities related to God as a society including the 'embedding' of social rituals and expectation of human flourishing in relation to the transcendent benevolence of God.

And as we contemplate our Australian context, we can identify evidence that mass media has played a significant role in forming momentum for social change, including the dynamic acceleration of change over the past century. As Australia embraced the emergence of mass media from early 20th Century, to the present reality of 'digital convergence' we may be able to identify evidence that our enthusiastic embrace has created huge strides forward in our technological advancement, but at the same time has created a parallel distraction from the concept of Divine transcendence. Recognising and analysing trends, including both positive and negative developments is very revealing. Valuable social science perspectives can be very enlightening as we correlate the influence and connection of mass media to the changing attitudes of the Australian people.

The Statistical Image of Australian Spirituality

After significant controversy over changes to the Australian Bureau of Statistics question that appeared in the 2016 National Census of Population and Housing, anticipation in the Australian Christian community was heightened, and leaders were bracing for an anticipated 'dose of reality' about the true nature of religious belief in Australia.

Up until 2016 the appearance of the Census question about 'Religion'[2] had listed Christian denominations at the top of responses, but this time the response of 'No religion' was relocated to the first option. 'No religion' is equivalent to 'Secular Beliefs and Other Spiritual Beliefs and No Religious Affiliation.

Barker[3] notes that whenever there is change to the way a question is presented there will be variant responses. In 1933 there was a drop in the numbers identifying with Christianity from 95% (1921) to 85% (1933). That variation was correlated to the additional instruction including the words, 'State the full name of the religious denomination'. Even then, 12.5% chose not to answer the question. While doubts may continue over the accuracy of the denominational percentage breakdowns, the concerns of a slide in statistical Christian adherence were realised with results showing a reduced footprint of Christian spirituality claimed by the Australian populace.

At the 2016 census, opponents of the dominance of Christianity were jubilant that the numbers had fallen, and while there were certainly concerned Church leaders, there was also a sense of 'relief' that the numbers in the census had more likely presented a closer to realistic statistic, given the relatively lower number of church attendances in recent decades.

A Diminished Religious Footprint

While statistical analysis continues to show Christianity as the 'most common' religion covering 52% (2016) of the population, the shock came in the statistical increase of an additional 2.2 million people who were added to the number ticking the 'No religion' box. While the rise of this category has been a trend for decades, this Census indicated that the number of people reporting 'No religion' was accelerating. Bouma[4] points to the intergenerational likelihood that parents who have 'no religion' are almost certain to have children who have 'no religion', so it's likely in the future that those who tick the 'no religion box' or the 'Nones' as they have become known, will continue to emerge perhaps increasingly becoming the 'new normal' in Australia.

What will be significant for our discussion about a rise in 'secularism' is the shift that has taken place since the 1960's to the present day. In the 1966 Census Christianity held a dominant statistical position with 88% of respondents claiming adherence to the Christian faith. The first major increase in those self-identifying as having 'no religion' happened in 1971. Barker[5] notes that the figure for those self-identifying the 'no-religion' category jumped from 0.8% in 1966 to 6.7% in the '71 Census with the inclusion of an instruction that stated, "if no religion write 'none'". However, this anomaly can't be blamed for later big jumps in the numbers of 'Nones' as was the case in the 2016 Census where the increase was from

22.3% to 30.1%.

Reasons for Change

There are substantial theories about change in the dynamics of religious affiliation. One of those is, the end of the White Australia Policy in 1966. While formerly migration policy had favoured Europeans, the number of new migrants began to increase from countries where religions other than Christianity were more prevalent.[6] This can't be the whole story, but the ABS figures show a significant acceleration of non-Christian religious affiliation since the half-way point of the 50 years since 1966. The influx of Other Religions almost tripled from 2.6% in 1991 to 8.2% in 2016. The figure may be corelated to the 'No Religion' increase from 12.9% in 1991 to 30.1% in 2016. A portion of the increase may be due to Government immigration policies that indirectly may be linked to the prevalence of secularization, though the creation of significant economic and ethnic preferential variation in the population could be viewed as a driver of the response of national policy makers in the endeavour to foster pluralist tolerance.

Towards the end of the 20th Century the movement of people 'out' of church was significant, but the reasons people used to justify their exit may not have been the usual responses. Jaimieson's (1999) research into why people leave Church from his context in New Zealand, is likely to hold true for those Australians who are 'close cousins'. His findings dispel what he calls 'myths' about why people leave church.

Across a series of 'myths', he discovered that it's not just traditional mainline churches losing large numbers of people, but also evangelical, charismatic and Pentecostal churches A steady 'back-door' loss rate as high as 10% indicates sizeable numbers. He also finds it is not just young adults or people on the fringe leaving church, with as many as 70% of leavers surveyed being middle aged (35-45 years).

Let's look as some of the 'myths', including the idea that:

1. It's all about what's happening in the home. The influence of positive parent bonds is weak, meaning that not all children readily capture the values of their parents, so it's no longer a guarantee that children will remain in church when they are old enough to make their own choice.
2. Lack of commitment is not the primary reason, with 94% of those surveyed having previously held significant leadership positions, and as many as 40% having been full-time Christian workers for at least a year.
3. Time pressures are not the reason, with many indications that time spent in church was replaced with other 'faith nurturing commitments.'
4. Neither do most of those leaving Church have personal issues, grievances or disagreements with church leaders, with many indicating that they left after a process of months or years, with the 'final straw' coming over only minor issues. Hopes that 'they'll be back' have been dashed too, though some indicated an attractive youth group may be reason for return.
5. And, the idea that people leave because they are 'backsliding' may also be another myth, with indications that leavers intend to continue in their Christian faith.

While Jaimeson (2001) warns pessimism has accompanied many a challenge throughout the history of the church, Christian leaders can't become complacent. In the worst-case scenarios from North Africa in places were Christianity was once strong, it has since been all but eradicated. It is not out of the question that the same scenario could develop in New Zealand, but he ventures that it could happen to the entire western world. He warns against underestimating the degree and depth of change that is occurring in society.

Age and Belief

Another statistical variant in the picture of Australian belief lies in the breakdown of 'Age and Belief'. Of adults in Australia those 18 to 34 years were more likely to report not having a religion (39%). Almost 12% of the 18-34 years adults were more likely to be affiliated with religions other than Christianity. Those over 50 were most likely to report an adherence to Christianity (70%). Figure 1.2 from the ABS shows a breakdown of Age and belief in Australia.

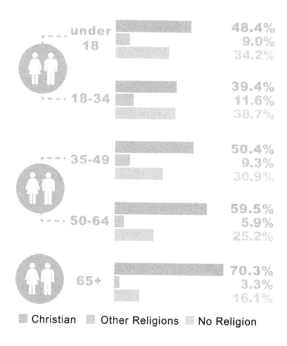

under 18	48.4%	
	9.0%	
	34.2%	
18-34	39.4%	
	11.6%	
	38.7%	
35-49	50.4%	
	9.3%	
	30.9%	
50-64	59.5%	
	5.9%	
	25.2%	
65+	70.3%	
	3.3%	
	16.1%	

Christian   Other Religions   No Religion

Figure 1.2 Religious Affiliation and Age, 2016 (ABS)

For Christian leaders, concerned for the future of an emerging generation, the news appears bleak. Bouma[7] suggests it is not atheism or rejection of religion that are the new norm. Young people are accepting of religious views, and spiritualities, but are suspicious of those who try to impose their teachings upon them suggesting the response of 'Be what you wish, believe what you find helpful, but leave me alone.'

It should be noted that Children are not the ones filling out the Census form, and it is likely that responses on the form reflect the parent's beliefs. Even so, the trend of disaffiliation by parents and their disconnection to the Christian church reveals a substantial problem for the propagation of

Christian faith where families have been the primary vehicle for passing on values for emerging generations. Christian leaders will register alarm that the 'fruit' of non-Christian aligned pursuit of secularized 'human flourishing' will likely influence substantially the agenda for social and ethical positioning of the nation through the coming decades.

Not everyone agrees that alarmist news headlines tell the whole story of religious belief in Australia. Barker[8] contends that while the 'Nones' make up 30.1% of the population they are still not the majority, nor the largest religious group. Overall religious affiliation is still over 60%, and that is twice as many as those identifying no religion. It means the 'Nones' are still in the minority, and there are still almost 10% of the population that chose not to answer the census question for a variety of reasons including the religious conviction of some Evangelicals and Pentecostals who have been motivated in their faith pursuit by the concept that Christianity is not a 'Religion' but rather a 'Relationship' and there are many who may not have answered the Census question because of their discomfort about aligning with 'Religiosity'. Even amongst the 'Nones' there is no category breakdown that identifies atheist, agnostic or humanist. There are many types of non-religion. Identifying 'no religion' needs to be differentiated from the concept that people within the category positively claim to be atheist or agnostic.

Endnotes

1   Taylor C. 2007 A Secular Age, Belknap Press of Harvard University Press, Cambridge, Massachusetts, USA and London, England. P.146

2   (Census Dictionary) www.abs.gov.au

3   Barker R. 2017, Religion and the Census: Australia's Unique Relationship to Faith and Belief, ABC Religion and Ethics, 5 Jul 2017.

4   Bouma G. 2018 Religion in Australia: What are the Implications of 'None' being the New Normal? ABC Religion and Ethics 28th June 2018.

5   Barker R. 2017, Religion and the Census: Australia's Unique Relationship to Faith and Belief, ABC Religion and Ethics, 5 Jul 2017.

6   Of those born overseas 47% reported an affiliation as Christian compared to 58% of the Australian-born population. www.abs.gov.au – Census Data Summary.

7   Bouma G. 2018 Religion in Australia: What are the Implications of 'None' being the New Normal? ABC Religion and Ethics 28th June 2018.

8   Barker R. 2017, Religion and the Census: Australia's Unique Relationship to Faith and Belief, ABC Religion and Ethics, 5 Jul 2017.

Chapter 6:
A Transition of Authority - Print to Electronic Media

For the word of God is alive and active.
Sharper than any double-edged sword,
it penetrates even to dividing soul and spirit,
joints and marrow; it judges the thoughts
and attitudes of the heart.

Hebrews 4:12

There can be no doubt, change creates a grab-bag of good and bad consequence. Leadership, be it good or evil, produces qualitative change where the subjects of rule accept conditions of change as normal. Bouma[1] calls the modern era 'Post-book times' suggesting that a key driver of the cultural shift, has been a movement away from a reliance on 'traditional' forms of authority to what he calls 'experimental' forms of authority. He identifies this change in the transition from print media to the variety of electronic forms of media. The advent of radio, television, internet and video began to replace print which had held the place of authority since the printing press shifted the knowledge industry from monasteries focused on 'copying' to universities that became empowered to produce and transmit commentary and knowledge.

In the 'print only' times of earlier generations, the 'gatekeepers' of society like clergy, lawyers and politicians could read, and 'literacy' was power.

Industrialization saw the power of print media soar through newspapers, magazines and books that found their way into the hands of ordinary people and in the century between 1850 and 1950 universal education reached its peak in the 'Age of Reason'. At this point 'truth' in print was perceived to be fixed and eternal. Since the 1960's the primacy of 'truth' in print has been in decline, with a new generation raised primarily on electronic media. Many churches had problems adapting to the transition of authority from print to electronic forms and styles of new media. In more recent times Pentecostal forms of worship have adapted better than others, but in the electronic context, 'truth' becomes more of an 'experience' with an internally held 'trust' basis for 'hope' rather than the external print form that required a 'rational affirmation'.

The 1950's 'A Golden Age' of Christian Influence—Australian Media.

From the time of Federation in Australia an internal migration was underway. Country people had begun a move to the cities. The pursuit of higher standards of living along with higher wages saw changes that began to shape the 20th century. As historian Manning Clark[2] reflects, in 1911 the figure of 38.03% of people lived in cities, rising sharply to 43.01% by 1921. In the 1920's the first Government broadcasting licenses had been issued to four companies, with two stations in Sydney, one in Melbourne and one in Perth.

It was around this time that dance halls became 'pleasure palaces' for the masses in an age of Jazz and the gramophone. Cabarets were the places to be seen. Clark notes the Christian attitudes reflected by priests and parsons held the feeling that 'God had been shouldered out of Australian life and replaced by paganism.'[3] With the appearance of exciting pleasures, like the picture show, the dance hall, the racecourse, the football ground and beaches, newspaper headlines announced that the 'sun' had defeated religion in Australia.

In the mid-20th Century Australia's post war population was

overwhelmingly Christian. As historian Meredith Lake[4] notes significant growth in the decade 1950-1960 in Church membership across all the major denominations suggested that there was more going on in Australia mid-century than 'simple secularization'.

Sunday school and Christian youth associations grew. Anglican confirmations swelled by 50%. Methodist membership grew by a quarter, and overall one in every three Australians claimed to attend church at least weekly. Among the many factors fuelling the increased spiritual activity, were the rise of school and university student groups and the notable presence of religion in film production coming from Hollywood making overt use of biblical narrative and scriptural settings. The motive of film producer Cecil B. DeMille was assertively in support of the Bible. He said, 'My ministry has been to make religious movies and get more people to read the Bible than anyone else ever has.'[5] DeMille was behind blockbuster films including *The Ten Commandments*, a film that is counted as one of the most successful box office productions in history.

The changing media landscape was affecting the 'visibility' of the Bible in Australian mainstream culture. Alongside the popularity of the movies in the 1950's, religious programming on radio was also in its heyday. A former war chaplain and ordained Anglican minister Kenneth Thorne Henderson headed up the first Religious Programming Department with the ABC. An extensive programming range including 'doctrinal, mythological, ethical, ritual, experimental and social dimensions of religion' were covered including the presentation of the Church at worship[6].

From the late 1940's virtually all commercial radio featured regular religious programs. Catholic Minister Dr Leslie Rumble hosted a weekly program spanning 40 years including a weekly 'question box', quoting the Bible in answers to listener questions. His replies were later published with global distribution selling millions of copies. Other notable broadcasters included Seventh Day Adventist Laurie Naden who hosted a program syndicated across fifty commercial stations by 1950, and the respected Methodist Alan Walker who produced Christian drama.

This level of spiritual fervour is likely to have contributed to the historic success of the 1959 crusade appearances of the American Evangelist Billy Graham who attracted 143 750 people to the Melbourne Cricket Ground, where the success including the overall response to Graham of 130 000 decisions, was a triumph of interdenominational cooperation, and 'the pinnacle of public religion in Australia'. This was the moment that Australia was closest to what may be described as national revival.

By the late 1950s the man known as the 'father of Australian religious broadcasting' Rev. Vernon Turner[7] led a team producing 800 weekly programs for 100 commercial stations in all states around Australia. He became editor of The Australian Christian World ecumenical newspaper in the same decade. He published a Christian magazine called Victory and later, his biography 'God gave me a microphone' went to four editions. It was Turner who gained an FM radio licence in Sydney and 2CBA-FM began broadcasting in 1979. Radio broadcasting became most surely a key platform for dissemination of Christian ministry into homes everywhere.

The 1960's Contraction

While the 1950's was a time when religious embrace suggested a kind of nation exalting 'righteousness', Meredith Lake[8] reflects on what was to follow in the 1960's decade, as a contrast to the previous 'golden age'. The golden age was followed by a pronounced contraction in the reach and influence of churches in the lives of Australians.

There are a number of reasons for the contraction. Among them, the population of Australia was increasing at an accelerating rate. By 1959 the national population had reached 10 million people, and over the next decade to 1970 historian Frank G. Clarke[9] notes, 2.5 million 'New Australian' immigrants had arrived and were settling into a new way of life.

Other issues fuelling the contraction include the changing media landscape reducing the visibility of the Bible in the mainstream, and lowering engagement causing a fall in biblical literacy. This crisis in Christianity including a large-scale disaffiliation during the '60's was not just an Australian phenomenon but was reflected across the Western world. Between 1961 and 2016 the proportion of adherents to the big Protestant denominations including Anglican, Presbyterian and Methodists dropped by half[10].

The whole of the Western world was changing. In the late 1960's deterioration of general acceptance of the Bible was being tested around the idea of 'religious neutrality'. The U.S. Supreme Court issued rulings[11], resulting in the restriction of state governments that opposed teaching the theory of evolution[12]. The court unanimously struck down an Arkansas law declaring it unconstitutional to ban the teaching of evolution in public schools. The ruling in *Epperson v. Arkansas* 393 U.S. 97 (1968) decided that forbidding the alternative to 'Creation' violated the First and Fourteenth Amendment's 'establishment clause' about promoting religion, because it sought to prevent learning of a viewpoint antithetical to conservative Christianity. The First Amendment not only bars the establishment of religion by the state, it guarantees 'religious neutrality' that individuals have the right to free exercise of their religion or their 'non-religion'.

A study in the Netherlands found Churches that adhered to a Creation view, slowed the decline in attendance rates. The research[13] focused on Clergy 'belief' regarding an historic view of the Genesis account of creation based on a 10-year comparison. The research showed that in churches where the Ministers adhere to the Genesis account, overall membership kept pace with the growth of the country as-a-whole. In Churches where Ministers reject the biblical creation as history, they were in serious decline.

Creationist leaders argue strongly that there is no-such-thing as 'religious neutrality'. Australian Ken Ham (Answers in Genesis) who founded the 'Ark Encounter' and 'Creation Museum' in the US state of Kentucky contends that while God, creation, and prayer have been thrown out of public schools, it doesn't mean that religion has been 'tossed out'.[14] It means that Christianity has been all but eliminated and replaced with the anti-God religion of naturalism/atheism.

Australian Creationist Dr Don Batten of Creation Ministries International traces present day radicalizing of students to the shift that began in the 1960's.[15] Once Christian countries indoctrinate young people in evolutionary thinking, students seek 'alternative self-authentication'. Under Darwin's model there is no direction, and no ultimate purpose or goal. Reinterpreted 'Fake History' takes popular thinking captive. Purpose is diminished, and adherents are left with no eternal hope or perspective.

The contraction in mainstream Christian church attendances may illustrate this transition of how people have now for decades, trusted 'truth', not according to a 'transcendence' view, but based only upon reason and experience.

Not all churches have declined over these recent decades. Notably, Charismatic and Pentecostal churches began to attract significant growth in the same period 1961-2016. This is perhaps best illustrated in the growth of some 'megachurches' including Hillsong in Sydney, Paradise (now Influencers) Church in Adelaide, Planet Shakers in Melbourne and Hope Centre in Brisbane. It may be that transcendence permeates every dimension of human existence, including the effects of concepts that are attributed to Charismatic and Pentecostal churches like expectation of miracles, healing, and often attention to other transcendence expectation like identification of biblical prophecy fulfilled, personal experience, and expectation of spiritual phenomena, like the 'Baptism of the Holy Spirit' and speaking in tongues.

Where the public reading and preaching of the Bible are minimised, people become disconnected from a sense of Divine transcendence. The populace isolated from 'transcendence' become more vulnerable to 'seeking alternative' ways of constructing their personal identities and contextualizing their life narrative, seeking new ways to understand their place in the world.

the 20ᵗʰ Century Media Trend

I believe we can see a dynamic fault line that emerged in the Australian context in the middle of the 20ᵗʰ Century, from a golden age in the 1950's, and a marked contraction in the 1960's that has continued to deepen and widen into the 21ˢᵗ Century. The demise of authority in print, to the rise in authority of the electronic experiential new media forms, has weakened the authority not only of the Church but also of governance and public sphere morality more generally. Since the 1960's people who trained in Christian spirituality have been forced to reinvent themselves to engage people in a conversation about faith in a much different world[16]. New adaptations using different technologies to engage, and appeal to different forms of authority, have become necessary if a substantial faith message is to engage at all.

It appears that the 'Golden Age' in the 1950's may be due to the crescendo that came with the peak of the 'printed trusted truth', and the testing of the waters where that same truth was received by mass electronic media through radio and the newly arrived television. We can identify the 'high point' as the late 1950's, where peak authority on the printed page 'overlapped' with the emergence of new electronic forms of media.

With the overlap came an unprecedented intensity, super-charging the message for a society steeped in the authority of 'print' and now moved by the emotive appeal of the electronic. No wonder there was a 'Golden Age' of Christian relevance, especially on radio, where the 'transcendent' truths of the Bible were held as authoritative, and the personalities bringing the Bible and theological insights to life were able to 'animate' those truths and principles of God in the everyday lives of Australians.

Heightened spiritual awareness, pointing to the event that saw the climax of the decade in 1959 with the authoritative charisma and oratory skills of Evangelist Billy Graham. He conducted the most significant display of public surrender to God in what was considered Australia's most significant period of national Christian revival.

Beyond this crescendo the arrival of new media forms in the 1960's appeared to cause 'distraction'. As a Western phenomenon, the arrival of new technology in new forms of media created a new revolution forging unprecedented social change. From this time forward the social revolution was supercharged by the new forms of mass media with enhanced production values captured the hearts and minds of a new generation not satisfied with keeping the status quo. Testing boundaries placed pressure on every facet of society including the way Government's legislated common morality.

Changes in Public Morality – Immanence as a measure of the 'Good'.

In 1968 the Australian Government changed the way it dealt with issues of morality in public broadcasting to a model that moved, from 'Censorship' to 'Classification'. The new system according to the Australian Law Reform Commission (1991) implied that nothing is banned, but only 'restricted' if necessary[17]. After a landmark 1968 case *Crowe v Graham* which involved the interpretation of the terminologies 'obscene' and 'indecent', the High Court upheld the use of a 'community standards' test. The test referred to the 'modesty of the average man', rather than the traditional common law test of obscenity based on the 1868 precedents on the tendency to deprave and corrupt. The Australian approach shifted from an 'interventionist' model of censorship and was intended to be a more open and accountable regime than simply the banning of material.

Before the *Crowe v Graham* case (1968), in Australia 'banning' was the norm, and since the 1970's the principle of 'classification' has reigned, and while there is still room for some censorship, based on what has come to be known as the 'Community Standards Test' the implication is that 'nothing is banned but only restricted if necessary'. Restrictions are now only imposed on those publications that push the 'upper limits'[18] of what is considered unacceptable by the general community.

A cooperative classification scheme was developed and underpinned by an Intergovernmental Agreement on Censorship between the Commonwealth and all states and territories. It provided for each state and territory to choose how and whether to implement classification decisions. The Classification Board and a smaller subset called the Classification Review Board[19] assumed the primary role of classifying films, publications and computer games in Australia. There is provision for as many as 30 members appointed by the Governor General with a general broad representation from across the Australian community.

Under the Broadcasting Services Act 1992, which replaced the longstanding Broadcasting Act 1942[20], a 'light touch' approach to regulation was adopted with a motive to promote greater competition, along with new technologies and the development of new services. Under the new system the development of program classification, and the handling of complaints were transferred to industry bodies operating in a co-regulatory framework through the development of industry codes of practice approved and registered with the Australian Communications and Media Authority. More specifically under the Act certain programs under dispute for classification were subject to Australia-wide qualitative and quantitative research on community standards of taste and decency in relation to classifications. The Act outlines what standards are subject to scrutiny:[21]

(3) In developing codes of practice relating to matters referred to in paragraphs (2)(a) and (c), community attitudes to the following matters are to be taken into account:

(a) the portrayal in programs of physical and psychological violence;
(b) the portrayal in programs of sexual conduct and nudity;
(c) the use in programs of offensive language;
(d) the portrayal in programs of the use of drugs, including alcohol and tobacco;

(e) *the portrayal in programs of matter that is likely to incite or perpetuate hatred against, or vilifies, any person or group on the basis of ethnicity, nationality, race, gender, sexual orientation, age, religion or physical or mental disability;*

(f) *such other matters relating to program content as are of concern to the community.*

According to Simpson and Potter[22] the shift in Australia recognises the subjective nature of judgement concerning what is indecent, offensive or obscene. Concerns about nudity and sexually explicit materials have been replaced by broader definitions of 'offensiveness'. The underlying policies in the Australian classification regime seek to protect people from 'unwanted' exposure to indecent or obscene content, while allowing a perceived 'freedom' for adults to see, hear and read what they want.

Before *Crowe v Graham* (1968) it was held that an indecent picture was one that is an 'affront to modesty', based on the belief that there does exist in the community a standard, or instinctive sense of what is either 'decent' or 'dirty'. According to the 'Hicklin Test' based on case of *R v Hicklin (1868)*, the test for obscenity was '*whether the tendency of the matter charged as obscenity is to deprave and corrupt those whose minds are open to such immoral influences and into whose hands a publication of this sort may fall.*' Simpson and Potter noted that this test is largely ignored by the courts who have simply asked whether an item transgresses the bounds of decency, and if so then its 'evil' tendency is taken to be apparent.

For me this illustrates changing culture according to the earlier metaphor, where the 'real world' living in the multi-dimensional 'light of transcendence' is deflated to the flatter lifeless form of 'reason alone' confined within the metaphoric immanent frame.

I believe we can effectively correlate the developments of Australian's subjective judgements, or 'classifications' of morality with the earlier warnings about the impoverishment of human experience that accompanies rationalism. A subtle break from the protection of morality grounded in broadly accepted Judeo-Christian ethical standards empowered by 'transcendence', opens the society to the likely danger of subservience for the entire populace, to the 'dark side' of charismatic elitist leadership.

Australia's modernity under the slogans of 'reason, progress and freedom' appears to be on the same trajectory as is inherent with the 'dialectical' view of modernity, where the 'reason only' view increasingly dominating the public sphere gives rise to self-interested ideologies. Reason alone is increasingly shown to be powerless to keep irrational, destructive or despotic forces at bay.

This is another instance, where the potential for 'contrast' coming from public Christian leaders, and modern-day Christian media is exceedingly important. By virtue of bearing the name of Christ as a descriptor of application, the moral expression of Public Christian expression in all forms of media, will frequently be diametrically opposite to new and emerging secular morality. We would wisely envisage a time, when there will come a point where accusations may test perceived contraventions of Section 3 (e) of the Broadcasting Act (1992) or of Australian Content Standards (2016) for public Christian expression including Christian Broadcasters which states:

> *Code 3.3: We will not broadcast material that is likely to stereotype, incite, vilify, or perpetuate hatred against, or attempt to demean any person or group, on the basis of ethnicity, nationality, race, language, gender, sexuality, religion, age, physical or mental ability, occupation, cultural belief or political affiliation. The requirement is not intended to prevent the broadcast of material which is factual, or the expression of genuinely held opinion in a news or current affairs program or in the legitimate context of a humorous, satirical or dramatic work.*

It is widely anticipated, that recent rationalistic changes in legislated morality, will intensify pressure on Christian biblical positions of morality, and present these orientations as intentionally endeavouring to incite, vilify, or demean the opponents of Christian morality. Transcendent views of human decency rely strongly on the words, actions and lifestyle of Jesus, and if they are reflected boldly by Christian media, new vulnerabilities will inevitably arise that will ultimately be tested in the courts.

As we analyse the evidence for secularization, our Christian attitude to the concept of 'inevitability' may be worthy to note. 'Inevitability' may be the catchcry of the godless atheist, but this ought not be the way biblical Christianity looks at negative change. An ability to acknowledge and even quantify change in our Australian context may be more appropriately categorised as recognition of 'disconnection' from earlier established markers that sought the good of a nation with Judeo-Christian aspiration.

Our optimism is re-energised when we acknowledge that current negative trends may reflect the godless Marxist pretence of inevitability. We are encouraged by the evidence for 're-connection' that comes with the growth of Christian media, along with the rise and formation other cultural markers like Christian schools, colleges, charities, hospitals, and even classically conservative political formations that seek to reflect a 'transcendent' view of reality, even though that view at times looks fragile.

Endnotes

1   Bouma G. 2009 Australian Soul: Religion and Spirituality in the Twenty-first Century. Cambridge University Press, Melbourne, Australia. p.103,104

2   Clark M. 1993 History of Australia, Abridged by Michael Cathcart, Melbourne University Press, Australia. p.496

3   Ibid p.497

4   Lake M. 2018 The Bible in Australia: A Cultural History, New South Publishing, University of New South Wales, Sydney, Australia. p.283

5   Ibid p.284

6   Ibid p.285

7   Source: Sydney Morning Herald 11th Dec 2006 https://www.smh.com.au/national/happy-mix-of-faith-and-passion-for-broadcasting-20061211-gdp0tr.html [Accessed 30th Jul 2018]

8   Ibid p.287

9   Clarke, F.G. 1992 Australia: A Concise Political and Social History, Harcourt Brace Jovanovich Group, Marrickville, Australia. p.269

10   Ibid. Lake p.289

11   A series of cases in which students challenged religious activities: Engel v. Vitale, 370 U.S. 421 (1962); Abingdon v. Schempp, 374 U.S. 203 (1963), Gibbs & Craze Co., L.P.A. 1995, Christian Law Association's Rights in US Public Schools. Creation.com.

12   Masci, D. 2019, Darwin in America, The Evolution Debate in the United States, Pew Reseaarch Centre, Religion & Public Life, https://www.pewforum.org/essay/darwin-in-america/

13   Tuinstra L. 2019 Unbelief Ushers in Unattendance (citing: Heerema, S., Kerken onderneem actie! logos.nl, 25 July 2017) – Creation.com

14

15   Batten, D. 2020, Radicalizing Young People, Creation 42(1): 6, Jan 2020. Creation.com

16   Bouma G. 2009 Australian Soul: Religion and Spirituality in the Twenty-first Century. Cambridge University Press, Melbourne, Australia. p.105

17   Source: Australian Law Reform Commission 'History of Censorship and Classification' https://www.alrc.gov.au/publications/2-current-classification-scheme/history-censorship-and-classification [Accessed 9th Aug 2018]

18   Ibid – Section 2.7 (Australian Law Reform Commission, Censorship Procedure, ALRC Report 55 (1991)

19   Ibid – Section 2.12 and 2.13.

20   Broadcasting Act 1942 https://www.legislation.gov.au/Details/C2004C02568

21   Broadcasting Act 1992 Part 6 (g) https://www.legislation.gov.au/Details/C2017C00201 [Accessed 9th Aug 2018)

22   Simpson S., Potter R. 2012 Restrictions on Freedom of Expression, Collections Law, Legal Issues for Australian Archives, Galleries, Libraries, and Museums.

Chapter 7:
Christian Music and Arts – Reflecting Transcendence

"'Love the Lord your God with all your heart and with all your soul and with all your strength and with all your mind'; and, 'Love your neighbour as yourself.'"

Luke 10:27

The unrealised potential for Christian Media, lies in the idea that it must neither be primarily devotional, nor academic, nor entirely activist in its approach to ministry. It must make provision for these dimensions, but it must effectively reflect an impression of the people of God in 'worship', connecting with God in His 'transcendence'.

'Worship' is a very broad term, but as James K.A. Smith[1] envisages, it is a deeper expression of relational connection. Worship is the idea of birthing a longing for the future Kingdom as a taste of the future 'powers to come'. Worship becomes a 'teaser' in the experience of a presently broken world. Worship trains the imagination to be eschatological. If Christian media falls into the temptation to 'secularize', with a view solely to entertain or to embrace programming strategy that is spiritually disengaged, the risk is that the people of God as consumers of Christian media may be isolated in their sense of transcendence in worship and subtly settle uneasily in the present, 'haunted by the brokenness of the now.'[2]

Popular broadcast media occupies a space where people listen for purposes of enjoyment, entertainment, news and information, and in the case of Christian media, one may assume authentic 'meaning-making' where biblical interpretation is applied to practical life situations and we experience a renewed and fuller dimension of our humanity. Skilled Christian programming expertise is developing as a specialized field that carries a significant weight of spiritual leadership responsibility.

It is my opinion having a long history in Christian broadcasting, that two pre-dominant types of contemporary Christian radio have arisen in Australia since the 1990's, though there may be a third which is a more neutral form which assumes a role as a neutral commentator on culture.

The first of the two dominant types could be categorised as Radio that sees itself as predominantly 'outreach', with a 'sensitivity' to the non-churched and a concern not to repel the non-believing listener by a negative religious portrayal of todays secularized realities. This form of public expression for Christian radio resists the focus of being completely different to the 'overall feel' of the most popular and commercially viable varieties of radio. In keeping with broad Christian values, cautious non-promotion of 'celebrity', carefully chosen 'personalities' or presenters, and a music-mix in keeping with contemporary music genres are presented as appropriate to a chosen demographic. These carefully selected content ingredients are held as virtues. A mix of contemporary mainstream music, with a carefully selected mix of more neutral and perhaps less confronting 'Christian' content produces an attractive product that won't 'offend' the listener. The underlying approach questions why you would cause unnecessary concern, and risk rejection by sponsors who may not be strategically aligned with a more direct presentation of the Christian gospel and discipleship principles.

The second of the two dominant types of Christian broadcasting aspires to 'discipleship' of listeners as the higher priority. Sometimes called 'in-reach', this form of Christian radio is not as concerned about whether the 'non-believing' listener will have their senses or morality challenged by evangelical realities or robust commentary based on biblical 'truth'.

There is less concern for populism, or the necessity to specifically target an unchurched audience. There is a higher willingness to approach cultural controversies where Evangelical biblical principles come into conflict with the secular sphere driven by 'politically correct' ideologies that appear to dominate the mainstream of modern Australia.

It's not that this second dominant type of Christian radio does not have the motivation for 'outreach' but it is more focused on directing skill, energy and resources to 'equipping' the listener to engage in the concept of personal discipleship including outreach. The image of contemporary Christian faith is more important to affirm and celebrate, rather than minimize for fear of being battered by the moody pressures from a demographic shaped by the secularised sphere who may demand conformity to a more rigid, two dimensional secular 'immanence'.

In contrast to the 'outreach' oriented form of Christian radio, the music mix for 'in-reach' radio is often intentionally 100% Christian, though in our modern day this is not easy to police with a legalistic dogmatism. Music inclusion is often defined according to the ontological alignment, and reputation of the artist's faith position more specifically than the lyrical content of songs. Lyrical content remains important and music 'choice' is still influenced by the popularity of the artist in the contemporary market. There is an underlying assumption that if the faith and reputation of the artists are biblically founded, their musical product will be aligned to a biblical reflection of righteousness. My observation is that this is a generally sound 'rule of thumb' principle to observe, given that the 'tick of approval' for musicians and their music, may be also seen as an endorsement of their future musical pursuits and enduring role-model lifestyle.

Teaching programs are usually screened to meet expectations of the station ethos, and evaluation processes look for what is 'trustworthy' in alignment with Christian/biblical cultural positioning of programming policy. Importantly, the criteria for selection of presenters/announcers aims to carefully nurture an alignment with a Christian integrity being built around Christocentric values, levels of maturity, and the ability to submit to the station's cultural 'ethos'.

A third category of public Christian media, may include the wider 'religious' broadcast media landscape that continues to become increasingly diverse, including the rise of Christian influence on new platforms. Not only are there expressions of evangelical, popular Christian radio, but also a host of production companies and program producers dealing with multiple dimensions of religious experience. The ABC's Religion and Ethics Report[3] is promoted as '*where religion and ethics meet news and current affairs in Australia and around the world*'. There is a strong emphasis on mainline religious engagement with issues.

Broader 'religious' programming on Community radio is not only Christian, but includes Jewish broadcasting, by J-AIR (Jewish Australian Internet Radio), and Melbourne Jewish Radio. Also, alternative Islamic expressions include Islamic Voice Radio Melbourne, and 2MFM in Sydney. There are numerous expressions of print and online publications, including Eternity Newspaper, and a growing number of Christian ministries producing their own online media content, like the Australian Christian Lobby, or the Centre for Public Christianity. Christian television is also growing in influence through the Australian Christian Channel, the Hillsong Channel and through companies that provide satellite Christian television with numerous global channels like TBN bringing international Christian programming to Australian audiences.

New internet Channels that are easily accessible on mobile devices feature a vast array of preaching, and teaching ministries. Numerous ministries are geared as production companies, creating content for other media, including Focus on the Family, Reach Beyond and CV Global. And many local churches podcast their preaching messages and generate significant social media networks. At the time of writing, Churches have been scrambling to stream Sunday services, youth events, children's ministries, and even digital holiday camps in response to closing churches responding to health concerns from a global pandemic. Thousands of churches are launching into the field of Public Christian media. This outline of other Christian media is by no means exhaustive but illustrates the variety of technologically driven platforms being utilised by Christian media professionals and enthusiasts. In these contexts, the issues in these chapters are of critical importance if Christian media is to be more than just another secular pastime.

The Functions of Music in Media

Because music plays such a powerful role in the everyday lives of people, for Christian radio broadcasting it may be useful to explore scholarly research on the functions and effectiveness of music choice.

A 2013 German study on 'The Psychological Functions of Music Listening' asked '*Why do people listen to music?*'[4] The study comprised a comprehensive investigation based on a survey of literature spanning 50 years, producing an exhaustive empirical study of more than 500 items concerned with musical use or function. From the responses after eliminating redundant items, a list of 129 distinct items were phrased '*I listen to music because ...*'. Eventually they were able to identify a 'Top 3'. While there is a long history of identifying possible functions of music the Schäfer, Sedlmeier, Städtler and Huron study found that people predominantly listen for these major reasons:

1. *Music offers a valued companion,*
2. *Music helps provide a comfortable level of activation,*
3. *And it creates a positive mood*[5] .

The first and second were found to be more Important than the third. The social importance of music was found to be overvalued.

The findings contribute to the various approaches to music theory ranging from social and emotional communication, social cohesion as in 'work and war songs', reducing social stress and tempering aggression, maintaining infant-mother attachment (lullabies), helping cope with 'life's transitoriness', and higher 'transcendental purposes' alleviating persistent human anxiety about death.

The researchers review of studies also noted other highly rated theories on why people listen to music including *'as something special, that defies the mundane, takes us out of ourselves, puts us somewhere else, and provides a means of escape'.* [6]

The researchers also noted the experience of flow states, peaks, and chills often evoked by listening to music. They classified these as forms of *'transcendence or escapism'.* Music is also theoretically connected with the manifestation of sexual selection and a means of social and emotional communication. Everyday uses revolve around entertainment, identity formation, and sensation seeking, activating associations, memories, experiences, moods and emotions.

Christians and Music – Social Identity Theory

Within the Christian community, historic debate concerning the use of music has frequently, produced 'Music Wars.'[7] Preferring 'substance over form', or 'style over structure' are as divisive as focusing on whether music should be 'cognitive or emotive.'

As a major point of departure from historic Church music (pre-Reformation 1517), Martin Luther is credited with a significant act that is recognised more as an afterthought to the ructions caused by his nailing of '95 theses' to the Castle Church door in Wittenberg. His focus in reforming 'the Mass' (later referred to as the Worship Service) was to 'give it back to the people.' Luther devised German text chorales so that the laity could express a collective religious identity through participation in worship. Traditional folk tunes were used, and people sang in the vernacular language (German) rather than Latin. Today across many denominations the difference between traditional and contemporary worship services is the style and instrumentation of worship music. The informality of a contemporary service is often accompanied by parishioners adding other dimensions like drinking coffee and eating.

In the evolution of contemporary Church it's recognised that music is an important form of communication, with an ability to 'transcend' social boundaries, and amplify messages designed to be captured in the formation of the group's identity. Johnson, Rudd, Neuendorf, and Jian note that in Social Identity Theory, subcultures develop when individuals distinguish themselves from the larger more prominent culture.[8] This can be a 'positive' or a 'negative' depending on an 'us-versus-them' mentality creating a dynamic emotional significance to group membership resulting in organizational identity being strengthened by 'structural inertia.'[9]

I expect that the same powerful dynamics that have been tested and observed in Churches may correlate to the strategies in which Christian musicians, and Christian mass media also builds its' audience from the formation of group identity. Johnson, Rudd, Neuendorf, and Jian[10] site a variety of research including examination of the identity of the contemporary Christian music community when boundaries begin to 'fade' between the secular and the sacred.

They conclude that in Church life, music preference strongly predicts worship style preference. Music is not only a form of communication, but 'music is communication' able to express socio-cultural norms and beliefs. Music shapes culture enabling the Church to communicate 'who we are, and what we believe.' And rather than concentrating on music style as the priority, there is clear advantage in pursuing the common goal of the organisation, using music genres to accomplish that goal.

As we endeavour to translate this understanding to Christian media, we may appreciate the power of music selections that are weighted towards the 'transcendent', rather than towards the more secularised 'immanent frame.'

There are important elements to consider in the way music is used, to achieve an aim in public Christian ministry whether it is in Church, for Christian musicians, or in Christian radio, television or online channels.

When the contrast of Christian media 'utility' (usefulness) is being focused broadly either towards 'Outreach' or 'In-reach' we might assume that there will be a different dynamic in music and content selection. For the 'outreach' station music selection is about 'proclaiming faith' (the Gospel). For the 'in-reach' station music selection is about 'strengthening faith' (discipleship). In both of these, whether the aspiration is to reach 'out' or 'in', the concept of transcendence is an essential element of what makes the music selection 'useful'. Schäfer, Sedlmeier, Städtler and Huron[11] settled their conclusions around those three reasons we humans have for listening: '*Music offers a valued companion, helps provide a comfortable level of activation, and a positive mood*'. For Johnson, Rudd, Neuendorf, and Jian[12] in their study of Christian music, their concern was for the identity of the contemporary Christian music community that tended to become more vulnerable when boundaries between sacred and secular begin to 'fade'. Their concept that music is not only a form of communication, but 'music is communication' leads to a cautionary warning to Content Managers in Christian media that the elements of 'transcendence' or the 'lack of transcendence' expressed in lyrical content may have an influential effect on an audience who are being shaped as to who they are, and what they believe.

The Good News = The Good Life

We can take this concept to an even deeper level. James K.A Smith[13] illustrates the dynamics of what is shaping people who are creatures of 'desire'. The power of not just music, but creative stories and pictures have influence in contrast to just propositions and doctrines. He says the telos to which our 'love' is aimed moves us to an orientation whereby the impression we receive of what constitutes 'the good life' or 'our desire for the presence of God' shapes, governs and motivates our decisions and actions. How these pictures of the 'good life' are formed in the mind of the listener, may be our clue here as to how not only the music, but the talk, testimony and every element in Christian media has capacity to enable us to 'co-mission' with God.

The songs we choose, the teaching we present, the stories we tell and the conversations we craft have the power to harness a glimpse of the power of 'transcendence' to meet the needs of human desire. Ultimately, a focus on meeting the needs of the 'heart's desires' may be the sledgehammer that breaks through the hard, outer frame that traps us in our own rationalist 'immanence.'

It's like letting the 'light' shine through the restrictive port-holes of the 'immanent frame' that traps us in the disenchanted secular, and actively blocks the Divine presence. Capturing a glimpse of God's transcendence allows our followers to open a new orientation to God's purposes. This is perhaps akin to how Jesus used Parables to communicate the deeper things of the Kingdom of God. This is how Jesus used parables as He explained in Matthew 13:13-17 [NIV]:

> *13 This is why I speak to them in parables:*
>
> *"Though seeing, they do not see;*
>   *though hearing, they do not hear or understand.*
>
> *14 In them is fulfilled the prophecy of Isaiah:*
>
> *"'You will be ever hearing but never understanding;*
>   *you will be ever seeing but never perceiving.*
> *15 For this people's heart has become calloused;*
>   *they hardly hear with their ears,*
>   *and they have closed their eyes.*
> *Otherwise they might see with their eyes,*
>   *hear with their ears,*
>   *understand with their hearts*
> *and turn, and I would heal them.'*
>
> *16 But blessed are your eyes because they see, and your ears because they hear. 17 For truly I tell you, many prophets and righteous people longed to see what you see but did not see it, and to hear*

what you hear but did not hear it.

Perhaps our most creative capacities as Public Christians are only just now being discovered, as we contemplate what it is in our program content that unlocks the transcendent power of God. Music, news, testimonies and teaching that unlocks the treasures of the Kingdom that consumers see with their eyes, hear with their ears, understand with their hearts and turn... that Christ would heal them.

Far from being a dry, laborious monologue with heavy-handed, self-righteous dictates of what some see as an oppressive form of Christian narrative, all Public Christian expression has an aspiration to bring 'Good News' that leads to a 'Good Life'. For Smith[14] what we 'love' is a vision of the 'good life'. The good life is an 'implicit picture of what human flourishing looks like'. It's an expression of what good relationships look like, what the stewardship of possessions and the environment looks like. It's what our vision of the economy looks like. It's what sort of recreation we choose and the idea of what a flourishing family or career looks like. The Christian media programming application of all of these elements will create a dynamic contrast to the way desires shape us when we are suppressed into the deflated, prison of the secular disenchanted 'immanent frame' that does not sense the fuller dimension of the Divine person, plan and purpose.

Popular Media Thrives on 'Desire'

Media and entertainment tap into the 'desires' of the broad populace. This is a dimension that creates a challenge to the typical Church approach of responding to cultural formation of 'desire' by confronting 'lower' passions with 'higher' ideas and belief.

While the secularized media continues a relentless bombardment of tapping into the heart as having an 'erotic core', shaping passion and desire towards the 'strange gods' of consumerism, and the alternative worship and other kingdoms, the Christian Church has often sought to try and quell the passions by bringing them into submission to the intellect.

Smith[15] observes that secular marketers 'get it' when they understand that, at the root foundations of humanity, we are 'erotic' creatures, oriented by 'love, passion and desire'. This critique suggests that many in the Church may have been 'duped by modernity' in the rise of secularization and settled for a model of the human person wrongly assuming, that an 'intellectual' focus on ideas and beliefs is the core of our being. Focusing on the 'head' alone, may be a misdirection of effort.

A more effective approach may be to consider what the marketing industry has discovered, that we are creatures of 'love and desire'. A ministry response with counter measures to the passions of the secular 'immanent frame' may find a new impetus with acknowledgment of our passional nature, and then approach the human status with an applied motive to re-direct it towards desire for God. On these grounds it is likely a truism that is ventured in the statement variously ascribed to G.K. Chesterton, St Francis, and St Augustine, but is only evidenced it the writing of Bruce Marshall[16] that, '...*the young man who rings the bell at the brothel is unconsciously looking for God*'. The search for God involves the search of that which is 'transcendent'. When we talk about marriage, we do well to reflect the mystical nature of God's relationship with humanity, in the way we talk about the intimate union of a husband and wife. When we talk about 'work', we do well to reflect the fact that humans are 'wired for work' in the way God works in creation. We are enlarged by the social science perspectives that pursue accuracy in the descriptive of humanity, but we become 'enriched' in the theological image of the picture of humanity that begins with our 'fallenness' and leads to alignment with a new identity and restoration through Christ.

Endnotes

1   Smith J.K.A. 2009 Desiring the Kingdom, Worship, Worldview and Cultural Formation, Baker Academic, Michigan, USA. p.158

2   Ibid p.158

3   ABC Religion and Ethics Report http://www.abc.net.au/radionational/programs/religionandethicsreport/ [Accessed 17th Sept 2018]

4   Schäfer T., Sedlmeier P., Städtler C., Huron D. 2013 The Psychological Functions of Music Listening, Frontiers in Psychology, August 2013, Vol. 4, Article 511. p.5

5   Ibid p.7

6   Ibid p.2

7   Johnson T.L., Rudd J., Neuendorf K., Jian G. 2010 Worship Styles, Music and Social Identity: A Communication Study, Journal of Communication and Religion, Jul 2010 p.144,145

8   Ibid p.148

9   Ibid p.150

10   Ibid p.152

11   Ibid p.5

12   Ibid p.152

13   Smith J.K.A. 2009 Desiring the Kingdom, Worship, Worldview and Cultural Formation, Baker Academic, Michigan, USA. p.53

14   Ibid p.52

15   Ibid p.76

16   Bruce Marshall (1945) The World, the Flesh and Father Smith. The American Chesterton Society https://www.chesterton.org/other-quotations/ [Accessed 11th Aug 2018].

Chapter 8:
An 'Eclipse' of Culture

So then, brothers and sisters, stand firm and hold fast to the teachings
we passed on to you, whether by word of mouth or by letter.

2 Thessalonians 2:15

The Eclipse of Anti-structure

People around the world are fascinated with a solar eclipse.
Daylight turns to night in what is for some a cosmic 'otherworldly'
phenomenon. As the moon passes in front of the sun, those in
the path are enveloped in the shadow. The sky darkens and the
temperature drops. The sun's appearance is transformed and at the
peak of the eclipse what is visible is the corona, or a halo of gas that's
not visible under normal conditions.

For some a total solar eclipse is something close to a religious
experience. But a solar eclipse is not the only eclipse we can envisage.
What concerns us in the coming chapter is the idea that culture can also
experience the phenomenon of eclipse. It may not necessarily be a bad
thing for some who anticipate what to expect and make plans to sustain
themselves through the experience. We can more easily comprehend
the way a cultural 'eclipse' might impact us personally, if we remain

adaptable and recognise the need to embrace personal transformation.

'Eclipse' appears to be a significant way to describe 'collective' cultural change. When change occurs, cultural reform displaces the former structures. Philosopher Charles Taylor who reflects on the idea of an 'eclipse of anti-structure'[1] argues that the changes that are now pervading societies are 'structurally' different to anything that has gone before. Antagonistic forces in a society are joining together, recognising their common grievances and uniting often under a force of 'nationalism'. He suggests that 'anti-structure' is very strong in a highly interdependent, technologically advanced and 'super-bureaucratised' world. These developments take the emergence of 'anti-structure' to a new level that he laments may be beyond the capacity of the modern age to deal with. The forces of 'anti-structure' unite against the common ideas of centralized control, regimentation, and the forces of conformity. The aim of 'revolution' is to replace the present order with a new code of freedom, and constructs of community, with a view to a new radicalism becoming the idealised norm.

'Anti-structure' is not so much a negative process as a necessary process in cultural change. As a descriptor 'anti-structure' translates to all revolutionary forms and whenever change occurs it is necessary to culture formation and cultural reform, be that it may have either a positive or negative set of consequences.

On the arrival of Christianity at the doorstep of the Roman Empire, the Apostles who were accused of 'turning the world upside down' (Acts 17:6) were heralding 'new structures' that would eventually permeate the prevailing social structure and render it obsolete. We may be witnessing the ebb and flow of social structures today. The emergence of pervasive present-day societal change in attitudes to passion, desire and sexuality may be the outcome of a centuries long eclipse of 'anti-structure'. The present day sexual and cultural revolution has come to obscure an earlier idealised position imperfectly shaped by a protestant Christian ethic. Thought dominated forces uniting, to topple a centralised structural

122

imaginary, have gradually brought about substantial change in societal attitudes. We'll look at these changes in a case study just ahead.

By the late 1960's philosopher Francis Schaeffer[2] had identified what he called a 'line of despair' that differentiated notions of understanding 'absolute truth', dating back to the loss he identified in the US to the year 1935. From this point he noted that a cultural drift caused people to think differently about 'truth'. A gradual shift spread geographically, from intellectuals, to the more educated, to workers, and the middle class. And the progression continued, beginning with philosophers and ending with theologians.

He identifies print media publications like Time, Newsweek, The Listener and The Observer as spreading something like a 'bad London Fog' that grew into revolution, starting with confusion, then bewilderment and before long people were overwhelmed. The basic problem he identified was a shift in 'presuppositions'.

The epistemological base had changed, and people no longer accepted absolute morals. They no longer accepted that if one thing were true, the opposite would be false. If one thing was right the opposite would be wrong. He argued that historic Christianity stands on the basis of 'antithesis' where the foundational antitheses is that God objectively exists, rather than the opposite of His not existing. Whichever one of these we choose, alters everything in the dimension of knowledge and morals and all of life.

Bringing these thoughts into the context of knowing the transcendent God, we might draw careful attention to the concept of exposure to the theological imagery of the Bible. When people become detached, either forcibly or by distraction, the glowing coals of their faith become cool and their sense of 'transcendence' is reduced to 'immanence' where the living God seems distant and powerless.

But the possibility of reformation is never far from the hopes and aspirations of Christian leaders. Evidence of this phenomenon is both around a 'decline' in religion under repression, and a 'resurgence' when exposure to religion is restored. The direct evidence for this possibility of 'resurgence' is found in reference to the religious revival experienced in Eastern Europe in 1989 where the resurgence or reaction to a time of repression under authoritarian regimes, was described as a 'U shaped curve'[3] following the fall of communism. Our immediate challenge may be to ensure that a deflated secular disenchantment does not lay hold of our own national governance and leave cultural leadership in the hands of secular elites.

An Eclipse of Sexual Ethics

Evidence for the way change progresses from one prevailing 'structure' to the gradual eclipse of a new 'anti-structure' can be identified in historic developments, that may be an important historic 'case study' of the progressive change of Western morality.

If indeed the passions of the 'Immanent Frame' are contrasted to the moderated passions contextualized under 'Divine Transcendence', the broadly popular presentation of those passions by the Christian church should be influenced by those 'higher ideas' and beliefs that come from the Divine source.

In examining the American context for dynamic social change Paul S. Boyer[4] describes a progression in developments culminating in the 20th Century where the dominant influence on 'sexual attitudes' shows a deviation from the mores established by Evangelical Protestantism.

This appears to be a useful illustration of developing secularization, that I believe may be corelated to a gradual generational 'loss of transcendence'. Identifying another dimension to changing attitudes in a rising sphere of secularization adds another layer of evidence for the movement away from those protective elements that Western societies with their Judeo-Christian foundations held as 'absolutes'. The result illustrates what Christians usually agree is a social deterioration that affects, individuals, marriages, families, communities and nations. Our view of 'human flourishing' is shaped by aspirations fuelled by our acknowledgement of a Divine transcendence.

The eclipsing anti-structure of changing attitudes to sexual mores illustrates the outcomes or consequences of the more 'flattened two-dimensional' picture of the pursuit of significance when captivated within the rationalist limitation of an 'immanent frame'. We may be able to rely on the assumption that what was happening in America, is also a reflection of developments broadly across the Western world and are applicable in correlation to developments in Australia especially as there has been an acceleration of secularization in the latter 20th century, and early 21st century.

It is worthy of note, that the role media plays, first as 'print' media and later electronic media as change develops. We may ask the questions, is the permeation of popular media broadly fuelling sexual attitude change? Or, are changes in sexual attitudes fuelling the depictions in modern media?

The Case Study – 18th Century Sexual Ethics

This story starts in the 18th century United States with the evangelical 'sexual ethic' originating from Protestant foundations. Founding law makers viewed procreation as a fact of 'Divine creation' and with definitive biblical demarcation of what constituted sexual sin. Fornication' and 'adultery' were inculcated as scandalous violations of the sanctity of marriage as a covenant consecrated by God.

Marriage was biblically reflective of the relationship between God and humanity. The protestant moral position on sex and marriage had since colonial times been reflected in Law and covered a wide gamut of sexual attitudes. But attitudes were always fluid, and as communications and distribution methods continued to evolve, eighteenth and nineteenth century Enlightenment writers began to highlight 'sexual adventures', along with reaction to the French Revolution and the emergence of the Romantic movement (18th and 19th centuries). Alternate writings brought a new emphasis on 'passion and emotion' that began to challenge traditional ideas about sex. Polygamous Mormons intensified their challenge to sexual mores especially in the US context through their political dominance in the State of Utah.

19th Century – Tensions Escalate

Urbanization in the late 19th century and European immigration brought increased prostitution to major urban centres. Boyer (2001) notes that the Evangelical response led to the formation of the Young Men's Christian Association (YMCA) as a counter measure to the perceived dangers of urban living including sexual temptations.

Women increasingly became moral guardians of the family, and 'motherhood' was reinforced as a special calling to be undertaken with purity and innocence. The Christianised image of motherhood became a measured contrast to the reality of working-class immigrant women bringing new fashions, and a challenge to the notion that the primary purpose of sex was only limited to procreation. The lack of sexual inhibition led to increased prevalence of venereal disease. Urban concentrations raised the ante in moral policy around bans on contraception, and there were fears that innocent women and children would be at risk from rising sexual immorality leading to the need for sex education for young people focusing on purity and abstinence.

20th Century - Media Accellerates Ethical Change

The arrival of the automobile freed young couples from rigid requirements of a chaperone and open discussion about sex in the Christian home was less about understanding, than it was the encouragement of abstinence and publicising its risks. Boyer (2001) notes that as sexual research advanced and condemnation of sexual practices continued, the post WW1 influence of Sigmund Freud brought a new authority on sexual matters where the dangers of sex were overtaken by discussion about repression and inhibition.

Terminology around sex was changing. Masturbation was redefined as 'autoeroticism', and psychosexual phenomena around dreams and fantasies began to be transformed from 'vice' to harmless inevitability. Campaigns to disseminate contraceptives championed by early feminist and women's rights activist Margaret Sanger (1879-1966)[5] who coined the phrase 'birth control' and worked towards its legalisation, encouraged women to accept their own sexuality fuelled by studies dismissing the idea that women 'lacked sexual desire and disliked sexual activity'. Margaret Sanger assumed prominence through writing a newspaper column called 'What Every Girl Should Know' (1912) in a campaign to educate women about sex.

The period between world wars saw the emergence of 'marriage manuals' encouraging experimentation and the 'enjoyment' of sex. Post WW2 Alfred Kinsey's writings in the *Sexual behaviour in the Human Male* (1948) and *Sexual Behaviour in the Human Female* (1953) became 'best-sellers' and were adopted by the media and popular culture as 'The Kinsey Reports'.[6] These books began a further revolutionising of attitudes to 'sex and gender' and brought a liberating effect including attitudinal changes to homosexuality, abortion, contraception and the sexual habits of prisoners.

In the 1960's the emergence of 'The Pill' as an oral contraceptive approved in the US encouraged women to relax control of sexual choices in terms of pregnancy, and further enhanced freedoms in female sexuality. Traditional roles were under greater challenge from popular countercultural movements throughout the 1960's with popular slogans including the iconic 'Make love, not war'.

The climate of the sexual revolution continued into the 1970's with reinforcement of public attitudes in Law through the US Supreme court decision to uphold a woman's right to abortion in *Roe v Wade* (1973) and the changes to diagnosis of psychologists and psychiatrists of homosexuality as a mental illness.

Nudity and explicit sex appeared more openly in movies, the courts relaxed pornography laws. The emergence of AIDS caused a reassessment of sexual freedoms, but 'safe sex' became the emphasis. The emergence of women as a force in defining sexual mores began to change the balance of male-female relationships with new laws around sexual harassment and more inclusive definitions of rape. By the end of the 20th Century social scientists were able to identify a major 'reformulation' of attitudes to sexuality and to the roles of men and women more broadly in relationships.

21st Century - The Eclipse Continues...

In the 21st Century the sexual and cultural revolutions have hit dizzying heights where even the definition of male and female have been blurred in a transsexual reformulation of sexual identity. Once Christian leaders are past the lament of how things have deteriorated, and the role of media in the process of change by 'eclipse', we are confronted with the question, as to whether social decline by print and electronic media, might also have the power to perpetuate the opposite effect, a reversal of the decline.

There is a new challenge before a new breed of modern media executives. The challenge is in how to 'utilise' present day mass media and 'new media' for a 'counter-cultural' expression of timeless transcendent Christian ethics as an injection into the 'immanent frame' of 'rational only' existence.

As 'new forms' of media on the variety of new platforms take social influence up to new levels the Public Christian leader has 'equipping of the saints' (Ephesians 4) in mind. Leaders use every opportunity to empower individuals and organisations who have the responsibility for influence, that has now become shared across more and more shoulders, to undertake the challenge to go 'counter-cultural' for a Kingdom purpose. What is required, is a structural eclipse of the 'alternate-kind' that re-imagines biblical values for the protection of generations to come.

Endnotes

1   Taylor C. 2007 A Secular Age, Belknap Press of Harvard University Press, Cambridge, Massachusetts, USA and London, England. P.53

2   Schaeffer F 1984 The God Who Is There, The Complete Works of Francis Schaeffer, Vol 1. 1968, Crossway, Illinois, USA. pp.5-8

3   Voas D., Doebler S. 2011 Secularization in Europe: Religious Change between and within Birth Cohorts, Religion and Society in Central and Eastern Europe, RASCEE 2011, 4(1) – p.41

4   Boyer P.S. 2004 Sexual Morality and Sex Reform, The Oxford Companion to United States History, Oxford University Press, Published online 2004.

5   Margaret Sanger – Activist and social reformer (1879 – 1966), https://www.biography.com/people/margaret-sanger-9471186 [Accessed 13th Aug 2018]

6   Source: The Kinsey Institute, Indiana University https://kinseyinstitute.org/about/history/alfred-kinsey.php [Accessed 13th Aug 2018]

Chapter 9:
21st Century Australian Christian Radio – Vision and Values

"Write down the revelation and make it plain on tablets so that a
herald may run with it."

Habakkuk 2:2

The significant emergence of dedicated Christian Radio in the 1990's
under a government relaxation of control over the Community radio
sector, has enhanced the opportunity for the emergence of what
for Australia was a relatively new orientation. Apart from just a few
exceptions in capital cities, dedicated Christian radio has been a relatively
new expression of Christian ministry in a landscape where Christian
expression on mainstream media had been in decline, perhaps since the
contractions of the 1960's.

Over the past two to three decades new expressions of Christian
broadcasting have emerged in Australia, largely thanks to the efforts of
key personnel from the Rhema Broadcasting Group in New Zealand,
who spear-headed efforts to encourage Christian leaders to pursue
Community Radio licences in Australia in the 1990s.

Christian influence in the community broadcasting sector has been expanding in influence and professionalism, as cities and towns have embraced the efforts of broadcasters with a Christian vision for their communities. The changing dynamics have given rise to new levels of Christian leadership as mature media operators rather than only program providers, or a reliance on limited or legislated airtime provisions of media regulation.

We might argue that detachment from the mainstream media, has its own downside, but for those enterprises who have seen opportunity, the testing of waters has for many begun to deliver a social dividend through loyal following and many stories of lives enhanced, and transformed by the assertive development of Christian radio.

The 'Vision and Values' of Australian Christian Radio

Australia has outstanding Christian radio expressions in capital cities, regional centres and even in remote outback communities. Sampling and comparing public expressions of Christian faith alignment is not intended to single-out or diminish the reputations of broadcast ministries. In the pages ahead I have endeavoured to select the most prominent Christian broadcasters with a view to reflecting on whether there is a prominent expression of 'transcendence' in Australian Christian radio. In contrast I was looking for a subtle settling for a deflated two-dimensional secular 'immanence'?

The public expression of 'Vision, Mission and Values' Statements, and/or website 'Statements of Purpose' may provide an important insight for our understanding of intent. What is expressed on public websites or in the documented mission and vision statements of Australia's prominent Christian Broadcasters in Capital cities and larger regional centres reveals their public motivations as expressions of Christian media.

The summary that I have put together here, is a surprise 'snapshot' taken in 2018. I've included a brief account of each station with relevant

132

content gleaned from the website presence of Australia's most prominent Christian broadcasters. You may be familiar with one or more of the stations that I chose, because they are perhaps the highest profile Christian radio stations in the nation of Australia:

1. **Sydney - Hope 103.2 FM:**[1] In 1953 The Christian Broadcasting Association Limited (CBA) was started by the Rev. Vernon Turner, as a non-profit content production facility in Sydney, providing programs for use on commercial stations. Today, Hope is one of the premier Christian broadcasters bringing a message of hope to the community through a family-friendly, safe listening environment. They're not quick to criticise or condemn, nor play on people's fears, but ready to celebrate what is good in society and culture.

   > 'Mission: COMMUNICATING HOPE TO TRANSFORM LIFE, FAITH AND CULTURE. *Vision: Hope Media aspires to be the Christian voice recognised as a credible and respected alternative to commercial and public media. Organisational Values: We believe: That all people are made in the image of God. That all people should be treated equally and should be dealt with justly. That all people live in need of God's love and grace and mercy. That all people are called to a life of faith in God through Jesus Christ. That we, together with all Christians, are called to share God's love with all people. That we are dependent on God for all things. That we are called to live in community and to serve the wider community. That we are called to be a reflection of Christ's love in all we say and do. That we are called to deal with others truthfully and with the utmost integrity.*

2. **Perth - Sonshine FM:**[2] 98five Sonshine FM broadcasts to 285 000 listeners weekly through FM and online, with countless stories of lives being changed for the better through music, words, wisdom, compassion and practical teaching programs that are broadcast every day. This is a 24 hour a day 'inspiration and celebration' station broadcasting the God-inspired words of the Christian

leaders of Perth every hour, together with inspirational music, practical lessons on life, relationship building and encouraging family and friends.

> 'To engage the people of WA with the positive message of hope in Jesus Christ.' 98five Sonshine FM and Sonshine Digital is a God-inspired, donor empowered mission that aims to bring the positive message of hope and the life-changing wisdom of God to every household in Perth, Western Australia and beyond. Values listed: Serving, Professionalism, Integrity, Community, Creativity. On the issue of Integrity: 'OUR PURPOSE IS TO DO WHAT IS RIGHT, NOT ONLY IN THE SIGHT OF THE LORD, BUT ALSO IN THE SIGHT OF OTHERS.' (2 Corinthians 8:21 GNT)

3. **Brisbane - 95five Family FM:**[3] Started in 1975, the founders met with a 'God-breathed' vision for Family Radio, broadcasting radio content that adds value, is suitable for the entire family and that ultimately makes Christ and His salvation as a normal and essential ingredient of a family life.

> 'At 96five our vision is that as people connect with us on air, via newsletters or our website they will feel welcomed, valued and appreciated and this begins a process of authentic engagement'... 'We believe Christ is made known through connection and engagement. We also partner with organisations that share these values and work together with a strong desire to make a positive difference across this city.'

4. **Melbourne 89.9 Light FM:**[4] Melbourne's Positive Alternative, dedicated to bringing positive, safe, family friendly, 100% clean content and a whole lot of fun. Anticipating a future, better than the present. Holding fast to Christian beliefs to guide their work, decisions and relationships. A community of God's people existing not for ourselves but for the sake of our mission.

'Our Vision is to see every life alight with Christian hope. Our Mission: We communicate Christian hope through remarkable content that positively impacts the personal journey of each member of our audience'. Our Values: We value creativity, seek original ideas & encourage thinking that is new & different. We seek to be remarkable in all we do including our content, relationships, workplace, by our actions & in our words. We dare to dream and imagine. We are authentic and inclusive. We are true to who we are, to God, and to who we serve.

5. **Adelaide 1079 Life FM:**[5] A 20-year journey to obtain a broadcast license for Adelaide came to fruition in 1993. The station is an interdenominational organisation run by a board of Christian business people. Programming serves the Christian community to be an outreach as part of the Church's wider commission.

> Mission: *'Life FM aims to challenge and influence contemporary thinking by presenting a Biblical worldview through broadcasting that leads people to a revelation of God's grace and encourages them to connect to the local Christian Church as followers of Christ.' Life FM delivers the vision by...Creating innovative, dynamic and relevant program content and personalities that connect with secular and Christian audiences. Using and exploring diverse technologies to effectively present the Biblical worldview. Supporting the vision with a team of diligent and dedicated staff who are committed to the Christian mission. Creating efficient and fully extended sponsorship and fundraising teams that fuel our mandate and impact future growth. Encouraging all Christians to engage in the vision through Life FM membership and financial support. Creating a brand that attracts our target audience to the station. Underpinning all endeavours with high quality and accurate research. Undergirding all activities with continuing and*

deliberate prayer.

6. **National Broadcaster: Vision Christian Media**[6] (700+ Cities and Towns[7]) The dream is to deliver 'Trusted Christian Media for Every Australian' and is not just the goal of Vision Christian Media, but an integral part of their DNA. Vision holds Open Narrowcast Licences, and broadcasts a program beamed by satellite from studios in Brisbane, to a repeater network in cities, towns and communities around Australia. Formerly UCB (United Christian Broadcasters) Australia. Vision FM was launched in the late 1990's. Radio is supported by popular devotionals 'The Word For Today' and Vision 180 Magazine, a youth radio online stream Vision 180, a resource arm Vision Christian Store, a confidential prayer request service Vision Christian Prayer, a national news service Vision National News, and tours to Israel through Vision Christian Tours.

> *Mission: 'To be a trusted, consistent and unifying voice in the Australian Community to challenge, encourage & affirm people in the Christian Faith. Vision: 'To see Australian lives and society redeemed and transformed through following Jesus Christ.'[8] Values: 'God is our provider' ...'Together is better' ...'We're here to serve' ... We love people.'*

7. **Canberra 1WAY FM:**[9] 1WAY FM is not a Church, but a Christian Community organisation holding to the statement of Christian belief known as 'The Apostles Creed'. In line with modern strategic planning practice, the Board has devised a Statement of Purpose,'[10] 1WAYFM presents a Christian message of hope and encouragement to listeners'. This carefully worded statement provides a "litmus" for testing everything we do in the station.

> *'Vision: Promoting a Christian Perspective across our community. Mission: Keeping the Christian message of hope relevant in the world today by presenting real stories by real people in real time'. Our Values: 1WAY FM aims to create a station envi-*

ronment governed by the values of Faith, Hope, Love, Humility, Wisdom, Servanthood.

8. Wollongong Pulse 94.1FM:[11] Living Sound Broadcasters was formed in 1983, originally Illawarra Christian Broadcasters. Part of their submission for a full-time license required a demonstration of the inadequacy of secular radio to meet the needs of the Christian community. Prayers were answered when they were granted a license in 1998.

> *Vision Statement: To serve the local community and church, by providing engaging radio content to our listeners, subtly communicating the message of Christ, through entertainment. Mission* Statement: To provide a local family friendly Christian community radio station via FM frequency, Internet streaming, mobile apps and podcasts; aided by social media *platforms; and being a positive alternative to all other local media, by designing our music and talk content to encourage and uplift the spirits of our listeners, aiming to motivate and inspire them throughout their day.*

9. Geelong – 96three FM:[12] A non-denominational Christian community radio station covering the City of greater Geelong, the Surf Coast and Bellarine Peninsula and surrounding towns of Colac, Ballarat, Gisbourne and much of Melbourne. Seeking to change lives by broadcasting hope and encouragement, positively reinforcing worth and building up the family unit based on sound moral and biblical guidelines.

> *From the beginning, our mission has been to "broadcast the reality of Jesus Christ" through a well-balanced blend of teaching programs and 100% Christian music. 96three is a faith ministry whose mission for more than twenty years has been to broadcast the reality of Jesus Christ by offering encouragement, hope and friendship all day, every day.*

10. Rhema FM Newcastle:[13] A Christian music and program provider.

The journey began in 1984 when a small group of Christians formed a group to begin a radio station. 14 years passed before a permanent licence was issued. Now more than 30 years on the station is careful to give God the Glory, Honour and Praise for sustaining the continuous growth from humble beginnings.

> *Mission: Rhema FM Newcastle is a 'home mission, with a mission to reach every home.' We aspire to reach those within our community and beyond, and to be a source of light by the will of God. We wish to assist the body of Christ across Newcastle and the Hunter, whilst providing quality and 100% Christian music and content.*

11. **Gold Coast Juice 107.3 FM:**[14] Operated by the Christian community to provide Good Taste Radio for the Gold Coast. In the broader community Juice suggests 'mainstream media doesn't seem to know what to do with the Christian faith.' Listeners indicate their love for great Christian music and artists that speak of hope and celebrate a depth and purpose of life that changes everything for the better. Also, unique programs that embrace the fulness of what it is to be human and explore what the Christian faith is in our culture today.

> *Juice1073 is proud to be a Community Radio Station operated by the Christian community to provide Good Taste Radio for the Gold Coast! In an environment where radio has become a little impersonal and disconnected, Juice1073 is proud to be operated by the local community and for the benefit of our city. Together, we provide local families with the best available programming, local information and music, all backed with a Good Taste Guarantee so the whole family can enjoy quality radio without any awkward moments.*

'Fine-Tuning' Christian radio?

Philosophical concepts of 'transcendence' are prominent in these publicly presented 'dream, vision, and mission' statements of Australia's Christian broadcasters. Some of the most common terms that illustrate this transcendence are in the words 'hope' and biblical 'worldview' indicating an 'otherness' to the broadly accepted mainstream notions of secularized immanence.

Other common terminologies include the concept of 'family friendly'. I suggest that this is not just because there is a desire to embrace all ages in broadcast content, but that the idea of being 'family-friendly' is a way of contrasting content to that which is increasingly prevalent in mainstream radio broadcasting where 'offensive' material 'bad language', 'inuendo' and sensually suggestive musical lyric content are pervasive. Perhaps this illustrates a disconnection on the part of mainstream broadcasters, from the values that Christians identify as 'family friendly' from biblical revelation of ethical behaviours that promote a 'godliness' model of human flourishing that defines relationships under Divine principles.

It is a common attribute in these expressions of Christian media to acknowledge the person of Jesus Christ as being central to their ethos. In a fallen world, the contrast of 'hope' is enlivened by the stark difference brought to bear by the character and example of the incarnate Son who is the perfect image of God and the central tenet of salvation. Christian radio demonstrates this aspiration to reflect the person of Christ, His character, and His teachings to a world while in its fallen state, and it does so by reflecting Christ's 'transcendence' through music, program content, teaching and news.

Collectively, those staff and volunteers that make up the teams that produce the on-air sound, are contributing to a biblical shaping, that confronts the 'social imaginary' widely expressed by secular culture. The result is a different, and often diametrically opposed cultural mix that is continually being 'fine-tuned' to create a mature biblically founded and dynamic presentation of a Divinely empowered Gospel in a mass media environment.

Some of the stations demonstrate their aspiration to have a deeper reflection, and engagement with current affairs, while others have a more devotional orientation. All are reliant on the growth in professionalism and maturity of staff, contributors and the availability of contemporary musical content that reflects the overall ethos of the Christian gospel.

What every station has in common, is that they have been driven by the generosity of determined and faith-filled Christian supporters and sponsors, who have enabled the foundations to be formed, and continue to enable the broadcast ministry to grow. Management, staff and volunteers have sown countless hours, endured significant controversies, hardships, and growing pains. Each has broken new ground, through the challenge of sowing vision, nurturing, and enabling their supporting communities to rise to the challenges of establishing functional and effective Christian ministry. Every operation started small, with people who responded to visionaries who rallied supporters, and in most cases, starting from a low base with little professional expertise to call upon, and because of this, each one could be counted as a miraculous occurrence. For the community sector it's a triumph when we consider the challenge to sort through choices for programming direction, and even in many cases to subordinate commercial considerations to the dream of authentic Christian radio for their respective communities.

Endnotes

1   Source: Hope Media Ltd: https://hope1032.com.au/about-us/history/ [Accessed 13th Aug 2018]

2   Source: 98five Sonshine FM: https://98five.com/about-us/ {Accessed 13th Aug 2018]

3   Source: 96five Family FM: https://www.96five.com/about-96five/vision-mission/ [Accessed 13th Aug 2018]

4   Source: 89.9 Light FM: https://www.lightfm.com.au/vision-mission-values/ [Accessed 13th Aug 2018]

5   Source: 1079 Life FM: https://1079life.com/about/vision-and-values/ [Accessed 13th Aug 2018]

6   Source: Vision Christian Media Staff Handbook: https://intranet.vision.org.au/externalintranet/intranet/index.html [Accessed 14 May 2018]

7   National Station list 700+ cities and towns https://vision.org.au/radio/station-list/ [Accessed 13th Aug 2018)

8   This Mission and Vision is dated 2018 – Ministry Plan Part 1 – Staff Handbook 2018.

9   Source: Canberra 1WAY FM: https://www.1wayfm.com.au/about-us/vision/ [Accessed 13th Aug 2018]

10   Source: 2017 Annual General Meeting – Chairman's Report p.2.

11   Source: Wollongong Pulse 94.1FM: https://pulse941.com.au/about/ [Accessed 13th Aug 2018]

12   Source: Geelong 96three FM: http://www.96three.com.au/about-us/ [Accessed 13th Aug 2018]

13   Source: Rhema FM Newcastle: https://www.rhemafm.com.au/about/ [Accessed 13th Aug 2018]

14   Source: Gold Coast Juice 107.3FM: https://www.juice1073.com.au/about-us/ [Accessed 13th Aug 2018]

Chapter 10:
The 'Gate-Keeper' of
Radio Content

But these are written that you may believe that Jesus is the Messiah, the
Son of God, and that by believing you may have life in
his name.

John 20:31

Does Christian Radio need 'Gate-Keepers'?

To more concretely identify Christian radio's strengths and weakness
and to ascertain trends in Christian radio programming decisions, I
sought to survey the top echelon of Australian Christian radio Content
Managers (2018). The Content Manager is the person charged with the
responsibility to make the 'hard calls' as to what content is broadcast and
to create policy that forms the day-to-day ministry culture.

In other expressions of Public Christianity, whether Church, para-Church
or Christian based not-for-profit Charity, a Pastor/Leader or appointee
will be responsible for the standards of day-to-day application of a faith
position to the operation. (In the coming chapters, we'll discover how
Christian ministries, and Christian business owners can make a similar
application through development of a new KPI (Key Performance
Indicator) to help in the management of Godly standards.

Usually a Content Manager is motivated by their own sense of 'call'
to serve through the Christian Radio expression in their city or town.

They are usually experienced and creative communicators. And they are generally street wise to what 'sounds relevant' to listeners in the station's demographic.

Their responsibilities usually include oversight of the strategic formation of the station's sound. While the 'Mission, Vision and Values' of the station are typically guided by members of a Board, much of the day-to-day executive decision-making including the selection and mix of music, talk, news, advertising style and teaching ethos is in the hands of the Content Manager, a role that Ahern[1] describes as akin to a company's Product Manager. If the product is good, it is usually due to the Content Manager's programming skill. If the product is bad, it may also fall at the feet of the Content Manager They are the ones entrusted with the 'levers' to fine-tune the station's sound according to the constraints of the mission, vision and values set by the board.

The music style and selection, program teaching content, news, advertising policy, and the oversight, recruitment and professional development of on-air talent (personalities) either typically, or eventually falls to the Content Manager. I believe the Content Manager as part of a functioning leadership team is to Christian Radio the most significant builder of station image for a chosen demographic and/or psychographic target market.

The Content Manager balances responsibilities for reaching and growing an audience, satisfying expectations of stakeholders in the ministry, being across the latest market research, and is often chief architect of new innovative programming initiatives. The effectiveness of Christian radio relies heavily on the capacity of the 'gatekeeper' Content Manager to leave no element of programming to 'chance'.

My survey (2018) sought to ascertain the 'views and attitudes' of Christian Content Managers in key Australian radio markets, including capital cities, and major regional markets where the maturity of a Christian Radio presence was already demonstrated as viable and fully functional. The

144

essence of the survey questions that the Content Managers were asked to respond to were centred around the most effective ways that God's presence and power (transcendence) is reflected in the programming elements used by Christian Radio.

Because stations place different emphasis on key elements of their programming strategy, care was taken not to manipulate or load questions with inferred criticisms of programming content, but to 'test the motives' for critical programming decisions, and to ascertain the value of attention to professional development standards that may be necessary in Christian Radio ministry.

Responses were sought on a Likert scale 1 to 5: **Very Low 1 – 2 – 3 – 4 – 5 Very High**. Respondents would remain anonymous, and for accountability purposes, and curiosity, a number indicated they would like access to the findings of this study on its completion. There were eight questions, and three requests for short responses.

'Gatekeepers Survey': Questions, Responses, and Analysis

Question 1. The Level of Pessimism about the Future of the Church

Given that Census statistics show a decline in those claiming Christian faith (52%), to what degree do you think people are pessimistic about the future of the Christian Church?

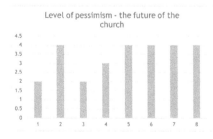

Very Low 1 – 2 – 3 – 4 – 5 Very High

What do these responses indicate?

The majority appear to reflect a significant 'negativity' of expectation for the future of the Christian Church. Only one of the respondents settled for the neutral option here. One might argue that a Leader requires a sober seriousness in their professional outlook and is careful not to assume that all is well. An alternative analysis may be that a cynical perspective from Content Managers may in fact be an advantage as one who is a watchman on the wall, conscious of impending danger. On the other hand, the perception that Content Managers as leaders may cause us to conclude that they feel as though they're 'fighting a losing cause', and that may be reason for concern.

Publicity around the Australian census figures (2016) showing falling church attendance may contribute to 'pessimism' even in Christian Radio leaders as it can be argued that a trend in declining church attendances will continue. We may also look to the personal eschatology held by individual Content Managers, where some may hold a negative outlook based on their interpretation of 'end times' biblical teaching. One view holds that having a negative outlook has an energising effect on the motivations of leaders not to accept the status-quo but take up the challenge using the tools in their hands to effect change in a pessimistic environment.

Question 2. Music vs Talk

Given that all Christian Radio wants to 'reach out' with the Gospel, to what degree do you think music selection is more important than the other, spoken elements?

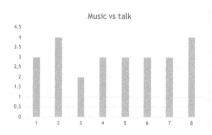

Very Low 1 – 2 – 3 – 4 – 5 Very High

What do these responses reveal?

On the question of the value of music and talk, the majority (5) of respondents are fence-sitters, opting for the more neutral option. Two of the respondents (25%) say the music is more important than talk elements of the program while just one of the respondents (12.5%) was comfortable to settle on the idea that talk elements of the programming content were more important.

The majority position choosing the neutral option on this question may lead to the assumption that Content Managers don't necessarily favour one side against the other, but that both music and talk are necessary for effective Christian radio. A reluctance to take sides on this question indicates an attitude of control over content within a fluid programming structure.

Question 3. Short vs Long-form Talk

Given that spoken word programs may be short or long, to what degree are short segments, testimonies or 'God Spots' more effective than longer teaching programs?

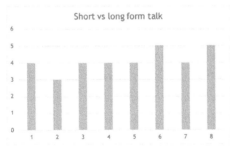

Short vs long form talk

Very Low 1 – 2 – 3 – 4 – 5 Very High

What can we glean here?

87.5% of respondents on the question of Short vs Long-form talk segments were either 'Highly' or 'Very Highly' in favour of short segments, testimonies or 'God spots'. It may be safe to conclude that Christian radio Content Managers in majority, prefer short, sharp and well produced

147

message segments, over longer talk format programs.

It may be of further interest and discussion to differentiate the 'longer talk' programs into those that may be monologue teaching programs, or long-form interview or Q&A style conversations or talk-back programming. Only one of the respondents was a 'fence sitter' here with the notion that both short and long-form talk segments were most effective.

It may be worthy of note to say that those surveyed were likely to be programming stations utilizing the FM band which has historically been a strong performer in music style programming, whereas AM stations often excel in talk programming. An important comparison may be useful in further consideration of 'short vs long-form' talk, where the national broadcaster ABC has news and information stations almost exclusively talk oriented with a view to fuller exploration of national news and current affairs presumably because 'understanding issues' is an important dimension in the relay of information. Christian radio in the future may need to prioritise how deeper Christian/biblical commentary may further equip listeners to engage the 'battle of ideas' that continues to rage in the public sphere.

Question 4. Transformation vs Apologetics

Given that many in the secular community deny the power of God, to what degree do you promote the miraculous and life transforming power of God, over the idea of apologetic arguments?

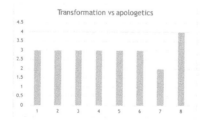

Very Low 1 – 2 – 3 – 4 – 5 Very High

Analysis

On this question, respondents were almost uniformly on the neutral position about the focus of the content of Christian radio. We might assume that a majority of respondents would promote equally those stories and testimonies of the miraculous and life transforming power of God, along with apologetic arguments that deal more with the cognitive aspects of Christian faith.

A neutral response might indicate equal value to both. This question is potentially about whether the 'head' or the 'heart' is a more effective focus. That the majority chose the neutral position means we may assume that respondents felt that both focusses are necessary to a balanced presentation of available content.

One respondent felt that miraculous and life transforming 'Power of God' issues were less important than apologetic argument, while another felt that they were more important. A reluctance to take a stronger position one way or the other may also indicate that we 'don't know' what is most effective and it's safest to sit on the fence.

Question 5. Encouragement vs Hard Core Biblical Issues

Given that much of our culture may be distracted from a focus on God, to what degree is your programming strategy centred on 'lighter' daily encouragement for individuals, rather than 'hard-core' Biblical mission issues?

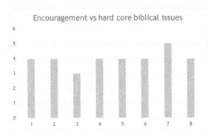

Encouragement vs hard core biblical issues

Very Low 1 - 2 - 3 - 4 - 5 Very High

Analysis

On this question, respondents were 'highly' or 'very highly' in agreement that 'lighter' daily encouragement of listeners was more important than 'hard-core' Biblical mission issues. The assumption here may be, that 'hard-core' Biblical mission issues are in the realm of the Church, or Bible Colleges.

Only one of the respondents took the neutral position, perhaps believing that Christian radio needed both the 'lighter', and at times a more 'intense' focus on Biblical engagement or mission issues.

Given the challenges of the 'Great Commission' there may be some concern here that Content Manager's attention to 'hard-core' mission issues is given a lower priority and are therefore considered less important.

It may be that a 'lighter' encouragement approach assumes that existing Christian listeners are already immersed in the idea of Christian mission. It may also be a response that assumes that the Christian radio ministry is 'itself' an expression of the Great Commission. There may also be an assumption that preparation for pursuing the Great Commission is itself only a light topic without the need for exploration in specific depth, either for a Christian audience, or for a non-Christian listener or seeker. Whichever way we look at this question, there may be an overall perception here that the lightweight option seems best, but deeper engagement with these important issues may be one of the most urgent and important elements expected from Christian media in the years to come.

Question 6. Politics and Ethics

To what degree is the discussion of politics and Christian positions on big ethical issues important for Christian radio?

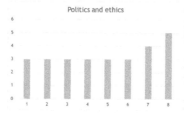

Very Low 1 – 2 – 3 – 4 – 5 Very High

Analysis

Most responses to this question indicate a level of comfort with the 'somewhat' half-way position to which we might assume that discussion of politics and ethics has a place, but not too often and not with higher intensity.

Two of the respondents took the 'high' and 'very high' preference for discussion of politics and ethics. Perhaps this is an indicator that Content Managers recognise that these issues cannot be left unattended as change continues to happen on significant social issues.

There may be a cautious recognition of 'risk' in presenting biblical positions on current issues, that some listeners may be offended by Christian truth or by the personalities that present political ideas. It may be of concern that a growing listenership should not be placed in jeopardy by presenting dissenting positions to the prevailing ethics being propagated by the mainstream media. The fence-sitter response here may also indicate that Content Managers hold doubts about whether Christians are supposed to engage in political debate, or that political commentary or debate is inherently partisan and therefore divisive.

Question 7. Influence on Values

Given that mainstream media sometimes has a negative influence on community attitudes, to what degree do you believe listeners 'values' are changed by of the influence of Christian radio?

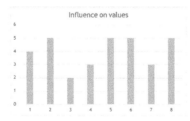

Very Low 1 – 2 – 3 – 4 – 5 Very High

What can we glean here?

Almost two thirds of all respondents on this question are 'highly' or 'very highly' confident that values are being challenged or changed by their ministry presentation on Christian radio. One third of respondents feel they have somewhat, or a low influence on values. It may be of concern that there is a low confidence in some Content Managers that their work is being effective.

Question 8. Preparedness from External Experience Alone

Given that professional development is important, to what degree does commercial, or community radio experience prepare presenters to function in the culture of Christian Radio ministry?

Very Low 1 – 2 – 3 – 4 – 5 Very High

Analysis

This question deals with recruitment and preparation for on-air presenters, asking whether basic radio training and preparation is enough to prepare on-air presenters to represent a 'ministry' pursuit in media. Most responses appear to show a 'high' level of agreement that basic radio announcing is all that is necessary to function in the culture of Christian radio. It may be that tight internal regulation around what presenters are permitted to say, or not say, keeps the communication of Christian content in the hands of well-produced, trustworthy segments carefully screened or overseen by the Content Manager.

The idea of a 'disc jockey' approach suppressing the spiritual dimension of the presenter, may also be a limiting factor in the capacity of the on-air presenter to communicate on a deeper personal relational level with the listener, adding weight to those things that are of greater significance.

This question may prompt further reflection on the idea that in Christian radio, even younger and less spiritually mature on-air presenters fill a vital role as ministers of the Gospel in their own right. We might assume that levels of polished professionalism honed, in a radio environment are favoured by Content Managers above recruitment of Bible College graduates who may have been through a Christian ministry 'formation' experience. There may also be a disconnect between Christian radio and Bible Colleges or their graduates who have sights set on serving in Church or mission contexts rather than on serving as a Gospel minister on radio.

Question 9. Your Station's Primary Values?

Question 9 sought a response from Content Managers on their station's Primary Values.

The final three questions of the Gatekeepers Survey asked respondents for short answers. After a process of 'coding responses', I was able to formulate an emerging cross-sectional sentiment. The final three questions asked about perception of the **'Primary Values'** of their radio station, in their role as the Content Manager. The last questions asked about perceptions of what it was, that made **'your station different?'** And, finally a question seeking **'closing thoughts'** as an opportunity to express a personalised contribution to the survey result.

The combined 'brief' thoughts of Content Managers in this exercise for Question 9 may be correlated to the overall public website display in the earlier comparative analysis of 'vision and values' of the most significant Christian stations discussed earlier.

Grouping responses, in the 'coding exercise' showed that the concepts of 'God centred truth', 'Relevant content delivered with integrity', 'Respect for listener vulnerabilities', and creating a 'Family fun positive' image of real-life experience are indeed the goals of Australia's Christian radio Content Managers.

For further development within the boardrooms and Executive meetings evaluating content, may be the question of 'weaknesses' or 'what's missing?' Broader encouragement to pursue issues of cultural engagement can be as 'simple or sophisticated' as the expertise available in the pool of talent at all levels of the ministry operation.

To deliver 'God Centred Truth' in 'Relevant Content' may require, at the discretion of Content Managers, frequent evaluation and expansion of content resources in order to effectively achieve the balance between what is 'family fun and positive, and vulnerable, with respect for the listener', and the weight of co-missional responsibility that leaders may have for 'God-centred truth in relevant content.'

Question 10. What makes your station different?

Content Managers responses to Question 10. delivered thoughts on what makes their station **'different'** by broadly identifying the contrast between Christian radio, and what is presented by the best rating mainstream secular radio in their communities. Three categories emerged in the coding process that may lead us to conclude from the responses, that:

1. The 'message of hope' points to its source 'relationship with God.'
2. Communities of belonging create a sense of 'well-being.'
3. And, the lived expression is indeed 'counter-cultural.'

The responses by Content Managers are in this question brimming to overflowing with a passionate desire for the fruits of what 'transcendence' promises to the ministry expression of Christian radio. 'Hope' is not just wishful thinking, but expectation of Divine deliverance not only in the future, but as a powerful force of security and motivation in the present. This word 'hope' in is in my view, one of the most powerfully charged 'transcendence' words in our Christian vocabulary.

Connecting listeners to a 'Relationship with God' is also vibrantly charged with the concept of 'transcendence'. What we see in this aspiration to relationship is the powerful desire for connection between the 'immanent and the transcendent'. This is the connection forged in the incarnation of Christ as *'The Word became flesh and has made his dwelling among us'*. (John 1:14).

Another important concept that emerged in the responses, is the aspiration to promote 'belonging and well-being'. As followers on a 'co-mission' with Christ we are confident that our 'well-being' is in His hands. We recognise that in 'belonging' to the wider body of Christ the functioning biblical expression of the Church has enormous benefits in bolstering our wellbeing, as we share insights into Godly wisdom, family and business ethics, and indeed expectation of a supernatural dimension of blessing that orients our pursuits to flourishing in every way.

A final insight in the responses from Content Managers on this question is in the orientation to be 'counter-cultural'. This expression in the context of the wider dimensions of what is contained within these chapters includes the aspiration of 'breaking free' from the pressures exerted by the 'immanent frame' discussed widely earlier. The counter concept of 'transcendence' is a present day 'counter-cultural' pursuit contrasted to the deflated single-dimensional Godless, pessimistic secularised mainstream media. The majority of thought expressed by Content Managers in this question either affirms the intentional pursuit of an orientation to transcendence, or the aspiration to increase the intensity of a transcendence for listening audiences.

For further discussion in the 'support networks' around Content Managers may be the question of 'how' ministry-oriented radio leaders facilitate the counter-cultural aspects of Christian Radio? And importantly, once a defined difference is established, how it is sustained when campaigns end, or the baton changes to new leadership. Sustainable professional leadership development will be a constant in the years to come, if momentum is to be maintained.

Question 11. Closing Thoughts of Content Managers?

The final question asked Content Managers for '**Closing Thoughts**?' These were open responses delivered by Content Managers having offered insights to the earlier survey questions. My process of analysing responses enabled me to focus thoughts and comments about some profound concepts being offered.

Being a 'Christian Voice' is a common sentiment. Further discussion may develop if we were to ask the question "is Christian radio 'a' Christian voice?' or is it 'the Christian voice?' The difference in responses may shed light on whether or not Content Managers have expectation that their station is 'only one of many expressions' of Christian truth perhaps taking a secondary position to the leadership of the 'Local Church.'

Alternatively, the Content Manager may see their programming role as presenting 'the only Christian voice' to many of their listeners. As you can imagine, when this is the case, we compound the importance of the maturity and skill of the Content Manager who may be charged with responsibility for discipleship and maturity of Christian listeners. And this may be amplified in importance if the primary pursuit is to connect with non-believing listeners.

The other responses of providing a 'Relational Voice', 'Resisting Compromise', and providing 'Balance' are also the products of ongoing evaluation of programming strategy. These may be enhanced by the soundness of the relationships of the Content Manager to his/her local church pastor, and encouragement provided by the executive leadership of the radio ministry. The protection and accountability of this relationship also has the powerful potential to 'bridge the gap' between the ministry of Christian radio and the ministry of the local Church. It's one significant way to ensure the ministry remains resistant to 'drifting' from the 'vision, mission, and values' determined by the board.

Endnotes

1   Ahern S. 2006 Making Radio, A Practical Guide to Working in Radio, 2nd Edition, Allen & Unwin, Crow's Nest, Australia. p.13

Chapter 11:
The Return of
Transcendence

How, then, can they call on the one they have not believed in? And how
can they believe in the one of whom they have not heard? And how can
they hear without someone preaching to them? And how can anyone
preach unless they are sent? As it is written: "How beautiful are the feet of
those who bring good news!"

Romans 10:14,15

To either predict, or strategise a comeback for the mass adoption
of a 'transcendence' fuelled social imaginary is not at this point, in
the ordinary conversation of Christians. However, to deepen our
understanding of the present, and to dream of possibilities, we can apply
relevant theory to the present circumstances as a starting point with the
view to inspiring strategy that may seed the possibilities of change.

In earlier chapters I have sought to identify the changing religious
landscape in Australia over the past century with a special focus on
developments since the 1950's. Understanding the rise and fall of
religious fervour is an important consideration, if we are to anticipate
another rise.

The value of understanding the perception of decline of the public role
of religion is addressed by European scholar David E.J Herbert[1]

He has sought to employ an explanatory framework outlining both growth and decline in aspects of the 'public presence' of religion. His aim has not been to deliver exhaustive data about Christianity, but rather to explore the implications for broader religious authority, symbols and religious discourse. An impression emerges, in Herbert's discussion that is one of optimism in the face of change, and a hypothesis that religion is predicted to 'adapt' to the increasingly hostile context of secularized societies. He describes how prevalent theories in modernity including Secularization Theory and Rational Choice Theory have 'over-simplified' religion, and failed to predict the more likely outcomes when a set of quantifiable conditions for 're-publicization' exist.

'Publicization' indicates the processes that create a heightened public presence of religion. In our own Australian cultural setting, we might identify the rise of religious presence in the decades leading up to the 'golden age' that I described earlier in the 1950's where the overlap of the authority of print media and the new developments in broadcast media worked in a synergistic way. They created a broad public acceptance of biblical authority and fervour for religious expression. We then discussed the way that the broad public acceptance dissipated from the 1960's.

In his assessment of observed changes especially in Europe, Herbert adopts academic neutrality in discussion of 'religion' using the term as a generic catch-all for the world's religions, highlighting the argument that in Secularization Theory 'all' religions become 'privatised', marginalised and devalued in the 'secular' public sphere. So, it's not just Christianity classified as a 'victim' in this deepening secularisation, but all religions experience the same decline.

Herbert's approach takes in expectations that include 'secularization' and the possibilities that we might welcome in an emerging 'post-secular' world. He engages the idea that 're-publicization' becomes the new spin on 'de-privatization' because according to Herbert it is a better description of the predicted expanding and adaptive public role of religion. The theoretical assumption is that religion can never truly be 'privatized'.

In contrasting the idealism of Secularization Theory, Herbert looks to redefine 'secularization' in terms of the expected decline of the social and political influence of religion.[2] He concludes that there is an 'over-estimated' expectation of secularization theory, and contrasts those speculations with the 'actual' decline of religion's influence. His method offers insight into 'why' this has occurred, and progresses to 'predictions' for future developments when a 'post-secular' environment leads to a new emergence, or 're-publicization' process.

Declining Power

Herbert relies on a definition describing the 'expected effects' on religion from secularization as 'declining power, popularity and prestige of religious beliefs and behaviour'. Additional problems include the complications presented in the IT driven social media communications revolution. While these 'new media' technologies enhance the appearance of secularism, Herbert's hypothesis includes another significant dimension. He argues that the accelerated development of media systems, especially 'audio-visual enrichment' acts contrary to secular expectations and lends 'optimism' to the enhancement of the transmission and transformation of religious symbols, traditions and discourse. This contrasting view has not been adequately considered by secularization theorists and is one worthy of deeper consideration for strategists who work towards the concept of re-publicization of Christianity for the masses.

Herbert's argument develops across a series of case studies in multiple cultural contexts to show that contrary to the perceived expectations of those who implement a secularisation theory, it is often the case that religion spawns an even more visible, and arguably a more powerful presence at a level of public discourse.

Conclusions lead us towards an expectation of 'increased' functionalised presence for religion playing a significant role in contemporary politics and the public sphere. Biblical metaphors of 'salt' and 'light' are never far from the thinking of Christian leaders who recognise the contrast of 'light and darkness' and the influential nature of what it is to be the 'salt' that should never lose its savour and sanitising effects.

The same technology forging a secularization of society is also available to every Christian. We are encouraged that increased distribution capacity in media systems has a positive effect on the potential of the Christian mission. New and increasingly sophisticated media platforms create opportunities for expanding the public profile of the same religious symbols and discourses that have been under attack from secularisation. Whether it is for religious worship, community service, commercial or political purposes.

New Forms of Authority

While traditional religious elites have regulated historical meanings, the concept of 'republicization' signals a transition to new forms of authority, contingent on access to new forms of media technology. Herbert has not confined his discussion of 'core' biblical culture created by Christians but is expressing a broad re-emergence of all religious expressions. For our discussion, Christianity surely is the main contender for public religious expression in the West, but other competitive religious expressions are also likely to be on the rise.

Evidence for the transition includes the rise of the religious 'Right' in the US and other Western nations including Australia. Church attendances are falling in some denominations contrasted with the rise of Mega-Churches. Also worthy of note is the rise of religious philanthropy, and the growing mediatisation of Christianity.

The Weakness of Secularisation Theory

What appears to be lifting this sense of anticipation about the possibility of 're-publicization' is the exposé of the weaknesses of secularization and neo-secularization theory that appear to underestimate the complexity of religion. Herbert[3] suggests that secularization theory operates with 'weaknesses' including the application of Rational Choice Theory. In this theory, it is assumed that within the limits of personal understanding, guided by preferences and tastes, people attempt to make prudent and logical decisions that will benefit themselves.[4]

Where does this weakness lead? While secularization is characterised by the symptom of 'differentiation', which is the idea of 'separation of religion from the secular', it is also loaded with potential for 'de-differentiation' in a religious 'free market'. Here Herbert argues that this is merely a stage before a coming 'regeneration'. It can be illustrated in the idea that cells under pressure can revert to an earlier developmental stage before an expansive regenerative process. In an environment where distribution mechanisms can rapidly carry religious ideas, symbols and discourse to the masses the conditions are being created for republicizing religion.

These principles are global. However, I believe there is room for creative application of thought and principle to specific contexts. According to these ideas the flow of history in nations like Australia would be shaped by trends in media, and in political history that should show quantifiable evidence between public and political agenda setting, including the publicizing effects of religion.

Everywhere that modernisation is occurring, should show the same results in principle. We can take at face value the progressive findings of the World Values Survey as grounds for the uneven phenomenon of progress towards re-publicization.[5] I have become increasingly convinced that understanding the limitations of secularization theory may be one key to assessing the place of religion in the context of secular culture. My hope for Public Christianity emerges in the potential for re-publicization through what we can agree will be a neo-secular phase.

While we may be encouraged by Herbert's anticipation of 're-publicization', there is also a warning to the broader Christian Church in mission. These same principles that apply to re-publicization of Christian religion, also apply to every other religious system. Under secularization, there is the same effect, that old religious authorities are losing strength, while new religious authorities are rising according to their use of modern media technology.

We are heartened by the concept that our dearly held Christian religious symbols are likely to undergo a re-publicization, contrary to the expectations of secularization theory. The challenging context we are presented with for the future, is in the upheavals that come with significant social, religious and political changes throughout the world. Herbert's thoughts sited here preceded developments of the Arab 'spring', religious revolutions, civil wars (Syria) and the political developments of the past decade but are illustrative of the catalysts for changing attitudes to religious authority.

New social structures have begun to emerge in Western nations, and ideologies that arguably accompany secularization (including 'cultural Marxism') appear to be taking significant ground once held by traditional Christian values. Our challenge is to become agile, and adaptable in the face of hostility, and to nurture Christian media's elevated importance in re-publicization.

Public Christianity – Resisting Surrender to Secularism

It's not difficult to imagine a drift towards the 'secular' in a scenario where newcomers to positions of authority in Public Christian institutions, or indeed in any Christian ministry or business, are elevated without a working understanding of the contrasts between what it is to be 'Christian' and what it is to be 'Secular'.

For those who are naively trapped within a secular 'immanent frame', the loss of transcendence will be felt in virtually every area of life, practice and ethics. There are those like Blamires[6] who in reflecting on mid-20th Century spirituality concedes that the Christian mind 'had already succumbed' to a secular drift which was unmatched in all Christian history. So the idea of discussing 'reform', 'renewal' or 'revival', retuning to a biblical way of thinking and acting is undoubtedly way overdue. Here is how we might recognise the contrasts between a Christian biblical way of thinking, and the now commonly held secular thinking.

1. A Christian subscribes to a different moral code to the non-Christian.
2. Christians rise to different obligations ignored by non-church people.
3. In prayer and meditation there is cultivation of a dimension that remains unexplored by non-Christians. This is the rich treasure we enjoy that the non-Christian does not access. This is particularly important because it is likely the case that many cultural Christians do not practice a discipline of prayer, meditation and study of God's word.

These ideas simply illustrate the observation that Christians in the modern world of the last century, mentally accepted a frame of reference 'constructed' by the secular mind, and a set of criteria reflecting secular evaluations. The mind of a Christian according to Blamires should be distinguished differently to the secular mind. The Christian mind has:

1. A 'supernatural orientation'.
2. It has an 'eternal perspective'.
3. The Christian mind has an 'awareness of evil'.
4. It has a 'consciousness of the battlefield between good and evil'.
5. The Christian mind has a conception of truth by revelation, not a human construction.
6. It has an acceptance of Authority.
7. The mark of the Christian mind is that believers are the visible vehicles of God's action in the world.

8. The Christian mind has a concern for 'the other person'.
9. It has a sacramental routine.
10. And a Christian mind denounces worldly sensuality.

Important for our contextual evaluation of disenchantment, the rise of secularism, decline in church attendance, and the adaptability of Christianity in Australia, is observation of movements in worship practices during the time we identified earlier as a 'golden age' for Christianity in the 1950's, and the developments beyond, that produced a contraction of the pervasive influence of Christianity.

Mega-Church sociologist Sam Hey[7] notes the rise of the 'Charismatic Movement' in Australia from the 1960's and into the 1970's was driven by changes in Australian culture that may be attributed to a disillusionment with Western rationalism and modernity. From the early 1960's global media began for the first time to take seriously, and report on the effects of the Charismatic movement. Interest in sociological changes in religion sparked articles reporting developments in worship style based on early revivals. Those reported reflected back to the early 20th century Azusa Street Revival in the US, and a similar effect that had grown from the Welsh Revival in the UK. Hey notes that respected media reporting on the Charismatic Movement began to awaken an acceptance of churchgoers to the experience called the 'Baptism in the Spirit'.

This is an important note, that a renewed quest for experiential spirituality was being sought by adherents to churches in a reactionary way as the forces of modernity began to advance. Commercial television broadcasting in the 1950's had also birthed the age of the 'televangelist'. Hey[8] notes early televangelists like Rex Humbard, Oral Roberts, Billy Graham and Robert Schuller used the 'new media' to fulfil revivalist goals, and with extended audiences came increased financial support and the enabling of formation of 'megachurches' became a possibility.

It was not just Christianity with an injection of life on a global scale. Peter Berger[9] notes in his 'about face' denial of the validity of the 'Secularization Thesis' that not only is the concept of a 'fatal blow to religion' that was forecast by the 'thesis' false in a universal sense, but also that globally the upsurge in spirituality had fuelled two major religious movements. He points to the rise of Islam, and the emergence of Pentecostalism affecting hundreds of millions of adherents around the world. Through the succeeding decades beyond the 1970's the spread of the Charismatic movement as a resurgence of classical Pentecostalism was spread through electronic media, on radio, television and through recording technologies like audio cassettes and video. In Australia as Sam Hey notes the former Methodist preacher Clarke Taylor expanded his ministry base through a weekly television program modelled on the American healing evangelist Oral Roberts. 'A New Way of Living' ran from 1977-1982. It was a contributing factor that accompanied the uptake of television contributing to the ways that Australians 'viewed their world, their place in it, and the ways in which they relate to each other'.

Sam Hey describes the Pentecostal and Charismatic movement as having grown significantly in both numbers and influence.[10] There are more attendees on any given Sunday in Pentecostal – Charismatic churches than any other Australian church denomination apart from Catholicism, and megachurches have become a major source of direction and influence upon the practices of all of Australia's churches. Historian Meredith Lake[11] notes another positive around attitudes to the Bible in the rise of Pentecostalism. The movement led to the historic formation of the nation's largest ever churches and subsequently enhanced an uptake of Bible reading.

Media Utility - The Formation of Public Opinion

Early forms of 'Public Opinion' were interpreted as non-political, but public opinion became 'useful', aimed at 'rationalizing politics in the name of morality'. The scholarship of Jurgen Habermas entitled *The Structural Transformation of the Public Sphere* (1962)[12] enlarged a focus on the Western European concept of 'Public Opinion'. Private people begin to engage in rational, critical, public debate aimed at 'absolutist rule'. Widely separated people shared the same views, exchanging ideas and reaching some levels of consensus.

In describing how theory transfers into practice, Habermas[13] reflects on the concept that installing a monarch to protect the 'natural order' of society required 'in theory' that the monarch does not gain insight into the natural order directly, but gains insights into 'laws' mediated for him by 'public opinion'. Habermas saw public opinion as an enlightened result of common and public reflection guided by the representatives of modern science – 'the Philosophers'.

'Public Opinion' does not rule, but the 'enlightened ruler' is constrained to be guided by the insights. In accordance with this theory, a political public sphere emerges to the same degree as the 'natural laws of the market assert themselves' with the aspiration that a balance of social rank and an equalization of civil rights will continue to be part of an evolutionary process of civil society. For Habermas this was the illustration of how the relation between 'theory' and 'practice' would guarantee the course of history, in the same way that the laws of physics guaranteed the course of nature. The consensus or common space eventuated through discussion 'in the media'.

In the 18th century it was books, pamphlets and newspapers read and discussed in social gathering places, for conversations, special events and public rituals, as well as more authoritative settings in policy formation of governing authorities. In these chapters we are looking to deepen our understanding of how modern media perpetuates this battlefield of ideas.

Philosopher Charles Taylor[14] describes the 'public sphere' as a mutation of the social imaginary, but in a positive sense is a necessary ingredient for the formation of a modern society. Habermas noted that the public sphere fell from a means of enlightenment to a 'means of education' when it began to serve the self-conceit of the state, and as such deserves to be as much respected, as despised.[15]

We can be enlightened by these insightful concepts recognising that Habermas appears right to identify public opinion as 'rationalizing politics in the name of morality'. But when morality is fast-changing in an intensifying secular public sphere, the idea of rationalizing becomes open to interpretation usually with the 'spin' of a public relations machine. We may rightly ask how Christian leaders rise to the challenge of engaging with the confusion that results when competing moral positions in the public sphere threaten long held moral positions within the Church and, what proactive engagements are now necessary to role-model biblical truth and transcendence against the propaganda of an antagonistic secularised public sphere?

Towards A New Theory – 'Winter-Spring Theory'

I propose that there is an ethical application for understanding the relationship of media and society viewed through the lens of 'transcendence'. In this view there is a goal to influence the effective formation of 'belief', and to be a catalyst for a Divinely influenced form of human flourishing.

The useful influence should have a 'regenerative effect' on both personal and societal human flourishing. Just like the 'Winter to Spring' seasonal transition, by necessity we must also acknowledge the orientation of the forms of media that produce a freezing over 'degenerative effect' on human flourishing, when settings are oriented according to the propagation of an 'immanent' rationalism.

This orientation functions in the same way that Habermas[16] theorized a political 'public sphere' emerging to the same degree as the 'natural laws of the market assert themselves'. The aspiration applies to how influence emerges when forces interact with balance and equalization of civil rights. Winter-Spring theory includes a notional 'Theory of Media Utility'.

The foundation of this theory borrows its orientation from the ethical theory of Utilitarianism developed by Jeremy Bentham and John Stuart Mill. It is often referred to as the 'Greatest Happiness Principle'. A theory of media utility activates a different orientation towards the power of media to produce 'good outcomes' of human flourishing, contrasted with bad outcomes of societal disintegration. Under Mill's theory[17], he held that '*actions are right in proportion as they tend to promote happiness, wrong as they tend to produce the reverse of happiness*'. For him happiness was intended to be '*pleasure, and the absence of pain*'. Morals are useful as they promote happiness, and detrimental as they cause misery.

Media has the potential for mass communication of alternate positions on morality be it good or bad. Therefore, if the settings of morality in media are calibrated poorly, the formation of public opinion creates either a positive or negative 'mutation of the social imaginary'. A 'Winter-Spring' theory aspires to the idea that mutations will either have a 'positive change effect', or a 'negative change effect' on human flourishing. To extend the concept of seasons as metaphor for societal transition, it may appear that seasons of decline can be described as 'autumn (fall) and winter'. A 'springtime' season of renewal would develop into a flourishing 'summer'. And for various reasons it may appear that the orientation of fallen human nature is predisposed towards autumn and winter.

How 'settings' work might be simply illustrated in the contrast between alternatives, 'Generosity vs Greed'. Generosity might be characterised as looking to the good of the 'other' vs 'greed' only concerned with 'self'. An 'Immanent' frame with its unshackled individualism, survival of the fittest, and personal empowerment, falls naturally towards the concept of 'greed' in the form of its individualism.

Early this century the Wall Street mantra of 'Greed is Good' triggered an indication of the 'fruit' born by the two-dimensional rationalistic 'Immanent Frame' where wealth is the highest sign of significance, and personal success. The alternative setting of 'generosity' favours the orientation of 'transcendence' where the restored 'image' of God the Creator has an effect that reorientates the concepts of 'significance and success', and models an alternative to materialist individualism.

A new model still has the individual in focus, but with a personal aspiration to a new collectivism where members have essentially a Divinely assigned value, and where an eternal perspective contextualises wealth as a tool for social wellbeing, elevated because of a commonly shared understanding of the restored 'image of God'. The simplicity of this illustration forms a platform for a fuller discussion of the 'Utility' of Christian Media in the pursuit of a Divinely appointed model of human flourishing that embraces not only the introductory Gospel message of personal salvation assurance, but also the discipleship goal of fulfilment of Christ-like wholeness in the pursuit of the biblical Cultural Mandate.

In this type of discussion, we should always stay close to a particularly sobering concept that keeps our aspirations grounded in the purposes of God for individuals. A well-known saying that *"God is more interested in our 'holiness' than our 'happiness'"* reminds us that there are those called to pay a high price carrying the transforming message of the biblical Gospel.

Hardships have a purpose too. Jesus reminded his disciples that Christian believers should expect hardship and persecution, *'If the world hates you, keep in mind that it hated me first. If you belonged to the world, it would love you as its own. As it is, you do not belong to the world. But I have chosen you out of the world. That is why the world hates you.'* (John 15:18). We're reminded of what hardship looks like in the experience of the Apostle Paul whose account of his pioneering of the early church leaves us in no doubt of the severity of personal hardship that some are called to endure. He wrote *'I have worked much harder, been in prison more frequently, been flogged more severely, and been exposed to death again and again.* (2 Cor 11:23) It may be that this form of hardship continues to the be lot of those who will courageously challenge the status quo in a 'winter season' with the aspiration of working for the new shoots of 'spring' that bring an environment of flourishing to communities that adopt the biblical image of a good life.

For Public Christians, leaders of Church, parachurch, ministry and business, media 'utility' (media as a useful tool) shapes a 'Good Life' according to the Content Manager's or product manager's worldview.

Embracing an understanding of media 'utility' enlarges the aspiration for Public Christians in their 'power to reinforce' and shape prevailing social imaginaries, or to counteract what is perceived as a mis-formed social imaginary.

Endnotes

1   Herbert has a career history in religion and philosophy, his academic pursuit appears to lead him to look at the broader issues contextualising all religion. His objectivity places the Christian church on the same footing, with the same scrutiny, and the same potential as the other significant world religions. D.E.J Herbert 2011 European Journal of Cultural Studies 14(6) 626–648, p.633

2   Ibid p.635

3   Ibid p.637

4   Stark R. & Finke R. 2000 Acts of Faith: Explaining the Human Side of Religion, University of California Press, USA, p. 38

5   The World Values Survey analyses data from countries where religiousness is predicted in-step with other factors including the levels of economic development and of social science indicators of human development.

6   Blamires H. 1963 The Christian Mind, How should a Christian Think? Regent College Publishing, Vancouver British Columbia, Canada. p.3

7   Hey S. 2013 Megachurches: Origins, Ministry and Prospects, Mosaic Press, Preston, Australia. p.73

8   Ibid p.136

9   Berger P. 2011 – Youtube Dr Peter Berger on Religion & Modernity, Faith Angle Forum on Religion, Politics and Public Life. https://www.youtube.com/watch?v=bv3aLp27sO4

10   Ibid p.82

11   Lake M. 2018 The Bible in Australia: A Cultural History, New South Publishing, University of New South Wales, Sydney, Australia. p.352

12   Habermas J.H. 1962 (Trans. Burger T. 1991) The Structural Transformation of the Public Sphere, First MIT Press, Massachusetts, USA. p. 102

13   Habermas J.H. 1973 (Translated by John Viertel) Theory and Practice, Beacon Press, Boston, USA. p.77

14   Taylor C. 2007 A Secular Age, Belknap Press of Harvard University Press, Cambridge, Massachusetts, USA and London, England. P.187

15   Ibid p.120

16   Habermas J.H. 1973 (Translated by John Viertel) Theory and Practice, Beacon Press, Boston, USA. p.77

17   Mill J.S. 1863 Utilitarianism, https://www.utilitarianism.com/mill2.htm, Chapter 2 What Utilitarianism Is.

Chapter 12:
The Dynamics of
Media Content

5 "A farmer went out to sow his seed. As he was scattering the seed, some
fell along the path; it was trampled on, and the birds ate it up. 6 Some fell
on rocky ground, and when it came up, the plants withered because they
had no moisture. 7 Other seed fell among thorns, which grew up with it
and choked the plants. 8 Still other seed fell on good soil. It came up and
yielded a crop, a hundred times more than was sown."

Luke 8:5-8

War of the Worlds: Injection Theory

In the United States, on 30th October 1938, Orson Welles and a formation
of the Mercury Theatre Group, used the occasion of the eve of Halloween,
to broadcast their radio theatre production of 'War of the Worlds'. It
became known as a *'Panic Broadcast'* that subsequently changed the
history of broadcasting.

The audience of an estimated 12 million people heard that Martians had
begun an invasion of Earth starting in the US state of New Jersey. Mass
hysteria caused people to flee cities for rural areas, stores began food
rationing, and the American nation was cast into a chaotic state.

Mass panic across an unsuspecting audience, created an opportunity for
social scientists to examine what happens when a 'bullet' fired from the
'media gun' is aimed directly at the audience's head. It appears that at

the time the audience was so caught 'off-guard' that many were not able to discern the actuality from fiction. O'Neill[1] notes that a post broadcast assessment by sociologists collected audience accounts in the immediate aftermath examining the context of the larger political and social upheavals.

People processed the 'crisis' in different ways with their predisposition to uncritically 'believing' what they were hearing, based on a combination of psychological personality traits including self-confidence, fatalism or deep religious belief. This classic example of radio's impact in social 'manipulation' of the masses, illustrates the immediate effect of radio's influence upon unsuspecting listeners.

Media theorists have been able to identify factors present in the 'direct influence' via radio that are still valid today. 'Injection Theory', also known as 'Hypodermic Needle Theory'[2] or 'Magic Bullet Theory' implies there is an immediate and powerful effect of broadcast media on audiences.

Concerns began to rise that media is a 'dangerous' means of communicating ideas because the audience as the 'receiver' is powerless to resist the impact of the message. The population is described as a 'sitting duck' while media material is 'shot' at them. The audience believes what they are told, when there is no significant source of 'alternate' information.

In the case of the 'War of the Worlds' the rise and popularity of radio was one factor. Subsequently, new lessons were learned providing impetus for the emergence of the powerful 'persuasion industries' of advertising and political propaganda which are deliberate and systematic attempts to shape perceptions and direct behaviour. Around the same time, studies were also being undertaken into the rise of cinema as a form of mass entertainment. Concerns focused on the effects on children including the effects of imitation of both positive and negative role models.

A question arises: Does the idea of 'firing a bullet' from the 'media gun' have the same influence if the intention is for a positive, even Christian outcome, rather than for entertainment, political or marketing manipulation?

Priming – for Evil or Good

In the 1980's it was discovered by psychologists that exposure to even a single word can have dramatic effects on thinking and behaviour. Researchers found that if a person had recently been exposed to the word 'Eat', they were more likely to complete the word fragment SO_P as SOUP rather than as SOAP. And the opposite effect would happen if a person had recently been exposed to the word 'Wash'. Under what is called a 'Priming Effect' we all become predisposed to responses in line with priming words like 'Eat', or 'Wash'.

Nobel Prize winning researcher Daniel Kahneman[3] describes the concept of 'priming' as being 'like ripples on a pond' where primed ideas have some ability to prime other ideas, spreading through a small part of a vast network of personal and associated ideas. All of this happens without any awareness of influencing our actions by the offering of an 'idea'.

Reminding people of 'old age' makes them act 'old' and walk more slowly. Reminding people of their mortality increases the appeal of authoritarian ideas, as in the cases of terror threats or global pandemic. If we force ourselves to 'smile' we can actually feel better. Where we cast a vote on polling day affects how we will vote.[4] People who are 'primed' around 'money' become more 'independent' than they would be without the trigger associations.

In an experiment, students were asked to construct a 4-word phrase that had a 'money' theme from a list of 5 words (high, a, salary, desk, paying). The outcome was the phrase 'a high paying salary'. Kahneman notes, 'money-primed' people had increased perseverance in solving difficult problems than people who were not 'primed'. They were not only more independent, but also more likely to be 'selfish'. In the experiment students were less likely to help another who pretended to be confused about a task. When the leader of the experiment dropped a bunch of pencils on the floor, the participants with 'money on their mind' picked up fewer of the pencils. Money 'primed' people were also more likely to show an increased preference for being alone. The theme of the findings was that 'money' primes 'individualism', with an increased reluctance to be involved with, depend upon, or accept the demands of others.

So controversial are the concepts around the power of 'priming', Kahneman notes that the remarkable research done by Kathleen Vohs, has been 'laudably restrained'[5] in discussing the implications of her findings. The research suggests that living in a cultural setting constantly permeated by reminders of 'money', has the effect of shaping our behaviours and attitudes 'in ways we may not be proud'.

On a national scale, 'priming' extends to cultures that provide prominent reminders of 'respect', others have mechanisms that remind people of their 'god', and a common feature of dictatorships is in the constant reminder to the masses to always admire large images of the 'Dear Leader'. The priming effect of images of the national leader convey the feeling that 'Big Brother' is always watching, and according to the 'priming' principle have the tendency to reduce 'spontaneous thought' and 'independent action'.

For the Public Christian, the concept of 'priming' and the ethics of 'leadership or manipulation' will always be an issue of personal motive. I have long held the view that the only identifiable difference between 'leadership' and 'manipulation' is personal motive. These motives are much more easily recognised when a leader is submitted to the transcendent God, than a personal governance under human rationalism. The biblical Christian is conscious of the personal application of what it means to '*not be conformed to the patterns of this world but be transformed by the renewing of your mind*'. (Romans 12:2) Public Christianity will always aspire to the welfare of its constituents in a process of discipleship where the context of loving God first is demonstrated in loving our neighbour as ourselves. It then becomes deeply important as to how the Christian submitted to the transcendent God, may hold to account those who are driven by their own rational passions, especially our governing authorities.

A Lesson in Media Leadership— Two Step Flow Theory

In briefly exploring this theory, we understand how important it is for Public Christians to see their role as Opinion Leaders. 'Opinion Leaders' pass on their own interpretation of mass communicated messages.

Earlier we noted developments over 200+ years in a study of the developing change of sexual ethics in Western culture. We noted the gradualism that brought about change, that accelerated as influence through print media, and then electronic forms of media attracted the attention of the masses, propagating alternative ideas until these ideas became pervasive. From the changes highlighted over two centuries we were able to draw conclusions as to how the progress of 'anti-structure' as an 'eclipse' can be allowed to happen gradually. We also noted, that with developments in mass communications, a 'counter-process' for change in a positive way can be imagined, empowered and even accelerated.

The 'eclipse of anti-structure' appears to intensify as the mass population is exposed to ideas that when articulated by authoritative and charismatic thought leaders, have capacity to shape not only individual worldviews, but also the prevailing social imaginary. Communications theory helps us understand how change permeates culture and may be the spark for 'counter-processes.'

In the 1940's a new communications theory called 'Two Step Flow Theory' was developed by Katz and Lazarsfeld[6] (1955) who illustrated their ideas with a conceptual model showing that information from the 'mass media' typically moves in two distinct stages. Firstly, 'Opinion Leaders' pay close attention to the mass media and its messages. And secondly, the 'Opinion Leaders' pass on their own interpretation in addition to the original messages.

The intervention between the media's 'direct message' and the audience 'reaction' helped researchers understand how 'Opinion Leaders' use personal influence to get people to change attitudes and behaviours. While opinion leaders do not replace 'The Media', they guide discussions of media messages.

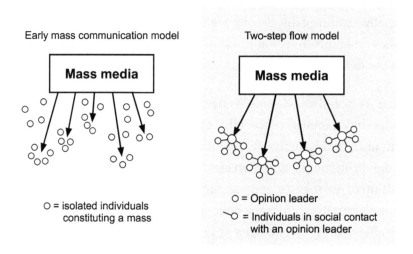

Figure 2. Source: Katz & Lazarsfeld (1955)[7]

The concept of Opinion Leaders even goes another step deeper from what we might call official leaders, to unofficial smaller subset groups. From isolated individuals influenced directly by the media, to individuals influenced by 'Opinion Leaders', Katz & Lazarsfeld[8] also identified a layer of 'Molecular Leaders' who were not necessarily prominent in their communities, but who were influential in their immediate small group environments. These included family, friends, and co-workers as interpersonal communication networks through which influential opinion flows. This identified group known as 'Opinion Leaders' have similar influential capacity to magazines, newspapers and radio, as potentially another medium of mass communication.

In these chapters I have been introducing a focus on the 'Utility' of Christian media, and the weight of influence that rests on the shoulders of

Public Christians, as leaders of Church, para-church or business that want to be a more prominent Christian lighthouse.

Ultimately the usefulness of the medium, be it radio and other electronic media, or social media, comes back to the settling of responsibility afforded to Content Managers, who are 'gate-keepers' for the content shaping the thoughts, opinions and attitudes of a listenership, a following or a customer base, and therefore their leadership influence must be considered higher on a hierarchy of Christian 'Opinion Making'.

We can't ignore the 'power' impact of opinion making at this level. It appears to have a capacity to either reinforce the 'target audience' in their 'captivity' to an 'immanent frame', or the opposite effect. It becomes imaginable that Opinion Making Christian leaders become a 'liberating factor' in the expression of 'transcendence' at all levels of the spectrum, including isolated individuals, molecular leaders, and highly influential opinion makers. And, because Christian Radio has the capacity to be a 24/7 companion to the masses, the opportunity to influence both individual and community flourishing cannot be overstated.

Who sets the 'Agenda?' – Agenda Setting Theory

In the 1960's, new research emerged shedding light on the powerful and even coercive impact of media on an unsuspecting populace. Two Associate Professors of Journalism sought to identify evidence that the choices and presentation of elements in mass media had an extraordinary effect on the shaping of political realities. Max McCombs[9] and Donald Shaw drew on the influence of Walter Lippman who in the 1920's assumed that 'pictures in the minds' of people formed images about public affairs.

Lippman coined the phrase '*The world outside and the pictures in our heads*'. McCombs and Shaw used a methodology that established a link between media and public opinion based on the idea that ideas and images in the media influenced the decision making of the public. They succeeded in matching the responses of 'the voting public' about the issues, with 'actual content' in the mass media. This Agenda Setting Theory was based on the application of statistical data from a sample of 100 residents surveyed before an election. By correlating their responses, they were able to ascertain the degree in which the News Media was able to influence public opinion.

Later their findings were reinforced in subsequent studies with larger samples and over longer periods showing similar strength to the Agenda Setting of mass media including a year-long study in the 1976 US Presidential campaign. And again, a decade long study of news magazines in the 1960s that found correlations between trends in public opinion and the content of news magazines. In that study they compared responses of the public with a Gallop Poll question, '*What is the most important problem that faces the country today?*'[10]

The significance of the measurable outcomes of research into Agenda Setting Theory continues to evolve. There is now recognition of greater applications additional to the idea of political campaigning. There are other obvious correlations to the broader advertising industry and moving the masses to purchase products according to marketing campaign strategies.

The evidence for altruistic campaigns conducted to influence and adjust societal behaviours like the 'Quit' campaign to stop smoking, or campaigns to 'Keep Fit', or 'Don't Drink and Drive' seem logical to the formation of public behaviour. However, I propose that the shaping of public values is just 'one way' of understanding the ways that media contributes to a pervasive influence on all forms of thought and behaviour.

Fortunato and Martin[11] argue that knowledge of a series of variables helps the process of understanding 'political communications' as the transference of the media agenda to the public agenda. The variables they use can be correlated not only to the concept of political communication, but I believe also to those forces, and values that shape the modern 'social imaginary':

1. Media organisations content selection and framing decisions.
2. Individuals and organisations with agendas to promote.
3. Technological capabilities of communication platforms to distribute and retrieve messages.
4. Audiences motivation to seek information.
5. Laws governing election campaign policies.

The media selects and frames messages, and as Agenda Setting Theory proves, it is shown to be a powerful influence on 'what' and 'how' the consumer public thinks. The 21st Century advent of 'social media' further complicates the communications process where advertising and viral messaging contribute to agenda setting influence.

If Agenda Setting Theory can be shown to influence the outcomes of political campaigns, I propose that the same forces of influence can also work in the formation of a society wide social imaginary either with growth and maturity towards Divinely inspired collective cultural wisdom, or with the less free, exploitable collective cultural sentiment driven by the agendas of factions within an 'immanent frame' model of society.

It may be in this contrasting comparison that we can identify grounds for Christian media influence upon public perceptions of 'truth and meaning' along with an agenda orientation to create what Francis Schaeffer[12] called a Christian based 'Freedom without chaos'. Until we understand the process of change, we remain closer to the 'winter' season of Winter Spring Theory.

Blurred Lines – Social Media Algorithms

Modern information mass media is itself shaped by the dynamics of the new challenge of the digital era's use of algorithms to sort information. The rise of social media platforms based on user-generated content has created the concern that information being accessed doesn't meet prescribed journalistic standards, or may be blatantly 'Fake News'. Algorithms sorting news preferences has the effect of 'blurring the lines' on the way all media is perceived and influences the way people 'trust' media in general.

Algorithms serve as demand predictors and content creators of news and information consumption, giving rise to limitations and restrictions on user access to the full variety of opinions in the marketplace. Cotter, Cho and Rader's[13] research into Facebook's use of 'algorithmic curation' automatically selecting and ranking content, found Facebook's reluctance to disclose their methods to be problematic. Each individual user accesses a personalised list of posts presented for consumption. Facebook appears happy to publish the 'why' of their algorithm method, disclosing their motivations, intentions and objectives for the system, but they are less likely to disclose the 'how' of their procedural logic and internal processes that may give users an ability to determine the accuracy, and fairness of content so that they can evaluate their reliability.

Further research into the extremes including 'information manipulation' may reveal the pressure for 'active censorship' of all social media and internet as appears to be happening effectively under communist regimes around the world. It's also applicable in Western nations where the 'morality police' on various platforms are quick to identify thoughts that are not in line with current standards of 'political correctness' that have a secularist Cultural Marxist foundation, resistant to biblical Christian positions on today's biggest ethical issues. Also applicable are the ideological intimidations fuelling a cultural divide along with the popular terminology of 'Fake News' generating tension between progressive and conservative political opinion in Western nations.

While it is argued that in the new environment where algorithm driven content may be detrimental, the new environment may also highlight the emergence of 'empowered elites' exploiting the 'immanent frame' as a method of control. It may also spark new initiatives to create opportunities for the awareness of the empowerment for counter-cultural Christian spirituality, for analysis of consumers attitudes, and new challenges to maximise potential for re-emerging 'transcendence' values creation.

For Public Christians, we understand that if we 'create values', we influence 'culture'. Culture includes our patterns of organised relational interactions at personal, economic, political, social and educational levels. Our challenge is to identify the contrast of our biblical Christian culture, and effectively communicate our culture, recognising the context of the pluralist and secularized environments that are awash with diversity and alternative choices. Even the Christian community 'social imaginaries' are heavily shaped not only by the 'sacred', but by the 'secular' forces of materialism, consumerism, and the Godless educational influences of the social sciences. Empowering a Christian ethos amidst these diverse alternatives through mass media and new social media helps the community adopt and defend biblical foundations.

Towards Re-Enchantment— Home Grown Australian Spirituality

The Challenge for Public Christian leaders is always in exercising wisdom in applying theory to effective practice. And there are numerous dimensions to consider in strategizing the application of new initiatives to enhance effectiveness. David Tacey[14] of the Australian Centre for Christianity and Culture reflects on Australian spirituality as split between thought and feeling, where feelings are often religious, but our communication is mostly secular. We can have religious feelings, though we dare not name that as such. He reflects on a 'fear of religion', as a 'fear of the unknown' or a 'fear of authority' where past experiences may have been tyrannical with an imposed conformity under threat of damnation. A rebellion against a style of religion, however, does not indicate a rejection of all religion.

It's not all bad. Where there is a 'strength of character' to reject enslavement to religious ideology, this may be worthy of celebration, as a pathway to presenting the biblical redemption of Jesus to the Australian cultural ethos. Tacey cautions not to assume that the 'sacred'

185

is dead in Australia recognising a long present disenchantment and loss of spirit in our official consciousness, that he believes is the product of tired intellectual and religious tradition that has lacked the courage to discover the Divine workings of the Holy Spirit in the present day. He holds hopes for a national 're-enchantment' but suggests what may be required is a new kind of Copernican revolution.

A new search for sacred mysteries, could include a new orientation which includes a positive outlook on a 'multicultural Australia' with ethnic and indigenous peoples. Tacey suggests that indigenous and multi-cultural Australians have an advantage in their spirituality, in that they are allowed to have a public 'enchantment'. It's contrasted non-indigenous Australians who remain in the shipwreck of 'reason', facing consequences if they venture into embarrassing spirituality like 'magic', even though that would be quite alright for indigenous or multi-cultural people.

I believe that at this time, the so-called non-indigenous Australians may have something of a lingering condescending attitude to ethnic and multicultural spiritualities, but a 'Copernican Revolution' may switch on a new search for sacred mysteries that take us beyond the mechanised life of the secular. Sudden economic, political crisis, or indeed the threat of global pandemic can jolt a community into a focus on shared values, bringing together communities beyond purely economic considerations, and opening engagement on 'myths and symbols' that foster new sets of ideals and shared meanings and religious conversations. It may be, that in the conversations about spirituality, a 'biblical thinking' on supernatural considerations and Christ-like behavioural ethics will find favour as the timeless Gospel is applied into new settings, and into the thinking of new generations.

At a time when 'Religious Freedom' is being hotly debated in Australia, I believe it is worthy of note that pathways to re-enchantment begin with respecting the reality of the sacred and the diversity of expression within communities that are an essential part of social cohesion. Tacey ventures that public enchantment requires a willingness to borrow,

186

exchange and integrate creating new hybrids or to use his metaphor, an 'interbred mongrel' which tends to be healthier than the thoroughbred. Christianity in his estimation has always had a vigorous history, learning to be eclectic and adaptable, while borrowing and absorbing influences from other traditions. What I have learned hosting talk radio on the national Christian broadcaster over the past decade is that listeners come from a wide variety of denominational backgrounds and shaping of their spirituality. Pushing a barrow of one flavour over another is not a good model. Including the best Christian commentary, from across the spectrum of denominational gifts and talents creates a new look for a 'united' body of Christ. Highlighting the strengths of rich tradition, with stories reflecting an enchanted transcendence, while maintain a Christocentric, high view of Scripture appears to be the way to win friends without compromising biblical dogma. Perhaps it's the cross-sectional 'talk-radio' platform that gives birth to the 'interbred mongrel' that may yet prove to be more agile, and street wise than the thoroughbred. In the days ahead, as Christian media reaches new phases in maturity, perhaps new depths of the wisdom of God will prove to be magnetic to the Australian people, with a yearning for more.

Retooling for a Secular Age

How do we start preparations to change perceptions of what we do as Public Christians preparing to 'lead' in an age that is increasingly secularized? Rodney Stark[15] notes key reasons why people embrace Christianity:

- Believers have a capacity to sustain a deeply emotional and existentially satisfying faith.
- Christianity has an appeal to 'reason'.
- It's inseparably linked to the rise of Western Civilization.
- For much of the world Christianity is seen as intrinsic to the idea of becoming modern.
- And, it is demonstrably essential to the continued globalisation of modernity.

Christians understand that there is a 'spiritual battle' to be fought. During the Old Testament captivity of the Israelites in Babylon, Daniel had enjoyed promotion through the highest ranks of authority in the Babylonian and Medo-Persian empires. Daniel *'prospered during the reign of Darius and the reign of Cyrus the Persian'* (Daniel 6:28), yet he fasted and prayed for his people and for the rebuilding of Jerusalem. It was not by 'political power' that the metaphorical 'chains of bondage' in Babylon would be broken. For Daniel it was a question of Divine intervention in answer to prayers that would begin the regeneration of his nation.

When Daniel read the words of the Prophet Jeremiah that the *'desolation of Jerusalem would last seventy years'* (Dan 9:2) and that Jeremiah had prophesied that Jerusalem would be restored, he was struck with the realisation that he was living and leading in that very time.

Daniel's prayer was one of humble repentance through detailed confession of the sins of his nation. The full confession in Daniel 9:4-19 includes reference to wickedness and rebellion, turning from God's commands and laws, ignoring the prophets, and unfaithfulness. He acknowledges that curses and sworn judgements written in the Law of Moses had been poured out on the Israelites and yet they had not sought the favour of God by turning from their sins and giving attention to His truth.

I suspect there are supporters, consumers and followers of your Public Christian organisation, Church or ministry with a longing for expressions of leadership, that acknowledge the darkness in the present day culture, and who make a genuine attempt to be catalysts for change.

Endnotes

1   O'Neill, B. 2011 Media Effects in Context. 10.1002/9781444340525.ch16. p.8

2   'Injection Theory', is also known as 'Hypodermic Needle Theory', 'Strong Effects Theory', or 'Magic Bullet Theory'. University of Twente, Communication Studies Theories, https://www.utwente.nl/en/bms/communication-theories/sorted-by-cluster/Mass%20Media/Hypodermic_Needle_Theory/ [Accessed 17th Sept 2018]

3   Kahneman D. 2011 Thinking, Fast and Slow, Penguin Books, London, England. P.53,54.

4   Support for propositions of increasing schools funding are more likely to be supported if a local school is used as a 'polling booth' on election day. Kahneman p.55.

5   Ibid p.56

6   Katz E., Lazarsfeld P. 2007 Personal Influence, Free Press, Gazi Üniversitesi, Ankara Turkey http://iletisimdergisi.gazi.edu.tr/arsiv/24.pdf#page=281 [Accessed September 2018]

7   Katz & Lazarsfeld (1955) https://www.scribd.com/doc/6446504/Lazarsfeld-Theory [Accessed 17th Sept 2018]

8   Ibid 2007 p.273

9   McCombs M. The Agenda-Setting Role of the Mass Media in the Shaping of Public Opinion http://www.infoamerica.org/documentos_pdf/mccombs01.pdf

10   Ibid. P.2

11   Fortunato J.A. Martin S.E. 2016 The Intersection of Agenda-Setting, the Media Environment, and Election Campaign Laws, Penn State University Press, https://www.jstor.org/stable/10.5325/jinfopoli.6.2016.0129 [Accessed 29th Aug 2018]

12   Schaeffer F. 1984 The Great Evangelical Disaster, The Complete Works of Francis Schaeffer Vol.4 1982, Crossway, Illinois, USA. p.309

13   Cotter K., Cho J., Rader E. 2017 Explaining the News Feed Algorithm: An Analysis of the "News Feed FYI" Blog. Michigan State University, USA. p.2

14   Tacey D. 2000 Re-enchantment, The New Australian Spirituality, Harper Collins, Sydney, Australia. p.240

15   Stark R. 2005 The Victory of Reason, How Christianity Led to Freedom, Capitalism, and Western Success, Random House, New York, USA. p.235

Chapter 13:
Towards a
'Transcendence'
Kingdom Culture

Surely the righteous will never be shaken; they will be remembered
forever. They will have no fear of bad news; their hearts are steadfast,
trusting in the LORD.

Psalm 112:6-7

The only organisations that are duty bound to centuries of 'religious
tradition' are Churches. Every other expression of organisation including
mainstream business that aspires to be 'more Christian' is faced with
the idea of adopting some form of 'ecumenical' business model. Skilled
employees will likely come from different religious backgrounds to your
own, or no religious background at all. It means that if you desire to lead
your organisation or department by adopting a more focused Christian
footing, you will be compelled to explore how a 'Kingdom' orientation
might be the rudder that steers your ship.

The biblical 'Kingdom of God' has practical implications for present day
organisational culture. The powerful metaphors of 'Hidden Treasure' and
'Pearl of Great Price' (Matt 13) used by Jesus to describe the Kingdom, call
for 'total abandon' of alternatives that have at their centre 'self-reliance'.
The Bible view is to embrace the Kingdom 'treasure'.

191

Our challenge in approaching the ethos of being a 'Public Christian' leading or working with a Christian organisation, is one of understanding deeper issues as to how the 'Kingdom of God' is expressed in forms of modern organisational culture. In the coming chapters I'll outline and review some of the common cultural approaches in Public Christian organisations, to address underlying influences that require attention if an organisation is to adopt or remain 'true to mission' and 'values consistent' with the biblical 'Kingdom.'

We'll broadly embrace Board level 'vision and mission' setting, Executive leadership, middle management, and how workers and volunteers can be on the same page working with a 'transcendence' focus on *missio Dei*, the mission of God. What remains true is that there are consequences of a distorted view of the Kingdom of God that have potential to either enhance of distort outcomes.

Fine-Tuning Organisational Values

In a substantial sense, a look at the way we function in a Christian organisation is a study in contextualisation. From creation to the cross, and from the cross to the present, culture is changing from nation to nation and age to age. As Don Carson[1] reflects, Christianity aspires to be understood in a 'transmitted pattern of meanings.' We find ourselves 'in continuity with, and in discontinuity with' Christians who live in diverse nations embedded in diverse cultures. This should be a straight-forward exercise, not loaded with controversy, and is likely to have few disagreements from leaders who hold the view that a 'work culture' in business and ministry should reflect gospel centred ethics, and those ethics should produce good fruit for your organisation.

I like the approach of Hilary Odiakaose[2] who contends that the motivation of auditing the dynamics of an organisation's culture should focus on the aspects that are 'positive in outlook and yield the greatest positive results' in terms of outcomes for the organisation. So, when we give attention to a 'transcendence' view of our organisation, when put into practice, it should mean a 'win-win' for all concerned.

Our Problem – Understanding 'Kingdom'

The concept of the 'Kingdom of God' is in both Old and New Testaments.[3] Carson and Keller[4] note that a good case can be made that the Kingdom is a unifying biblical theme that holds both Testaments together. There are many metaphors, including the mustard seed, leaven in flour, a hidden treasure and a priceless pearl. However, there is one parable of the 'Kingdom' that makes a marked distinction as to the authority of God in the concept of His Kingdom. The Kingdom is deliberately exemplified by Jesus in His parable (Luke 19:11-27) describing a nobleman's journey to a far country to receive for himself appointment as King over a kingdom and then return.

He was made King and returned home where he then held to account those entrusted with stewardship of his property (ten minas[5]) while he was absent. Those who invested and managed increase to the Kings wealth were rewarded – 'take charge of ten cities.' But the one who hid the Kings mina (property) because he knew the Master was a harsh man, had his mina taken away, and given to the one who had ten. This is frequently a passage used to reflect on stewardship, but there is also a disturbing consequence revealed demonstrating the seriousness with which we pray 'Your Kingdom Come' (Matt 6:10).

What sounds harsh to our 21st century senses that cannot be ignored are the consequences for the Kings enemies (v.27) who rejected his rulership. Jesus then says something that is perhaps less emphasised. He declared the outcome for the King's enemies with words that don't sound like the words of a gentle Jesus meek and mild. He says of the enemies of the King, 'bring them here and kill them in front of me.'[6]

This idea is confronting to our modern sanitised Western thinking about rulership and our perception of individual rights. Wilson[7] observes that in nations that are ruled by 'democracy', rather than monarchy there is an ambiguity to the meaning of 'Kingdom' that leads to some confusion. Our perception of workable earthly forms of government like the democracy we endeavour to maintain, must be contextualised against the idea that 'Kingdom' in the Bible is different, and should be seen at times to be diametrically opposed to 'democracy'.

In a democracy membership has a 'vote', but in the Kingdom of God, New Testament subjects are called to subordinate themselves entirely to their King - Christ. This is illustrated in the parables Jesus told of the 'The Hidden Treasure' and the 'Pearl of Great Price' (Matt 13:44-46) where the man *sold all he had* and 'in his joy' bought the field in which the treasure was hidden, and in the same kingdom grouping, the merchant *sold everything* he had and bought the Pearl of great price. The implications for pursuing a 'transcendence' Kingdom culture are challenging to modern 'self-centred' culture, and are worthy of our theological reflection as we consider our personal submission to King Jesus, and how his Kingdom culture might look as we apply biblical insights about organisational culture into our ministry workplace.

This appraisal of the deeper meaning of Kingdom, is not intended to say that 'democracy' is not a valid form of earthly government, or that a congregational style ministry leadership is altogether wrong, but it does reinforce that ultimate authority in relational leadership is in the person of Christ who is the perfect image of God. Just as we can see the transcendence principle work in the court witness being compelled in a promise to 'tell the truth, the whole truth and nothing but the truth – so help me God', or in the foundations of the 'Rule of Law' workable in context of God's transcendent law, so we are challenged as to how our organisation may function in light of the Kingdom of God.

On a national governance scale Carl Henry[8] argues that constitutional democracy offers opportunity for 'self-determination' and therefore the development of righteous Kingdom rule. However without the concept of Divine 'transcendence' governments and organisations are reduced to the deflated, disenchanted singular dimensional 'immanence', where the wisdom of God is minimised and charismatic elites arise to take the nation or organisation into a direction not submitted to Divine rule. Alternatives set a trajectory to deterioration ethically which as we discovered earlier leads not to flourishing, but oppression and destruction.

In broader business organisational contexts, as in many churches, a board, congregational or an eldership 'vote' may be an appropriate way of practicing discernment of God's will, but it remains true that the concept of Kingdom values, and mission are not 'self-determined'. For the Christian organisation, vision and mission are never separate from biblically consistent *missio Dei* - the mission of God. For further reflection on Kingdom models Howard Snyder[9] proposes eight dimensions helpful for discerning a present-day framework for conceptions of God's reign.

1. The Future Kingdom: The Kingdom as Future Hope.
2. The Inner Kingdom: The Kingdom of God as Inner Spiritual Experience.
3. The Heavenly Kingdom: The Kingdom as Mystical Communion.
4. The Churchly Kingdom: The Kingdom as Institutional Church.
5. The Subversive Kingdom: The Kingdom as Counter-System.
6. The Theocratic Kingdom: The Kingdom as Political State.
7. The Transforming Kingdom: The Kingdom as Christianised Society.
8. The Utopian Kingdom: The Kingdom as Earthly Utopia.

These dimensions may be helpful in reflection, strategizing or 'sorting through' concepts of practical meaning of the Kingdom, as applied to organisational culture.

The 'Synthesis' Challenge

Our assessment of how we recognise the importance of placing God in His rightful place is compounded by the challenge that Christians and the Church are constantly drawn to a 'synthesis' of Christ and contemporary culture. Richard Niebuhr[10] warns against synthesis. One who makes this accommodation of Christ to the prevailing views of the time *'erases the distinction between God and man by divinising man or humanising God'*. In picturing Christ-centred Kingdom Culture, the real difficulty comes where present day culture conflicts with the ideals of 'selling everything' for the sake of following Christ, turning the other cheek to the violent, humbling ourselves and becoming servants, abandoning family or forgetting tomorrow. A synthesised cultural Christianity does not match the call to radical embrace of Kingdom of God culture.

What we are left with is an 'aspiration' towards a Kingdom culture in our organisation that will rise or fall on the personal character of those appointed to lead, according to the set mission, vision and values designed by prayerful leadership starting at board level.

Culture Determines Outcomes— Divine Kingdom or Secular Tyranny

Where the exercise of a ruler's power is limited by law it is a 'Kingdom', but if not, it is a 'Tyranny'. As Beasley-Murray[11] builds definition for 'Kingdom' he embraces a 'lawful exercise of royal power', in contrast to 'tyranny' which is characterised by unjust use of authority.

In the Old Testament for the Prophet Isaiah, the arrival of the Kingdom of God was the picture of the emancipation of the people of Israel. In the New Testament the Kingdom of God is used in the context of the fulfilment of God's promises given in the Old Testament where the 'royal power' is promised to end injustice and oppression by evil powers. Jesus came '...*proclaiming the good news of God ... The Kingdom of God has come near...*' (Mar 1:14-15). The intended outcome of the mission of Christ was to fulfil the promise since the creation, of the inauguration of the Kingdom bringing liberation for oppressed humanity.

Jesus opened the scroll in the synagogue to read from Isaiah 61 to apply the Old Testament prophecy to Himself.[12] As New Testament followers of Christ we can corelate our role in the mission, to do as Christ has done. We make His mission, our mission in respect of what characterises our personal and 'organisational purpose'.

Culture Evolving—

A Critique of Hofstede's Secular Model

There is a subtle but profound difference in organisational culture when a Kingdom focus is applied. Societies have a remarkable capacity to conserve distinctions in culture through successive generations. Hofstede, Hofstede and Minkov[13] describe culture as 'Rising from its ashes like a Phoenix'. They use a biologic analogy of new human body cells continually replacing the older cells. A 20-year-old adult has not retained a single cell from infancy. The body exists as assembled cells because the cells all possess something in common - they share the same 'genes' and genes share DNA. Even though there may be dramatic changes over time, distinctive culture is created and maintained in the deepest layers. As the analogy is applied to societal culture there will be indication of a similar 'genetic capacity' that passes on in organisational contexts. What becomes 'nested in the mind' shapes basic issues of human social life.

While Hofstede forms his analogy based on a limited 'biological evolution' model. The picture of a perpetuating concept of Kingdom of God culture should be imagined at a level where the Spirit of God shapes a people for Himself. This is the model we see in the formation of the Children of Israel, and later in the emergence of the New Testament Church as a 'new humanity' (Col 3:9,10).

Hofstede's model is useful, but inadequate for a fuller description of a developing 'Kingdom of God' culture. For Hofstede the future of culture is restricted to humanity's capacity to create its own future. He sees Philosophy and Religion as divorced from the material, biological world.[14] His ways of seeing culture develop, are based only upon a materialist perspective without consideration for a Divine dimension that God's people experience in the Old and New Testament historic dealings of God with His people. As Charles Taylor[15] argues in 'A Secular Age' materialism alone shaping the cosmic imaginary only deepens a mechanistic view of the universe. It leaves no room for other kinds of meaning and ultimately leads to a lack of purpose in a disenchanted world. It's another example of how we might view the contrast between the 'transcendence' view of culture, compared to the 'immanent' deflated disenchanted Godless model.

The Divine Kingdom – The Royal Image

Humanity created in the image and likeness of God is made in the 'Royal Image'. J. Richard Middleton's[16] hermeneutic of the Genesis creation account (Gen 1:26-28), describes humanity as formed in the *imago Dei* reflecting a 'Royal Image'. It's expressed in the empowerment of man to be 'God's multi-sided prism in the world'.

This 'prism' metaphor in contrast to a pure reflective description in the function of a mirror, highlights the '*reflecting and refracting of the Creator's brilliant light into a rainbow of cultural activity and socio-political patterns that scintillates with the glory of God's presence and manifests his reign of justice*'. That sentence beautifully reflects the vibrancy with which we might aspire to see the world through a 'transcendence' lens.

While other scholars exclude the corporeal body from the 'image', [17]the limitation of neglecting the physical and sensory appreciation of God's workings through individuals and organisations tends to devalue the life of the body in relation to spirituality. The link between the *image* and the mandate to 'fill the earth and subdue it' (Gen 1:28) in this sense includes a 'corporeal representation', or the embodiment of the Divine presence. [18]

The 'Royal' function, with God as King presiding over heaven and earth includes a humanity created in *imago Dei* co-missioning with Him as creator, judge and redeemer to subordinate all things to Himself.

Middleton[19] acknowledges critics including feminists and environmentalists. Feminists claim the 'Royal Image' is 'patriarchal'. Environmentalists fear a distortion of 'dominion' and the triumphalist advocacy for 'reconstructionism' which holds the potential risk of oppression.

While *imago Dei* as 'Royal Rule' has potential for misuse as an ideology, the opposite effect of 'liberation and empowerment' appears to be the contrast presented in Genesis, especially to the prevailing Mesopotamian or Babylonian[20] cultures and their accounts of origins at the time of writing. It's also noteworthy that Israel understood the concept of 'monarchy under God' as an institution with strict limitations as laid out in Deuteronomy 17:14-20.[21] With such distinct biblical attention to 'Kingship' rule, we are poorer to ignore Old and New Testament reflections, and how we may interpret those more efficiently in our modern day.

A Divine Model of Culture Formation

The concept of 'Kingdom' and 'Kingship' continues in the portrayal of Jesus as 'Messiah' (Matt 26:62-64, Mark 8:29), and as the one who is the incarnate *imago Dei* – 'image of God'. The writer to the Hebrews (1:3) said the Son is *'...the radiance of God's glory and the exact representation of his being, sustaining all things by his powerful word.'* Jesus is 'King', however in the first century there was a new contrast of Kingdom of God culture, to the first century Roman empire 'culture of kingship'.

In response to the first century prevalent culture, Jesus counselled the disciples not to exercise power as the 'Gentiles do'. Rather as Middleton[22] expresses, the concept of ruling was contrasted from 'Lording it over' to the paradox of 'Serving one another'. 'Rulership' is therefore exemplified in compassionate service, not in oppression and control. Because Christ is head of the church, the church as the 'Body of Christ' inherits his revelatory mandate and calling, to imitate his sovereignty not for self-gain but for compassionate self-giving across the entire range of human life.

The Transcendence Effect – Shared Leadership

When we form our organisational culture under God, the culture ultimately shapes us. James K.A. Smith[23] observes that the culture in organisations is typically of 'human making'. We 'make' the organisation, and at some point, the organisation starts to 'make us'. When the input of individuals

199

collectively forms an institution, the institution itself takes on a life of its own. People begin to share their talents, share values and before too long a kind of 'opposition view' develops to a point where humans change places and become 'the product' of the cultural institution. 'Systemic power' gives influence in the culture that ultimately is not just the thing being 'shaped', but the organisation itself becomes the shaping influence.

On the question of governance in Christian Organisational Culture, we can identify the emergence of 'lateral shared leadership'. Banks, Ledbetter and Greenhalgh[24] note that 'shared leadership' became the functional model of 'servant leadership'. The Apostle Paul redefines the idea of status where servanthood replaces rank, and others are valued above self-interest.[25] It's hard to imagine how an 'immanent frame' model that relies on the shared values of exclusive humanist rationalism could function when self-interest and individualism are the usual outcomes when transcendent objectivity is neglected or rejected.

What this may mean in practice, when applied to a growing business, and a flourishing workplace, is the aspirational outcome of a harmonious workforce where 'servanthood' replaces self-interest, demonstrated from the top down.

A Brief Summary— Kingdom Organisational Culture

From the brief overview so far, we can glean some significant biblical and theological guiding principles towards what a 'Kingdom of God' culture looks like in practical application[26] to government, organisations, and Church including Christian Media. We have discovered so far:

1. 'Kingdom' is not democracy. Jesus models 'total abandon' to God's will. Independent 'self-determination' is contrasted to the Biblical understanding of 'Kingdom'.
2. The King's power is limited by laws. Tyranny is the result of leaders seeing themselves as being 'above' the law. This principle

relates to all levels of organisational leadership. Where Christians pro-actively aspire to 'legitimize power', biblical principles can be actualised in broader society.

3. The Royal Image is best expressed in organisational culture as the empowerment to be 'God's multi-sided prism in the world'.

4. We link the Divine *image* and the Divine cultural *mandate* to 'fill the earth and subdue it' (Gen 1:28) by recognising that God's people are also His modern-day representation.

5. The fruitful outcomes of Kingdom Culture are 'liberation and empowerment' of righteous rule.

6. Kingdom of God is a 'counter liturgy' to secular liturgies, as Smith[27] understands the formation of disciples who are taught not only 'desire for God and His kingdom', but also an elevated capacity to 'resist the formation of alternative secular liturgies'.

7. 'Kingdom of God' organisational leaders reflect Jesus' model of 'serving others' in 'humility', foregoing rights and privileges to serve the interests of one another.

8. Biblical New Testament 'governance' principles for today incorporate a collective contribution of leaders (shared leadership) where servanthood replaces rank, and others are valued above self-interest.

Endnotes

1   Carson D.A. 2008 Christ and Culture Revisited, Eerdmans, Michigan, USA. p.86

2   Odiakaose ODOR, H. 2018 Organisational Culture and Dynamics, Global Journal of Management and Business Research: Administration and Management. Vol 18, Issue 1, Version 1.0 2018. P.2,6

3   'Kingdom of Heaven' (Matt 18:3), the 'Kingdom of the Lord' (1 Chron 28:5), and the 'Kingdom of Christ' (Eph 5:5), 'My Father's Kingdom' (Matt 26:29); and simply the 'Kingdom' (Psalm 45:6; Matt 9:35).

4   Carson D.A., Keller T. 2011 Gospel-Centred Ministry, The Gospel Coalition Booklets, Crossway p.9

5   A 'mina: a unit of weight, valued at one 16th of a talent.

6   Carson and Keller (2011 p.9) speculate, it is possible that in this parable Jesus was thinking of the parallel story of Herod who went away to Rome, securing Caesar's blessing so that he might return to Judea and reign as King Herod.

7   Wilson T.R. 2014 Reclaiming the Kingdom of God Metaphor for the Twenty-First-Century Church, D.Min Thesis, George Fox University, Oregon USA. p.4

8   Henry C.F.H. 1992 Reflections On The Kingdom of God, Journal of The Evangelical Theological Society, 35/1 (March 1992) pp. 39-49

9   Samuel, V. & Sugden C. (Editors) 2009 Mission as Transformation, A Theology of the Whole Gospel, Chapter 7, Howard Snyder, 'Models of the Kingdom', Wipf & Stock, Eugene, OR. USA. p.120-130.

10   Hynd suggests under Niebuhr's Christendom mindset, it is difficult to make issue by issue judgements as to how we respond in ethics and mission and does not allow a graduated menu of practical options. Hynd D. 2008 Public Theology After Christ and Culture: Post Christendom Travectories, https://www.csu.edu.au/__data/assets/pdf_file/0006/789225/Hynd.pdf p.11

11   Beasley-Murray, G.R 1992 The Kingdom of God in the Teaching of Jesus, Journal of the Evangelical Theological Society, 35/1. p.20

12   'The Spirit of the Sovereign Lord is on me, because the Lord has anointed me to proclaim good news to the poor. He has sent me to bind up the broken-hearted, to proclaim freedom for the captives and release from darkness for the prisoners. To proclaim the year of the Lord's favour...' (Luke 4:18,19 NIV)

13   Hofstede G, Hofstede G.J, Minkov M. 2010 Cultures and Organizations, Software of the Mind, Intercultural Cooperation and Its Importance for Survival, McGraw Hill, New York, USA. p.26

14   Ibid p.475-477.

15   Taylor C. 2007 A Secular Age, Belknap Press of Harvard University Press, Cambridge, Massachusetts, USA and London, England. P.366-367

16   Middleton J.R. 1994 The Liberating Image? Interpreting the Imago Dei in Context, Christian Scholars Review 24.1 (1994) 8-25. (pp 12,24,25)

17   Origen & Augustine.

18   Middleton highlights 'the that the semantic range of tselem, the Hebrew word for "image" in Genesis 1, typically includes "idol," which in the common theology of the ancient Near East is precisely a localized, visible, corporeal representation of the divine.' (1994 p.11)

19   Ibid p.15,16

20   An alternative, replacing the battle of the gods found in the account of Enuma Elish and an alternative to Babylonian astrology in creation of the cosmos. Middleton (1994 p.18)

21   On possessing the Promised-Land the Israelites were to: (a) Be sure to appoint a King the Lord your God chooses. (b) The King must not acquire a great number of horses for himself. (c) He must not take many wives. (d) He must not accumulate large amounts of silver and gold. (e) He must make a copy of the Law. And (f) He must not consider himself better than his fellow Israelites. (Deut 17:14-20)

22   Ibid p.23

23   Smith J.K.A. 2009 Desiring the Kingdom, Worship, Worldview and Cultural Formation, Baker Academic, Michigan, USA. p.72

24   Banks R.J, Ledbetter B.M, Greenhalgh D.C 2016 Reviewing Leadership, A Christian Evaluation of Current Approaches, 2nd Edition, Baker Academic, Michigan, USA. p.136

25   Contrary to many criticisms, the Apostle Paul became one of the strongest advocates for equality of women with men.   In his letter to the Philippians (2:5) he ventures the notion that all have the 'same mind', in marked contrast to the cultural milieu of the first century where hierarchy was prevalent, especially in the defined 'class systems' of the day.

26   We may benefit from employing various discernment models like the Wesleyan Quadrilateral to crystalize biblical principles as they function 'in practice' taking in scripture, tradition, reason and experience.

27   Ibid 2009 p.126

Chapter 14:
Transcendence in Your
Organisation's Culture

Examine yourselves to see whether you are in the faith; test yourselves. Do
you not realize that Christ Jesus is in you - unless, of course, you fail the test?
6 And I trust that you will discover that we have not failed the test.

2 Corinthians 13:5,6

Modern Secularism is a Competitor of the Gospel

Because the integrated Christian organisation is a mechanism for multi-
dimensional influence in personal, spiritual, family, business, church,
ethical and political formation, it is therefore a vehicle for either nurturing
an effective 'transcendence centred' leadership paradigm, or succumbing
to the subtle diversions that ensnare leaders into a secularised ethos.

In an organisation aspiring to be 'More Christian', leaders have special
reason to focus on the primacy of a Divine 'strategic purpose' in formation
of contemporary organisational design. New leadership joining your
organisation will come with industry skills, and corporate wisdom
gleaned from the non-Christian sector, and it takes time to instil your
expectation of how organisational culture should be shaped for the idea of
a 'best practice' Christian workplace.

Consequently, contemporary Christian organisational design aspires to be functionally grounded in 'co-missional wisdom' sourced and sustained in a clearly articulated biblical foundation. The organisation will have a built-in resistance to core motivations of a prevailing secular and humanist social science ethos for shaping leadership in business and ministry.

Unlike conventional secular business, organisations under our care are essentially considered a 'possession under God's ownership' and we are effectively 'stewards' of His enterprise. Motivations are counter to a secularised model exploiting resources for advancement of power, wealth, rank or honour for a controlling few. In the chapters ahead we'll explore the administration of the Great Commission in the enterprise of ministry and business as a 'Divine' pursuit (1 Cor 12:28) with emphasis on safeguards to 'mission drift'.

'Mission true' organisations do not merely use biblical ethos as a 'front' for secular human endeavour. Rather there must be an aspiration to shape your ministry as an ethically sound biblical enterprise that functions 'hand-in-hand' with Divine purposes, both for leaders, and for the organisation aligned with the mission of God.

The product and influence of Christian business and ministry organisations begins with an internal 'co-missional' leadership approach. The foundations are firstly incarnational[1] in line with the widely understood and oft espoused Lord's Prayer invocation inviting 'your Kingdom come...'. Next, there is a 'gospel centric' approach to biblical truth, not only applied to your products, or published content, but also to the internal structures of the organisation. Then we apply those principles to the formation of people, whether they be staff or volunteers as the ones who will reflect the ethics of your enterprise to those you are reaching. Those working for us and with us ultimately interpret what they perceive is grounded in our organisational approach to Christian management integrity.

Let's be honest about the way we do ministry in our Christian organisation. If it all looks 'secular' and lacks the courage and vitality to apply the wisdom that comes from a 'transcendence' culture, it's probably missing some 'kingdom orientation' that needs to be brought into leadership discussions within the organisation. Our strength will be founded on what reliable biblical wisdom we can glean and apply to our present working model of ministry or business.

We can make an effective comparison of what is 'biblical', then apply it to our current business model. We'll look to define a biblical hermeneutic of administrative leadership from Old and New Testaments, and consider how these principles can be applied to administrative leadership essentials required in the wider context of the organisation. A further contextual avenue to explore is also of critical importance. It's how we shape the essential connection of a Christian organisation to the functions of the Christian Church as the fullest expression of the 'body of Christ' (1 Cor 12:27).

Hastings[2] observes that modern 'secularism' is the competitor of the Gospel and is an alternative confession, often borrowing capital from original Christian roots. Because much of what we already do is good, we can tick the boxes on existing practices that affirm what is strong and commendable. But let's also be open to highlight those elements which are vulnerable or 'at risk', denouncing those values that conflict with the movement towards a higher Divine purpose of redemptive influence.

The Contemporary Purpose of Co-Missional Leaders

As a Christian leader you may be able to appreciate a marked difference between your business goals, and what you think God's will is. In an organisational sense, the 'transcendence' of God can permeate your success pursuits. His presence can be exercised, practiced and articulated by those key executive figures leading the organisation. These days a 'Kingdom View' is becoming more and more a 'Counter-cultural View' of prevailing ideas that bring success.

By example, contrasting Christian media in the context of 'getting on the same page with God', with the prevailing secular view of business, ministry and 'success' will foster the formation of conclusions and recommendations that we may never have previously considered. Recognising the difference between the two is inspiration for moving towards a biblical 'co-missional framework' for organisational management. Central to the 'motivations' that galvanise the people of God to invest time, finances and energy in the pursuit of God's mission will be the establishment of a 'primary purpose' with a fresh look at motivations through a 'co-missional lens'.

For co-missional leaders, formation for our organisation engenders a 'transformational' relationship with the triune God. We recognise the ongoing power of God through the indwelling presence of the Holy Spirit who is superintending our formation as leaders according to His eternal purposes. The Apostle Paul demonstrated the rich empowerment that God brings to the life of the leader where the leader identifies with 'participation' in the very nature of God. It's easy to think of 'church leaders' requiring this level of relationship, and it may be a stretch for some to apply these same principles to our own role leading a business or organisation. Paul does not hold back the necessity of surrender in the internal issues of the heart. He said *'I have been crucified with Christ. It is no longer I who live, but Christ lives in me.'* (Galatians 2:20). The outworking of that statement for every boss, employee or volunteer is not supposed to be left inside the door of your local church on Sundays. We pray for the success of our business, but as Blackaby & Blackaby[3] discerningly state, the purpose of Christian leaders is not to achieve 'their goals', but to accomplish 'God's will'.

It is possible for leaders to achieve all their goals but miss God's will and purpose. Those Divinely valued people then within our influence are not merely the 'means', to achieve our goals as leaders. More specifically those 'people' we are called to lead, and those we are called to influence are 'the end'.

Under this approach to leadership those who achieve their personal goals but have carelessly allowed people to suffer and fall to the wayside in the process have failed. Where a company or ministry reaches its revenue targets, but key personnel lose their faith, marriages, family, or mental health the leadership has failed.

Where the Christian organisation fails to identify a Divine purpose for their enterprise, it is merely a secular pursuit. The *how* of management is just as important as the *what* of management. For the co-missional business or organisational leader, the end does not justify the means.

In Christian organisations, as in Church ministry the consumers are 'God's people', and the ministry personnel including staff and volunteers are valuable assets we identify as 'gifts' to the body of Christ. Our staff, be they paid or volunteer, are not an exploitable faceless force without reference to personal value. The motive for the co-missional Leader is to effectively mobilise the people of God as created in *imago Dei* (image of God), to use their gift in pursuit of *missio Dei* (the Mission of God).

Administrative Leadership – Order From Chaos

While scripture begins with chaos where creation is 'formless and empty' (Genesis 1:1), the unfolding narrative paints a picture of the intentional formation of 'order'. Order from Chaos is a key Kingdom orientated goal for all leadership. What begins with the spoken word is completed as an accomplishment and is categorised as 'good'. What begins in the garden has its culmination in the city. The Genesis 'creation' is the earliest demonstration of an organisational framework where the administrator is God.

There are numerous identifiable organisational streams in the biblical narrative. Notably, Abraham implemented the beginning process for the formation of the nation of Israel with a call to Haran, and then on to Canaan, with a promise that his descendants would possess the land (Acts 7:2-8). And later, Joseph proves to be a model of a Divinely appointed administrator elevated in the house of Pharaoh after suffering mistreatment (Acts 7:9-19). Deeper reflection on these biblical characters and their achievements will show that God's purposes were multi-generational. His ways are higher than our ways.

In God's timing, we are captivated by the Exodus, which we may consider as an 'administrative assignment and organisational development' with Moses as the leader. He is 'called' by God in the wilderness to deliver the Israelites from slavery in Egypt, and to shape the formation of a people 'belonging' to God.

While the immediate managerial goal after the Exodus may have been to 'possess the land' of Canaan, the concurrent strategic goal was 'God's agenda' of separating a people to Himself, and forging a unique cultural framework under a Divine covenant. As Blackaby & Blackaby[4] contend the Israelites spent 40 years wandering in the wilderness so that God could establish a relationship of faith with them. They would be for God a 'treasured possession', a 'kingdom of priests' and a 'holy nation' (Exodus 19:5-6).

The purposes of God become even more clear in the New Testament, where the Apostle Paul links God's purposes with the Israelites of the Old Testament, to the formation of a 'new humanity' in the creation of 'one new man out of two' reconciling both the Israelites, and the Gentiles to Himself through the cross (Ephesians 2:15,16). Consequently, Gentile believers in the New Testament are not foreigners, but fellow citizens with God's people and members of God's household.

> [19] *Consequently, you are no longer foreigners and strangers, but fellow citizens with God's people and also members of his household,* [20] *built on the foundation of the apostles and prophets, with Christ Jesus himself as the chief cornerstone.* [21] *In him the whole building is joined together and rises to become a holy temple in the Lord.* [22] *And in him you too are being built together to become a dwelling in which God lives by his Spirit. (Ephesians 2:19-22* NIV*).*

The formation of a 'new humanity' is noteworthy in the context of how we lead Christian organisations today. This illustrates the connection between God's original purposes with Israel, linked with his global purposes to the present day. This same passage not only solidifies the connection between Israel and New Testament believers, but also pre-empts an organisational framework for the 'new humanity' with the metaphor of building a 'holy temple' with Christ as the chief cornerstone and a foundation of apostles and prophets. The building is joined together and rises to become a dwelling in which God lives by His Spirit:

The New Testament construct of Divinely appointed administrative leadership begins with Christ, who fulfils the original covenant and under a 'new covenant' initiates the formation of a 'new humanity' with Himself as its head. He extends the redemptive purposes of God beyond, but not separated from His originally chosen people using a strategically Spirit empowered missional action, through 'witnesses', '... in Jerusalem and in all Judea and Samaria, and to the ends of the earth' (Acts 1:8). As this primary purpose unfolds beyond His death, resurrection and ascension, the prominent stream of supervisory administrative leadership is carried by the apostles and prophets. It may be a challenge to our present-day models of business leadership in organisations to suggest that our senior managers fit some form of modern definition of being an 'apostle' or 'prophet'.

New Testament Administrative Leaders – Today!

The formation of Paul the Apostle to the Gentiles is remarkably similar to the formation and commission of Moses. Both were Hebrews. The education and formation of Moses in literature, languages, history, transport, commerce and military strategy is foreign (Egyptian) emanating from the house of the Egyptian Pharaoh.

Paul, also a Hebrew was shaped by foreigners (a Roman citizen) from the city of Tarsus the capital of Cilicia and centre of Roman culture, philosophy, skill and craft. Paul was trained by renowned Jewish scholar Gamaliel in the 'law' (Acts 22:3).

Both Moses and Paul have a distinctive supernatural encounter and 'call', where Moses at the burning bush (Exodus 3) hearing the voice of God can be compared to Paul's encounter with Christ on the road to Damascus (Acts 9). Importantly for our discussion centring on Public Christians in organisations, in Church ministry, business and Christian media, both Moses and Paul being shaped by alternative foreign cultural formations, were used by God in their context, character and gifting to bring structure to the formation of the people of God for His purposes.

Both Moses and Paul confronted the prevailing authorities and sought to solidify God's revelation. And both strategically 'published' historic, prophetic and pastoral accounts of God's dealings with His people. These elements of formation, character development and 'publishing' have critical meaning and direction as principles necessary for present day leaders of Public Christian enterprises. To use the media example to illustrate the difference, you know you are trapped within the secularised, 'immanent frame' if you argue that Christian media is more about 'entertainment' than these strategic elements of formation, character development and the heralding of God's dealings with His people today.

Moses and Paul— God Preparing a People for Himself.

While leadership lessons are evident throughout scripture Moses example is outstanding. He shouldered leadership and supervisory responsibilities in the formation of a 'nation' under God, so we might theorise that lessons learned from his journey carry Divine validity in our consideration of Godly organisations today.

The elements of Moses leadership reveal insights into Divinely appointed principles that may be assimilated as foundational to leadership philosophy and administration in the shaping of both the ancient Israelite nation, and therefore modern nation contexts as direct illustration of the purposes of the Spirit of God.

We understand that God was preparing a people for Himself, so in the 'setting apart' of a people, the establishment of a 'transcendent' rule of law, the organisation of tribes, the value of a priestly class, political representation, civic governance, health protections, and education are founded on principles of strategic administrative leadership, and hold timeless value in all pragmatic Christian leadership, forming foundations for culture anchored in Divine wisdom.

Administrative leadership through the Apostle Paul also carries Divine weight with New Testament applications for the structural framework for the 'building' of the body of Christ as a 'new humanity' (Ephesians 2) set apart with Christ as head. As the organisation grows the integration of 'gifts' enlarges. The influence of your organisation also grows in directions you planned and beyond your expectations. The potential for new initiatives means the culture you have worked hard to build expands, and personnel that you have raised as 'administrative leadership disciples' explore new arenas of influence.

Under your watch, the Great Co-mission continues to win ground. What becomes decentralised geographically, continues to be empowered by the same Spirit that brought order to chaos at the beginning, is now bringing order from chaos in your enterprise. Just as new believers enter a cyclic discipleship model, so does your organisational enterprise, where the fruit of the Great Commission sees the flourishing of God's kingdom on earth. We recognise the parallel between the Genesis commission for Adam and Eve to 'multiply', with the Matthew 28:18 Great Commission for believers to multiply.

Connecting Your Organisation to 'the Mission'

An important pillar emerges for the motivations of Christian business leaders, influencers and media practitioners, where there is pragmatic connection to the motivations of the 'Great Commission'. Pioneering Missiologist Donald McGavran[5] in his seminal work in church growth, ventured that world evangelisation is concerned with the billions who are yet 'completely unchurched' under domination of sub-Christian and anti-Christian ideologies, value systems and religions.

Churching people cannot be the product of unplanned, 'kindly' Christian activity. Where the proclamation of the Gospel and gathering of believers (planting of Churches) is the first dimension of the Great Commission, the second part is the 'teaching' of everything that Jesus commanded.

Firstly, there must be 'many' churches, then only where practicing believers form sizable minorities can they expect their presence to effectively influence economic and political structures. What he notes specifically, is that the formation of local churches is not only a good goal, but necessary on a large scale for influence in the wider society.

McGavran[6] contends that planned 'church planting' must never be abandoned in favour of creating a vague community of justice and goodwill alone. These convictions present a challenge for Christian media as 'para-church' ministry and for Christian business enterprise that sees itself separate to the work of the local church. It must be an important relationship, to discover 'co-missional' dimensions of supporting endeavours for 'church planting' and to develop resistance to the potential for 'mission drift' away from remaining committed to the ultimate commission.

Aligning Church, business and media in a strategy for community transformation requires an intelligent plan for 'seeding the countryside' with strong, growing and effective Church congregations. This remains important for increasing potential to influence today's secularised culture. It's my opinion that a vulnerability for Christian organisations is in their propensity to retreat into the pursuit of 'kindly Christian activity', or in the case of Christian media, that their ministry operation, because of its potential reach, is more important than the concept of the 'Local Church.'

Jesus the Strategic Team Leader

We might expect nothing less than 'profound' leadership and

administrative principles in Jesus, the Son of God.

The 'team leadership' of Christ is the penultimate expression of the multi-factorial and quintessential elements of the co-missional leader and administrator. Gangel[7] identifies Jesus' team leadership as the 'genius' of the New Testament. It is exemplified in Jesus formation of the disciples and continues through the ministry of the Apostles.

Jesus appeared to the Apostles saying to them *"'Peace be with you! As the Father has sent me, I am sending you.' And with that he breathed on them and said, 'Receive the Holy Spirit.'"* (John 20:21,22) Where the same Spirit of Christ dwells in His followers, 'co-mission' takes on new value connecting Christ, the Apostles, and all who believe and receive the Holy Spirit. As the Father has *sent* Christ, Christ has *sent* the Apostles and all who believe and receive the Holy Spirit are also *sent*. This 'sent-ness' of followers creates the administrative imperative for purpose and strategy embodied in all Christian leadership.

In the New Testament the Apostles, particularly Peter and Paul hold places of eminence, but the place of pre-eminence, even in the subsets of leadership and administration always centres on Jesus Christ and His promised Holy Spirit. At the Jerusalem Council in delivering the important administrative 'decision' resolving a dispute over rules governing Gentile believers, the decision is formally announced co-missionally as 'It seemed good to the Holy Spirit and to us...' (Acts 15:28). It's Him and us together.

The concept of an unfolding Divine 'plan' is interwoven throughout scripture, affirmed in John 1:3,4 where through Christ '...*all things were made; without him nothing was made that has been made. In him was life...*' (John 1:3,4 [NIV]) The plan for humanity from creation is evident and affirmed in a timeline through the events of the flood, Abraham, Moses and the exodus, the Tabernacle, Joshua taking the promised land, Solomon's construction of the Temple and Nehemiah rebuilding the walls of Jerusalem after the exile. The culmination of 'prophecy fulfilment' is affirmation as the biblical terminology for a Divinely appointed 'Strategic Plan' that had its telos in the fulfillments of the coming of Messiah at the birth of Christ, and in Jesus' redemptive appointment at the cross.

Today's leaders and administrators recognise the present and future strategic/prophetic telos as affirming the sovereign purpose of God. We should also expect His faithfulness in future eschatological fulfillments. To ignore these affirmations is to retreat into the secularised deflated disenchanted 'immanent frame' that captivates Christian leaders into 'secular thinking' and minimises the full depth of the transcendence of God in his Divine purposes.

Decentralisation – Leadership of the Laity

In the New Testament, the dynamic of leadership is part of an 'expansion plan' beyond those who lead the Israelite nation, with the sweeping 'decentralisation' goal extending the redemptive purposes of God to present day far-away lands:

> *But you will receive power when the Holy Spirit comes on you; and you will be my witnesses in Jerusalem, and in all Judea and Samaria, and to the ends of the earth. (Acts 1:8).*

The Apostle Paul identifies Divine 'gifts' who are placed in the Church, not only of those primarily aligned with a Clergy/Priesthood class, but of functional leadership gifts exercised by the Laity.[8]Special ordination is not a pre-requisite to serve in the expansion of the Kingdom of God.

The egalitarian nature of a mass of new believers develops the need for 'function specific' leaders beginning with those who are devoted to prayer and proclamation, and those who would be commissioned to serve the practical needs of the people. Those serving practical needs are required to be nonetheless gifted as 'full of the Spirit and wisdom' (Acts 6:3).

Formalisation of leadership as the early Church matured saw the emergence of elaborate corporate structures[9], and formation of a priesthood which appears to harken back to an Old Testament priestly model. Under the New Testament pattern Church leadership is constrained to the Divine 'co-missional' telos of equipping the body of Christ:

> '...until all reach unity in the faith and in the knowledge of the Son of God and become mature, attaining to the whole measure of the fullness of Christ.' (Eph 4:13)

Later into the early 16th century Protestant Reformation, as 'reform forged renewal', the reformer Martin Luther (1483-1533AD) taught the notion of the 'priesthood of all believers'. In his view, the 'ploughboy and milkmaid' could do priestly work, and according to Luther, ploughing and milking were in fact 'priestly work'. As Lindsley[10] notes, both Priests and Laity were doing the work of God as they exercised their gifts. The implications are significant. Christians connect their 'beliefs' to everyday 'action'. Leaders, bosses, employees, and volunteers are equipped to serve in the one 'Great Co-mission' through their daily work.

In the Church, Paul identifies 'those with gifts of administration' (1 Cor 12:28) working in cooperation with other leaders including apostles, prophets, teachers, and workers of miracles. For further reflection is the placement of the 'gift of administration' included at number seven in a list of eight gifts in 1 Cor 12:28. This placement in the lower order on the list, may not be because the gift is a lower valued gift. I suggest that It may be because the gift does not always require public prominence. The true value of the gift of Administration may be in that without the effective function of administration those 'higher' or more prominent gifts are left vulnerable through weaknesses in formal contextual stability in strategic direction.

The administrative leadership is strategically important. New Testament administration κυβέρνησις[11] (kubernésis) is metaphorically described in the image of a 'helmsman' portraying 'the responsible decision maker on a ship' (1 Cor 12:28). A person with this gift will be identified as one who is drawn to directing the tasks and ministries of others.

Human Skillsets – Are They Enough?

The secular model assumes our rational abilities and well-developed skills are what makes us successful. But as Christians, we may be compelled to analyse this more deeply. We might begin with a question as to whether human skillsets alone, were responsible for the series of nation shaping dynamic developments described in Old Testament scripture.

In Moses, a series of Leadership foundations are identified showing that a combination of Hebrew Theology and preparation in Egyptian politics was not adequate for the formation required to do the work of God in the Exodus. Gangel[12] identifies the task of 'nation building' was impossible to do in Moses' own strength (Ex. 2:11-14).

The contrast is stark, between the person of Moses as a Divinely 'called' and 'commissioned' leader in the wilderness, to his earlier Egyptian leadership formation in the house of Pharaoh. In the wilderness Moses' isolation highlighted his own inadequacies with time to reflect upon and contextualise failures.

His experience of the 'call' and 'commissioning' by God (Exodus 7:14-18) became the necessary springboard for his capability to persevere through the coming adversities including the pressures, and risks to personal safety in the confrontation of Pharaoh, as well as the formation of organisational structure for the new nation, and later the resilience to cope with the 'murmuring' and complaints of the people. This type of pressure takes more than a 'set of skills' and experience. The impossibility requires the empowerment of God pursuing His purposes through flawed human agents like Moses.

Counting the Cost

In Moses, we could see that the 'call and commission' of God come with a cost. In the New Tetament Jesus instruction to *'count the cost'* of discipleship (Luke 14:28-31) requires intimacy with God in 'planning and administration':

1. *'Suppose one of you wants to build a tower. Won't you first sit down and estimate the cost to see if you have enough money to complete it?'* (Luke 14:28 ᴺᴵⱽ)
2. *'Or suppose a king is about to go to war against another king. Won't he first sit down and consider whether he is able with ten thousand men to oppose the one coming against him with twenty thousand?* (Luke 14:31 ᴺᴵⱽ)

The context of Jesus' use of these metaphors, of building a tower, or going to war, is in the call for believers to bear their own 'cross' and come after Him as disciples (Luke14:27). For the administratively gifted leader, Jesus is not merely 'part' of the strategic process, His 'mission' is the motivation for a planning process. Not only does the whole resource belong to God, but so does the mission strategy. The elements of sacrifice and surrender in the bearing of our 'own cross' illustrates that mission endeavour, while meeting our own needs, cannot be purely for the furthering of personal interests.

Biblical Culture in today's Workplace

The nurturing of biblical ethics in an organisation takes place in the business environment. It's one thing to theorise, but the reality is that wisdom and experience come from resolving the problems that arise on the 'shop floor'. The challenge for leaders is to create or affirm a 'biblical values culture' as the driving force behind the processes of decision making at all levels of the organisation. The transformational leader works with a view to developing what Powers[13] describes as a 'transformistic' organisation with aspiration to transform the wider community. The Christian church has traditionally been organised as a hierarchy with Ordained leaders towards the top and the followers at the bottom. But as Powers argues there is a move away from what was known as a 'ladder of perfection'. Current thinking suggests a gravitation towards renewal, where only the layers and structures that are necessary for the fulfillment of the mission are required.

Organisational design has become flatter in structure rather than deeply hierarchical. Programs have become dispersed rather than centralised. Leadership has moved from 'Pastor and Staff' to 'Ministers and Teams', and a picture of success as a happy church has moved from 'growth with good programs' to 'growth and people on mission.'

There may be conversation within business enterprise aspiring to be more Christian, and Christian media organisations over what this means for mission orientation. Does Christian media hierarchical structure need to emulate secular models to function efficiently? Is there a truly unique biblical model that is more effective than worldly wisdom applied to the Kingdom pursuit?

Where 'secularism' is the competitor of the Gospel and is an alternative confession, priorities for the contemporary ministry organisation are realigned, to begin with the orientation of 'Leaders' both strategic and administrative. Formation of our leaders is firstly surrendered to relationship with the triune God recognising the transforming indwelling Holy Spirit who is able to superintend the formation of the leader according to His eternal purposes. The leader with insight into the 'transcendence' of God and his purposes sees a bigger picture than the leader still trapped within an 'immanent frame.

A New Testament organisational framework becomes the administrative goal for leaders with a transcendent God's-eye view of Divine purpose. The biblical New Testament image of purpose emerges with the goal of leading a 'new humanity' with the metaphor of building a 'holy temple', with Christ as the chief cornerstone and a foundation of apostles and prophets. The building is joined together and rises to become a dwelling in which God lives by His Spirit (Ephesians 2:19-22).

Elements of formation, character development, and publishing have critical importance to the principles necessary for present day Christian organisations with application to business enterprise aspiring to Kingdom purpose. Where the same Spirit of Christ dwells in his followers, our 'co-missional' cause takes on new value connecting Christ, the Apostles, and all who believe and receive the Holy Spirit. As the Father has *sent* Christ, Christ has *sent* the Apostles, and all who believe and receive the Holy Spirit are also *sent*. This 'sent-ness' of followers creates the need for purpose and strategy embodied in administrative leadership.

Endnotes

1   'Your kingdom come, will be done, on earth as it is in heaven.' Matt 6:10 (NIV)

2   Hastings R. 2012 Missional God, Missional Church, Hope for Re-Evangelizing the West, IVP Academic, Illinois, USA. p.52

3   Blackaby H & R. 2011 Spiritual Leadership, Moving People on to God's Agenda, B&H Publishing, Tennessee, USA. p.122

4   Ibid p.128

5   McGavran D.A. 1970 Understanding Church Growth, Eerdmans, Michigan, USA. p.439

6   Ibid p.443

7   Gangel K.O. 1989 Feeding and Leading, A Practical Handbook on Administration in Churches and Christian Organisations, Baker, Grand Rapids USA. p.27

8   The term laymen is credited to Clement of Rome (c. AD 95) who described laymen as full participants in the life and work of the Church, including the liturgy. Welch R.H. 2011 Church Administration, Creating Efficiency for Effective Ministry, BH Publishing, Tennessee, USA p.14.

9   As the church became wealthy and the dominant institution, elaborate churches stood as 'monuments to God.' By the 20th Century the concept changed to a meeting place, though society generally accepts a Church as a sacred place. Ibid. Welch 2011 p.190,191.

10   Lindsley A. 2013 The Priesthood of All Believers, Institute for Faith, Work & Economics. P.1

11   Strongs Greek 2941: kubernésis: properly, someone who steers (guides) a ship; (figuratively) the divine calling which empowers someone to lead in affairs relating to the Church. It should be noted that this is the only occurrence – 1 Cor 12:28.

12   Ibid 1989 p.17,18.

13   Powers B.P. 2008, Church Administration Handbook, Third Edition Revised and Updated, B&H Publishing, Tennessee, USA. p.13-17

Chapter 15:
Transcendence
Culture – in Practice

See, I am doing a new thing! Now it springs up; do you not perceive it?
I am making a way in the wilderness and streams in the wasteland.

Isaiah 43:19

Let's use Christian media organisations as a 'case-study' to examine
how transcendence looks in practice. Christian media organisations
are of interest as an illustration, because they fall somewhere 'between'
the sacred structure of the Church and the conventional operation of
business. Christian media in Australia typically functions within the Not-
For-Profit sector.

Administratively they operate as a service provider of Christian content.
Spiritually they are typically non-denominationally aligned, and therefore
not under obligation to traditional religious oversight. If fact, over my
many years in Christian media, indeed I have seen policies that bar
ordained clergy from positions of influence. The 'image' projected to
supporters including any formal denominational alignment, has been
concerning for some. And the downside has been that essential Christian
'rules' and leadership ethics have not applied in the same mature way
as Church denominations might. So, when choosing Christian Radio
as a case-study subject for talking about how to be 'more Christian' in

business it is a valid choice, and a good model to explore.

The 'values' identified and propagated by organisations are the essence of the 'framework for the culture' of the organisation. Leaders decisions will either reflect a biblical approach to God's purposes or will reflect alignment with a secularised view.

Identifying Context – Christian Media

There are three broad overlapping contexts in media. For example, our case study example Vision Christian Media is related in context to a broader expression of Christian media in Australia. This expression is in turn related in context to the larger and much more pervasive 'mainstream media' industry made up of all streams of secular and religious media. The more recent rise of 'social media' is also an important consideration of how co-missional leadership is necessary far beyond the boundaries we might use to identify what is 'Christian media' and what is not.

The context of all Australian 'Christian' media, includes Christian newspapers, television, magazines, publishers, web based ministries, welfare agencies, the music and production industries, and the online presence of numerous para-church expressions. At the time of writing, in Australia Churches are undergoing a revolution in the way they deliver services through 'on-line streaming', as a consequence of bans on meeting together because of the Coronavirus pandemic.

The broader national 'mainstream' media typically with an ethos autonomous from religious influence, is broadly secular. While neutrality may often be stated as an aspiration, this is not a realistic possibility given the social imaginaries that have shaped individuals with editorial influence or control. At the time of writing, it is broadly accepted that mainstream media outlets tend to be 'left of centre' politically, secular, and increasingly either embarrassed by, or are becoming even hostile to Christianity.

Administrative Issues for Theological Reflection

It may be confronting to suggest a 'review 'of the way Christian organisations strategize for success. However, discussion about these issues may be an important Board and Executive level conversation. The Church obsession with strategic planning has been described as a pursuit of 'human control' contrasted to the essence of a community that is gathered together through the Holy Spirit in the life of Christ and is sent by the Holy Spirit to represent the kingdom of God. Hastings[1] ventures to suggest that there is an epidemic of control through modern 'strategic planning' that can have the counter-productive result of keeping the church from missional effectiveness. He postures that the kingdom of God is not about human control, but God's reign.

We might ask the question in the context of our organisation how much strategic planning is enough? Or, if an unhealthy reliance on strategic planning is detrimental? I propose that the solution to the question of 'human control' is addressed in the requirement of 'both' detailed strategic planning, and concurrent submission to the purposes of God.

The deeper issue may not be in the process of strategic planning at all. If you fail to plan effectively, you effectively plan to fail. The challenge may not be the process, but in the 'character', and Christian maturity of those responsible for the planning process. This may highlight the true value of a co-missional Leadership. Where human strategic planning is identified as contrary to, ignorant of, or designed to subvert the organisation's pursuit of *missio Dei,* the leadership needs to be able to identify that failure, even if the face of the organisation shows an appearance of flourishing. For the organisational leader wanting the organisation to reflect a more Christian ethos, the inclusion of mature Christian 'leadership' personnel around the strategic planning table will be a necessary inclusion in the process of setting your plan.

Where executives and individuals are 'empowered' to serve, embrace change, and absorb shock under a principled strategy, including sound administrative stewardship of the resource and theologically reflective strategic planning, the ministry could be affirmed as a 'success'. We remember that 'success' before God is more about faithfulness to his purposes than a sole attention to the 'bottom line'.

Transcendence orientation in discernment for strategic direction, includes expectation for Holy Spirit inspired capacity to envision, and plan for future scenarios in preparedness for change. The capacity for successive ministry Leaders benefiting from the reinforced attention to co-missional strategic planning aligned with *missio Dei* forms part of a basis for sustainable leadership, and is an important ingredient for succession planning or the intentional discipleship of emerging leaders.

Scenario Planning

The concept of 'Wind Tunnelling' a range of scenarios for the future appears to be especially important for co-missional strategic planning for Christian organisations. The prospects for changes in legislative environment, technological innovation, audience movements, or an increasing tendency towards litigation, allows vulnerability under pressure to soften or abandon biblical truths. The same wisdom applies to all conventional business aspiring to be more publicly Christian. God's wisdom is required for mergers or takeovers, multicultural necessities, shifting belief trends, hostilities towards the broader Christian church, the threat of war, conflict or terror attack, and the more seductive insidious 'mission drift'.

The concept of 'wind-tunnelling' tests scenarios up to five, ten, fifteen or twenty years from the present with anticipation of both defensive and entrepreneurial responses to the likelihood of 'shocks' and change scenarios. According to Schoemaker[2] managers who exercise imagination for a wider range of possible futures enhance their positioning to anticipate unexpected 'opportunities' that arise. These often include elements that can't be formally modelled such as new regulations, value shifts or new innovations. Uncertainty is only high relative to the Leadership team's ability to predict change and make necessary adjustments.

Secularisation trends sweeping the West assume a marginalising of religion to downplay its relevance and remove it from influence. However, the body of Christ continues to work for the 're-enchantment' of Christian faith in every societal context, and has at its disposal every modern platform for communication (Christian Media) available to the secular competitor. Co-missional leaders prepare for change.

Leaders must rely on Divine strategy to stem the tide with an anticipation that secularisation will wain and eventually fail. As Smith[3] argues the thing that characterises secularism and the secular age is the reliance on exclusive humanism as a way of constructing a social imaginary without any reference to the transcendent God. The Christian organisational leader relies on the transcendent God for the re-formation of a social imaginary according to His missional purpose.

In constructing 'strategic scenarios' for Christian media, a motive to chart middle ground resists the risk of 'under or over-prediction' when imagining issues like economy, interest rates, political elections, faith or family trends. Simplified outcomes are sufficient for scenario planning. The value of scenario planning and wind-tunnelling in an environment where prayerful openness to *missio Dei* is enabled, means that the result of the exercise may highlight the inspiration of the Holy Spirit in the forward movement of the ministry organisation. How we hear and identify where God has spoken, may be in the idea that prayerful strategic planning has focused achievements that can only have one reason for their accomplishment, that it was the hand of God at work in building His organisation.

Whether the scenario 'wind-tunnelling' works with quantifiable results is not the only importance. The stretching and refocusing of thinking will have the effect of correcting a typical bias towards over-confidence for the future. Creating an environment where leaders are expectant but not over-confident, and being mindful of future scenarios will be a useful spiritual exercise including the openness to 'Divine Strategic Planning'. Like the positive expectation that is aroused when we study biblical prophecy, we anticipate with a new confidence that God can be sought in a co-missional sense for administrative empowerment of the organisation.

Calling, Preparation, and Staffing with Attention to *Missio Dei*.

There are many biblical examples for key leaders to 'identify with' in the concept of having a Divine 'calling'. It will be useful to focus attention on how the development and function of skillsets can be aligned to 'gifting'. Aspirations for Christian media leadership are towards a view that encourages staff and volunteers to pursue their role as a 'vocation aligned with God's mission'. In other words, the people Leading departments in your organisation ideally don't see their role as 'just a job'. Not only is there a servanthood, sacrificial dimension to this level of service/leadership, but a requirement for applied principles of stewardship in both professional and personal life.

Because of the nature of, and relatively brief history of Christian broadcast media in Australia, there is not a significant body of formalised co-missional mediacentric studies on specialised leadership. A transformational (working alongside) approach to Christian media skills is the predominant methodology for maturing leaders in co-missional organisational culture.

As sophistication grows this process of transformational leadership may be accelerated by defined inclusion in the responsibility of department leaders to develop documentation that describes the co-missional nature of their pursuit as a 'Christian vocation', and not just a 'job' working for Christian media.

The Value of Personnel – 'Gifts' to the Church.

Because the people of God are considered a 'treasured possession' of God, Rodin[4] contends that when working relationships are valued,

228

communities are endowed with 'meaning' that reflects our created state before the triune God.

Acceptance of staff and volunteers, each as a 'gracious gift', nurtures a protection from the influence of the secular model which in contrast seeks meaning found in the hoarding and consumption of resources. The secular model will often be marked by the symptomatic exploitation of staff and volunteers.

One of the temptations for Christians in the ministry workplace is to fall back into the secular way of thinking that does not value a 'priority of grace' where people are joyfully treasured. Stewardship of relationships in public Christian workplaces is contrasted with the secular idea of acting as 'owner' of the organisation where relationships are used to self-centred benefit. A transcendence 'priority of grace' will permeate the way employees are valued and will therefore serve your vision as service for God, not just a human employer.

Connectedness to the Goals of the wider Church.

An aspiration for all authentic Christians is to be the visible fruit of the Great Commission. It's in the idea of being marked by a discipleship formation in groups of believers and disciples. The missional concept of Church formation and sustainability requires careful attention. How powerful it is, that Christian leaders may be formed and released not only within the walls of the Church, but in the enterprises of people connected to the Church.

Christian media and many other Para-church ministries sometimes see themselves as 'alternatives' to personal participation in a 'local church'. This thinking is deficient in biblical foundation. Connection to personal participation in the 'local church' requires continuous attention. Where the New Testament concept is to decentralise and spread the 'good news' across the world, the task of substantial discipleship continues within the concept of a physical gathering of believers. As Smith[5] observes, humanity is made up of 'embodied persons' rather than just 'thinking things', and people become attuned to 'practices' rather than just ideas. It's this personal participation in Christian worship that engenders an alternative cultural formation.

Participation in the worship practices of the Church as Jesus commanded through communion, baptism and discipleship, are critical to the formation of practices of belief and the sustainability of the Church generationally.

Without this connection of empirical practices like 'planting and growing churches' McGavran[6] laments that only a vague community of 'justice and goodwill' is created which may be contrary to the pattern of the New Testament.

Resistance to Mission Drift

When the Triune God is the 'true Leader', the context of the organisation is built around Him. From this foundation, administration theory translates into administrative practice, including stewardship. One of the vulnerabilities for Christian media lies in the pressure to implement private sector strategies for social sector success.

Sponsorship and advertising bring in crucial 'dollars' but they are often accompanied by ethical challenges. Dart's[7] qualitative case study research identifies four elements for distinction between business and non-profits. He includes:

1. The goals of programs.
2. The organisation of programs or service delivery.
3. Organisational management.
4. And organisational rhetoric.

On one hand, business is a sustained activity by an organisation to blend profit motivation with the use of managerial and organisational design tools in a business setting. In contrast, the non-profit motivation typically rests on moral principle, mutuality, trust and a common cause, and is organised around a set of prosocial and voluntaristic values with few references to the financial resources by which these values are enacted.

While financial issues may often be the predominant issue, the potential for 'mission drift' in Christian media ministry organisations is enhanced by the misuse of 'organisational rhetoric'. Biblical mission is weakened where leaders primarily adopt industry jargon borrowed from business and management theorists[8] as the priority description and discussion of the mission or in the programming.

For the co-missional leader, a preferred rhetoric in building motivation for *missio Dei* will favour the promotion of both 'biblical examples' and 'current testimonies' for explaining and promoting the dimensions of organisational activity.

These thoughts should not to be misconstrued as seeing the potential for advertising and sponsorship as being bad, or ungodly. The primary motivation in discussing this revenue stream is to remind us that Jesus warned that we cannot serve 'two masters', and tight policies will be needed in the context of preventing 'mission-drift'.

Summary and Implications— The Organisational Framework

A 'transcendence' approach to organisational leadership causes us to look at the role of our business or ministry organisation in light of the purpose of God in the growth of the Church grafted into the vine, as one 'new humanity' (Eph 2:15). The metaphor of a 'dwelling' being built by God in which He lives, may have implications for all Christian organisational design for ministry and business.

A significant resistance to secularisation culture, may be functionally realised through the appointment of a mission caretaker at executive level, with an eye for biblical standards. We might call that person a 'Director of Quality and Standards' responsible for the development of internal co-missional culture. In a practical sense, there is possibility for a leader or team to be appointed as part of the hierarchy to safeguard a transcendent co-missional ethos in all levels of administration, policy, process, legislative compliance and best practice, to draw people into the aligned purposes of the organisation, and to develop the strengthening concept of *imago Dei* in the workplace.

An organisational framework like that of Ephesians 2 has been made possible by Christ, and may determine leadership decisions on organisational design and structure:

> [19] *Consequently, you are no longer foreigners and strangers, but fellow citizens with God's people and also members of his household,* [20] *built on the foundation of the apostles and prophets, with Christ Jesus himself as the chief cornerstone.* [21] *In him the whole building is joined together and rises to become a holy temple in the Lord.* [22] *And in him you too are being built together to become a dwelling in which God lives by his Spirit. Ephesians 2:19-22 (NIV)*

Imagine your own organisation being built on the 'foundations' in scripture. Where people are 'built together' to become a dwelling in which God lives by His Spirit, deep implications for every organisational framework, and indeed every department within the broader organisation may be realised.

For co-missional leaders in Christian media, the design of governance, business models, strategic planning, and day to day relations with staff as treasured 'gifts', may be a foundation for broader influence. The idea of connecting faith to life in people, or the aspiration to sow seeds of the wisdom of God begins in the organisation doing the seed sowing. Aspiring to be the ministry/business example of a Divinely transformed entity forms the foundation of a workplace culture. That exercise confidently espouses the look of a renewed 21st century people, who are Christlike, not only in word but also in practice. As a Christian organisation we are to be a dwelling in which God lives by His Spirit, and we are received as 'partakers' in the fullest expression of *missio Dei*, so that we might effectively model this for our clients, and our supporters.

Endnotes

1   Hastings R. 2012 Missional God, Missional Church, Hope for Re-Evangelizing the West, IVP Academic, Illinois, USA. p.67

2   Schoemaker P.J.H. 1995 Scenario Planning: A Tool for Strategic Thinking, MIT Sloan Management Review, Winter Edition, USA. pp.1-5

3   Smith J.K.A. 2014 How (Not) To Be Secular Reading Charles Taylor, Eerdmans, Michigan, USA. p.26

4   Rodin R.S. 2011 The Steward Leader, Transforming People Organisations and Communities, Intervarsity Press, Illinois, USA. p.35

5   Smith J.K.A. 2009 Desiring the Kingdom, Worship, Worldview and Cultural Formation, Baker Academic, Michigan, USA. p.35

6   McGavran D.A. 1970 Understanding Church Growth, Eerdmans, Michigan, USA p.440

7   Dart R. 2004 Being 'Business-Like' in a Nonprofit Organisation: A Grounded and Inductive Typology, Nonprofit and Voluntary Sector Quarterly, Vol 33, no.2 June 2004, Association for Research on Nonprofit Organisations and Voluntary Action. P.239,302

8   In one example a comparison is made between a non-profit counselling service and a hamburger franchise, where clients are compared to people waiting in line to purchase hamburgers. Connecting sets of behaviours and approaches can misrepresent the value or needs of the clientele. (Dart p. 302)

Chapter 16:
A Transcendence
'Management
Framework'

But one thing I do: *Forgetting what is behind and straining toward what is ahead, [14] I press on toward the goal to win the prize for which God has called me heavenward in Christ Jesus.*

Philippians 3:13-14

The case study that I have continued to discuss in the chapters of this book focuses on the organisational pursuits of Vision Christian Media as a market leader in para-church Christian ministry. Rather than just a theoretical proposition, or dealing with a series of hypotheticals, I've had the privilege of observing the practical function of principles at work. In the coming chapters there will be much to fuel the conversation among organisational leaders about setting direction and safeguarding from 'mission drift.'

Mission and vision 'Setters', and vision 'Casters' will be concerned with whether settings in the organisation are clear, with built in protection from 'mission drift.' It's especially important for Public Christian organisations ensuring that all departments are moving in the same strategic direction.

Constructing an Integrative Management Framework creates a visual application where the Strategic Manager is aware that 'Mission Drift' can easily permeate the organisation. Because the business, ministry environment, and political landscape are changing so quickly, built in mechanisms for resisting the 'secularising' influences are useful. Where the rubber hits the road in delivery of ministry and services, it is valuable to keep prominent, a 'transcendence' culture in the organisation along with a way to monitor pathways to 're-enchantment' for stakeholders and the wider community.

While broader philosophical issues for a co-missional approach to the task of 'media mission' are contrasted to the secularised mainstream media industry, this evaluation introduces a co-missional integrated framework for total quality management as it applies to the Christian media organisation. The construction of the 'Framework' will form the foundation for an implementation plan and a biblical 'stress test' for the strategic direction of the organisation.

Towards a 'Co-missional' Integrated Management Framework

Applying a transcendence view, and a co-missional lens to the 'best practices' pursuit of Christian media organisations, introduces us to the need for quality of management in the ministry organisation. Where 'motive' is as important as 'action', what we do in practice should be consistent with biblical scholarship. The total quality management concept promises 'economic' gain through continuous improvement.

Jesus emphasised the dimension of 'thoughts and motives' as an important precursor to actions.[1] If these thoughts and motives are useful for personal transformation, they are clearly useful for setting directions for business and ministry. God is interested in priorities for leaders. Thoughts, motives and actions are all part of how we might think about safeguarding the 'co-missional' alignment of the organisation, to the already established mission of God (*missio Dei*).

The task of 'benchmarking' best practices should become commonplace for Christian organisations as a reference standard. Becoming increasingly co-missional will also yield 'new indicators' of applied biblical stewardship to management practice. When this happens the 'Goodness'[2] of God translates to followers and clients who are also called to be 'good', cling to 'good', be evaluated on their behaviour, and to do 'good works'.

Where biblical passages shed light on relationship with the triune God[3] and one another, we can infer that many key biblical passages that relate to the 'body of Christ' in the life of the Church, also translate to ethical behaviour in business practices.

Issues of the Heart - in your business pursuit.

The co-missional Leadership ethos begins its expression in organisational management where Leaders allow God's presence to permeate the 'inner life'. This may be especially important for senior leadership in Executive Management. Applied wisdom has its foundation in understanding Divine oversight of His mission.[4]

Jesus' barometer of the condition of the 'heart'[5] shapes the pursuit of the intimate spiritual 'inner life' of leaders. We do well to nurture one-another and continue in practices of encouragement. This encouragement for executive leadership and staff, is likely to stem firstly from healthy connection in a local church. Pastoral care is much easier in the life of your organisation, if leaders and staff each have their own local church connection, as an external way of nurturing Christian spirituality and fellowship with others. The writer to the Hebrews expressed the need for '...*not giving up meeting together, as some are in the habit of doing. But encouraging one another – and all the more as you see the Day approaching*'. (Hebrews 10:25 [NIV]). A steady diet of real-life biblical application to men, women and families enriches your ministry and business pursuits.

Where practical biblical examples of stewardship have direct influence upon best practice, these can rightly be considered an application of Divine 'management wisdom'. An example of an adjusted alignment of 'inner life' because of faith translating to practical application can be found in the narrative describing Jesus and his encounter with Zacchaeus.[6] Here was a real world example of a corrupt business man whose transformation illustrates the contrast between the secular world[7] operating in greed, extortion and deception, to one who was willing to restore his relationships with those he had defrauded, and to correct his injustices. Martin[8] notes that as a rich business operator leading a team of unjust tax collectors, a new 'transcendence' business model emerges from the encounter with Jesus. The new model reflects repentance and restitution for past wrongs, and an aspiration to make things right. These attitudes show a change of heart in Zacchaeus that we might judge as the fruit of a changed heart reorientated by the Spirit of God.

While attention to the inner lives of Christian ministry leaders will not always correlate to that of Zacchaeus, the principle of a transformed life and maintenance of a renewal focus will be an ongoing essential foundation for managerial motives, and will form part of the 'outcomes' criteria that may be monitored and potentially measured.

Just because we may at this time be part of a Church or para-church ministry, we are not always better protected from mission drift, or less obligated to the highest standards of integrity in the governance of our own business practices. The same obligations exist for the broader Church and at all levels of leadership participation in the body of Christ.

Practices that lead to Superior Performance

The individual 'inner life' of senior leaders will always remain important for continued health of the entire organisation. But I'll suggest that there may be some ways that the fruitful delivery of day-to-day business practice can maintain a focus on the practical application of the 'inner life'. Business leaders are no strangers to the concept of Key Performance Indicators (KPI's) showing the efficiency of delivery of products and services to clients and stakeholders, and so to initiate a new KPI is not something foreign to monitoring the health of the organisation.

Best practice policies for content delivery are essential to the consistency of high-quality services and for long-term sustainability. As Benke & Benke[9] note, basic purposes are not independent from higher purposes. They are an interrelated 'symphony' synergistically extending ministry to new heights. Where Purposes, Policies and Practices can be refined relative to a co-missional Integrative Management Framework, there will be a new capacity for an effective evaluation of success or failure. In other words, where key performance indicators can be identified and monitored in the same way as traditional business models, we can make relevant day-to-day adjustments to the way we view outcomes. It's a way that Christian organisations can align with a compass pointing to a set of standards we can confidently say is a truer model of 'flourishing', a Divinely centred model with a 'transcendence' orientation.

Towards an Integrative Management Framework

The Figure 1 'radial cycle' diagram (below) makes explanation easy for how each of the core processes in your organisation revolve around the central characteristic of ministry and business – God.

Even as your business or ministry organisation grows more complex the addition of an Integrative Management Framework will draw separate elements together in co-relation.

In my case study example at Vision Christian Media, the *primary processes* include the delivery of a multiplex of services including a terrestrial broadcasting network - Vision Christian Radio, an online youth channel called Vision 180, a daily devotional arm called The Word For Today, a youth focused devotional publication called Vision 180 Magazine, a national prayer line - Vision Prayer, resources distribution through Vision Store and international tours to Israel in Vision Tours. As is the case with all mature organisations there are significant complexities. There is need for *support processes* including governance, human resources, finance and administration. Each of the governance and administrative support mechanisms have an aspiration to align consistently with the *planning process* including the strategic plan, operational plans and the budget.

In all the complex dimensions of the organisation, the central figure in the day-to-day function of the organisation is God. In the context of all of the departmental functions the challenge of the culture of the delivery of services is understood in terms of God and His mission – *missio Dei.* Because humanity is created in the image' of God, this image is an important theme in mission and defines its aim. Getting it wrong or ignoring the need to fine-tune our 'motives and practices' may constitute a continued inappropriate use of resources or missing the goal that you set out to reach in taking the helm of an organisation as a Christian leader. The audience, clients and stakeholders of the organisation don't need entertainment, as much as they need for leaders to recognise the core needs of humanity that can be met in the life transforming power of the Gospel. Hastings[10] distils an understanding of humanity as the product of three influences:

1. Humans are created in the image of God (Gen 1:27) ***imago Dei.***
2. The 'fall' has defaced and distorted the image; and
3. there is a process of restoration of the image in Christ, ***missio Dei.***

The process of restoration is emulated in all forms of effective mission. The Apostle Paul describes a 'new humanity' conformed to the 'true' image of God embodied in Christ (Eph 2:14). It is by faith that people are brought into participation in restoration. It is by the Holy Spirit that we are nurtured into the fulness of the image of God in Christ. The role of the Public Christian leader therefore must be to raise up human instruments of mission, to work as God works, just as reigning over creation is in communion with God as His co-workers.

The following diagram connects the aspects of the functional Christian organisation with the mission of God. Here we discover that an ability to 'think Theologically' has broad effects for the starting point in the organisation. It will be in the formation of the 'Mission' of the organisation that begins at Board level, and sets the culture for how everything will be motivated. And if this has not been the starting point for your organisation, it will never be too late to refine your focus.

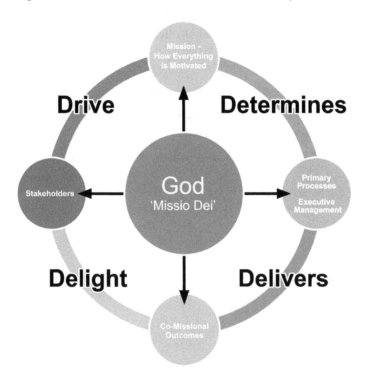

Figure 1. *A Radial Cycle – Integrated Management Framework where God and missio Dei become the primary influence on the purpose of the business.*

It should be noted that 'administrative theological reflection' on the mission of God in terms of restoration of the image by the Spirit is in keeping with the broad evangelical concepts of the 'new birth' (John 3) and processes of 'discipleship'. It also encompasses outcomes described by the Apostle Paul using the metaphor of God's household as a 'building', joined together to 'become a dwelling in which God lives by his Spirit' (Eph 2:22).

The radial cycle Integrated Management Framework (Figure 1) illustrates how the elements of the Strategic Plan, form into one meaningful process. Each element is interdependent on the primary elements of *missio Dei*. While the 'Mission' will be generated by the Board and key Leadership, the implementation is executed in the 'Primary Processes' through the department Managers. What is delivered as co-missional 'Outcomes' including the increasing pursuit of micro-interactions should be influenced by the co-missional application traced back to formulation of the mission.

All of the processes of delivery of your service is to the delight of 'Stakeholders' who support your organisation either because of your ethos, or the way that your product or service is delivered according to a higher level of business ethics and practice. The Strategic Direction can be regularly reviewed to ensure the organisation remains 'mission true.'

Endnotes

1   The Widow's mite (Mark 12:41-44) – Many were giving money, but Jesus focused not on the action of giving, but also on the motive. The motive of the woman was remarkably different because she sacrificed her own wellbeing in her action in giving to God.

2   Matt 19:17 'Why do you ask me about what is good?" Jesus replied. "There is only One who is good. If you want to enter life, keep the commandments." (NIV)

3   Matt 22:36-40 (NIV) '37 Jesus replied: "'Love the Lord your God with all your heart and with all your soul and with all your mind.'[a] 38 This is the first and greatest commandment. 39 And the second is like it: 'Love your neighbour as yourself.'[b] 40 All the Law and the Prophets hang on these two commandments."

4   Proverbs 16:2 "All he ways of a man are clean in his own sight, but the Lord weighs the motives". (NIV)

5   Matt 12:34 'For the mouth speaks out of that which fills the heart.' (NIV)

6   Luke 19:1-9.

7   Jews opposed the Roman taxes because they were exploited to support the secular government of the Romans and their pagan gods.

8   Martin D. 2005 On Secularization, Towards a Revised General Theory, Ashgate Publishing, Hants, England. pp.1-4

9   Benke W., Benke L.N. 2011 Church Wake-Up Call, A Ministries Management Approach that is Purpose-Oriented and Inter-Generational in Outreach, Hayworth Press Inc, Binghamton, NY, USA. p.74

10 Hastings R. 2012 Missional God, Missional Church, Hope for Re-Evangelizing the West, IVP Academic, Illinois, USA. p.150

Chapter 17:
Applying A Transcendence Strategy

'In everything set them an example by doing what is good. In your teaching show integrity, seriousness and soundness of speech *that cannot be condemned, so that those who oppose you may be ashamed because they have nothing bad to say about us.'*

Titus 2:7-8

Missio Dei Measured as a Key Performance Indicator (KPI)

While elements of a Mission Statement are often deliberately broad, the idea that broad can be 'vague' infers that the mission is not measurable. While Christian organisations will monitor, measure and rely on Key Performance Indicators (KPIs) in daily operations or 'business as usual', the concept of applying a co-missional paradigm in the primary processes of Executive level management will enhance the quality of service delivery in line with *missio Dei*.

Objective evidence and client feedback are two critical measures of performance, but they are not the only ones that matter. The idea that nobody is complaining about what we are doing is not good measurement for aligning to the purposes of God.

Along with sophisticated 'business metrics' that track and assess processes, 'marketing metrics' track campaign and program statistics, 'sales metrics' prompt the pursuit of new opportunities from leads in the database, and 'executive metrics' focus on big picture financial indicators. For many business operations data is readily gathered and used to create elaborate measurements charting progress. E.g. 'individuals and moving range' (X-MR) charting is often used to judge whether change has led to improvements in outcomes. KPI reports and 'digital dashboard's provide Executive Management with real time indicators. A new 'co-missional' application to organisational management has the potential to add an important dimension in the business and ministry function of the organisation.

Towards a Co-Missional Evaluation of Key Performance Indicators

In light of a 'new view' of the world, allowing the transcendent presence of God into 'day to day' organisational management, we might find real value in spending time reflecting on the differences that applied Christian thinking brings to the organisation.

The following table is not an exhaustive example of contrasts we can identify. The table has more particular focus on the Media organisation, but the same principle comparisons apply to any organisation that sets it's sails to be publicly Christian. You can add to this list, those specific elements that are unique to your organisation, or in your department. The list in the table below, identifies differences that could be introduced in the application of a Christian 'co-missional' framework, contrasted to the outcomes in a traditional (secular) model.

Key Performance Indicator	Secular	Christian (Co-Missional)
Co-missional Ethos	We make 'our own' plans	Aligned to God's mission
Profit - Balance Sheet	Did we make a profit?	Ethically generated profit?
Costs	Reduce and Manage	Wise Stewardship
Audience Numbers	More listeners	Growing disciples/Church
Readership (TWFT)	Raw Distribution	Growing Network
Customer Satisfaction	Make them happy	Extra Mile - Servanthood
Workplace Efficiency	Contractual	Covenantal - Relational
Sustainable Leadership	Hire skillsets	Professional Development
Objective Feedback	Customer satisfaction	All Stakeholders + Bible
Resource Sales	Increasing Numbers	Numbers and quality content
Stewardship	Owners discretion	God owns the resource
Geographic Coverage	Most profitable	Most mission strategic
Staffing / Volunteers	Essential to Operations	Essential to Mission
Seasons and Cycles	Profitable Seasons	Church Growth Seasons
Donors / Supporters	Statistical	Personal Relational Valued
Marketing	Investment and Return	Kingdom Investment
Social Media Strategy	Metrics measurement	Mission Interactive
Data Collection	Strategic Growth	Strategic Mission
Survey Ratings	Market Share	Share + Influence
Census Data - NCLS	Program Strategy	Faith and belief evaluation
Demographics	Targeting an audience	Audience Influence and trust
Psychographics	Reflecting who they are	Shaping what they can be
Church Connection (Staff)	N/A	Pastoral Care & Vitality
Family Stability	Work/Life Balance	Wholeness/Wellbeing

The Growing Challenge - Micro-Interaction

Revolutionary change in the media landscape calls for adaptability for traditional broadcast, and print content. Psychographic influence on style, attitude and feel, is in the radio context, an outcome that Kassof[1] describes as a 'stationality'. Stationality resonates with 'personality' and is empathetic with emotional needs of core consumers.

However, the increasing digital environment demands the increase of personalised micro-interactions. Delivering the right content to the right audience at the right time is among the biggest challenges for the future effectiveness of marketing your Christian organisation.

A synthesis of biblical mandate combined with information gleaned from client interactions has the potential to help shape services delivered to users through a growing reliance on automation and content tools. As Pophal[2] highlights when describing new opportunities in multi-channel marketing, granular customer data gleaned can enable marketers to deliver micro-services, micro-experiences or 'experience as a service' to consumers.

Beyond websites and apps, the use of Artificial Intelligence (AI) and machine learning may fuel the potential of the existing technologies to deliver personalised content. Imagine a day coming where your Public Christian business/media App working on mobile devices, has sophisticated 'mood-tracking' along with the potential to deliver specific content to the individual App user. That day is close, as this technology is already being used to support those suffering mental illness, and can 'track moods' to the point of triggering content for the user, and a series of micro interactions including a trigger point where a message is sent to 'trusted friends' that the mood is low and the App user needs an encouraging phone call.[3]

Understanding audience psychographics, demographics, and behaviours increases potential for personalisation. Christian ministry administration is about 'people' in the light of Christ and therefore delivers content in dimensions rich in theological and pastoral ethos.

For Christian broadcast and print media, these dimensions of service delivery are both internal within the organisation, and external embracing stakeholders[4] including consumers at all levels. An Integrated Management Framework connects the 'co-missional strategy' from its origin and has the potential to reach every dimension of service delivery, including the 'ethos content' to the most minute of individual micro experiences.

Workplace Cultural Development—
The Biblical Concept of 'Covenant'

Relationships with a 'transcendence' view of God take on a new level of priority. It's not only the micro interactions with listeners, readers, consumers and clients that are affected by the 'Top-down' influence of the Integrated Management Framework and monitored through a Key Performance Indicator. Managers, staff, volunteers, and supply chain connections are equally important in the broad influence of the Public Christian organisation. It's not just the end receiver who is important on this journey, so are the people we entrust to deliver our services.

A deepening appreciation of an enhanced 'value' for Managers, Staff and Volunteers as 'Team' within the organisation will enhance the missional effectiveness of the ministry strategy.

There are numerous biblical examples of teams apart from what Macchia[5] calls the perfect team within the triune Godhead. He includes men and women who have shared a common heart for God including Adam and Eve; Noah and his family; Moses and Jethro; Aaron, Hur and Moses; Jesus and the disciples, or the early Church including Paul and the Apostles. However, there is a noteworthy example of an Old Testament allusion to the issues of 'employer/employee' relations from which we can glean an amazing workplace principle. It comes from the book of Ruth.

In Ruth Chapter 2 we see demonstrated, a model that may be useful in applying the concept of 'covenant' to relations in modern business and ministry. When Boaz (the Boss) arrives in his fields, he greets his harvesters (Employees) with the words 'The Lord be with you.' What follows is the reciprocal response from the harvesters, 'The Lord bless you!' (Ruth 2:4). Both the greeting and response reflect a demonstration of 'leadership attitude' and a motivation to serve in a 'covenantal' way.

The remainder of the chapter shows the demonstration of transformational leadership from Boaz to his foreman (vs. 6) expressed

249

in the application of an initiative through his leaders and staff to deliver an outcome in the protection and provision for new 'hard-working' staff member Ruth who at the beginning is considered a 'stranger'.

There are applications of this 'covenant' concept for modern church, ministry and aspiring Christian business settings in the development of covenant-based loyalties to God and ministry/business mission. Thomasma, Niejenhuis and Kallemeyn [6] infer that relationships between Christian employers and employees speaks of more than 'contract', it speaks of 'covenant' built on promises and enriched by trust. The concept of 'brothers and sisters' in Christ, 'partners in the Gospel' and 'family of God' enhance the value of all who are called to use their gifts in the service of God.

The practical application of this level of 'covenantal relations' on display in the Public Christian business/ministry including all forms of ministry, business and media. We may begin with a review of 'how' staff evaluations are undertaken. An employee evaluation becomes an opportunity for gracious and candid conversations that reinforce the clarity of the mission of the organisation.

Anticipated outcomes from an evaluation process are extended to include aspirational movement towards a shift in personal priorities for staff; a desire for new educational or learning objectives in the coming year; a contrast between secular thinking on their department and a 'transcendence view' of the operation under God; fine tuning of job descriptions better honouring employee gifting; and affirmation of how the staff member is contributing to the co-mission of the organisation. [7]

Best Practice – Broadcast, Online and Print Ministry

A co-missional evaluation process could involve a departmental 'criteria' for biblical 'Best Practice': The following evaluation processes may also be useful as 'workshops' helping staff appreciate the contrast between the view of their work as a 'secular pursuit' and one that is influenced by the 'transcendent' presence of God, who is active in their lives, and the Christian workplace.

1. God is 'Good' – (*agathos* Greek: Good in character). Because God is good, followers of Christ are also called to be 'good' (Rom 12:9; I Thess 5:15), and to do 'good' for others (Rom 15:2; Gal 6:10), and to do 'good works' (II Cor 9:8; Eph 2:10; Eph 4:29; Col 1:10) Note: We are not called to be 'nice', we are called to be 'good'. How is goodness expressed in my role? _____

   _____

   _____

2. Motivations of the Heart – Zacchaeus and his changed business ethic after an encounter with Jesus (Luke 19:1-9). How should my attitude change in alignment with motivations that come from my service for God? _____

   _____

   _____

3. Personal Agendas – Rivalry vs Goodwill. (Philippians 1:15-17; Ruth 2:4). How can I express goodwill in my workplace? Will that improve my advancement prospects? _____

   _____

   _____

4. Justice – The whole law summed up in 'love' for God and one another. How we treat others is how we treat God. (Matt 25:34-40) How can I be more focused on love for others in a practical sense?

   _____

   _____

   _____

5. Performance - Business / Ministry – measuring the outcome of the practice using business related measures. Skillsets (gifting) exercised faithfully and fruitfully. (Luke 16:10-13) What can I do to improve my skills to the glory of God? _____

6. Stewardship[8] – Departmental and financial (Luke 19 and Matthew 25 includes: Zacchaeus, Parable of Ten Talents, and the Parable of the Ten Virgins) What areas in my department could be streamlined, and resources allocated to the best Kingdom oriented outcomes? _____

    _____

    _____

There are not necessarily 'right or wrong' answers to these questions, but an opportunity is created to highlight the contrast between a secular way of thinking about work and relationships, vs the more transcendent way of assessing the functions of working together in the mission of God.

Personal Mission Evaluation— for Management, Staff and Volunteers.

A set of questions can introduce a new alignment to 'participation' in God's mission. This may have broad application in staff performance reviews or in a weekly staff gathering for encouragement.

1. What is my connection to the Mission of God - *missio Dei*? (My Calling)
2. What skill has God 'gifted' me to serve in the Body of Christ? (My Purpose)
3. How do my relationships within the organisation affect my commitment to the mission? (Great Commandment – God and Others)
4. Do my work colleagues understand the essential elements of the mission? (Discipleship, Transformational Leadership, Theological Reflection)
5. How does my work interact with other departments, and external clients? (Interaction)
6. Is it my desire to become more proficient in using this gift to serve the mission of God? (Professional Development)

Towards Implementation of a Professional Development Strategy

Balancing internal 'transformational' leadership development (measured by Department Manager feedback and in staff evaluations) with an individual or group plan should identify improvement needs. It may also require an internally developed Professional Development track that is specific to the individual ministry departments under the banner of your organisation. A more advanced goal may identify a set of external accredited courses and incentives for professional development. This may require research and negotiation with course providers according to the special needs of your organisation.

As part of a resistance to secularisation culture, a measure I suggested earlier may include the appointment of a Director, or a Committee responsible for 'Quality and Standards'. The role of the Director or Committee would include development of internal 'co-missional culture' and may also identify specific development tracks for departments.

In the case of Public Christian enterprises specific departments where frontline personnel are responsible for the direct connection of ministry to the provision of services and online consumers, a formal development track may include:

1. Basic level ministry studies equipping staff in biblical foundations. This is something we often think Churches do, but why not our workplace?
2. Biblical Christian ethics; and
3. Engagement with the history and direction of the diverse Australian church.

In a workplace with a 'transcendence' aspiration, basic training in these key fields may be the foundation for a new culture to arise.

Sustainable Leadership— The 'Fruit' of Professional Development

For the future of Public Christian organisations, the quality of succession planning in senior and departmental leadership will be dependent on attention to professional development of faithful and gifted leaders. Key administrative roles are also spiritual leadership roles.

The concept of sustainable leadership in succession planning is important for the viability of the continuity of fruitfulness, and as a defence in the challenge of remaining 'mission true' into the future. Laniak[9] portrays Joshua as an 'anointed' human leader used by God to lead His people. Succession planning for a Public Christian organisation is no less important than the transition from Moses to Joshua where the goal is sustainable growth and missional effectiveness.

Effective Leadership continued after the death of Moses, because God enabled Joshua as His chosen successor. We should not assume we have the sole responsibility with respect to spiritual preparation, but we are compelled through a discipleship mandate to steward the formation of successive leaders.

Elements of a Professional Development Model

A culture in the workplace that reflects 'Transcendent' wisdom over the immanence of the deflated disenchanted secular wisdom, will be entrusted to executive levels of management with a view to improving the quality of the missional aspects of the organisation. From shifting stubborn secular paradigms, to the practical application of developing skills, leaders have a vital role in making the organisation Christ-like.

1. Internal attention to the application of a co-missional paradigm for departments.
2. Identifying future requirements for administration/ministry/ production skills.
3. Identify appropriate formal training / seminars / conferences / networks / resource materials.
4. Incentives or requirements for management/staff to develop

professionally.

Where 'Theological reflection' sheds light on relationship with the triune God, we can infer that key biblical passages that relate to the 'body of Christ' also translate to ethical behaviour in business and 'co-mission' oriented ministry practices. The increasing maturity of para-church ministry in the growing field of Christian media organisations is therefore under similar compulsion to adopt the highest standards of governance integrity as any other administrator serving God in the wider body of Christ.

Where strategic direction and policies are refined relative to a co-missional Integrative Management Framework a new capacity is created for an effective evaluation of 'success or failure' according to a biblical cultural mandate. Christian Media as a human instrument of mission is called to work as God works, in communion with Him as co-worker.

The reference to the 'radial cycle' diagram (Figure 1) earlier illustrates the 'centred status of God' and His mission, deepening the appreciation of how 'Primary Processes' of management pursue co-missional outcomes benefiting and inspiring all stakeholders to drive the mission of the organisation. Application of co-missional leadership principles to the organisation's Strategic Direction presents an immediate opportunity to 'pressure test' the Strategic Plan Summary, with seeds for further development and refinement of the elements in light of a biblical reflection of *missio Dei*.

This reflection can be taken to further depths of application with the proposal that Key Performance Indicators (KPI's) may be measurable when assessed in contrast to standard 'secular' indicators that drive the majority of business models.

Recommendations for a re-aligning to a biblical mission:

1. Introduction to a Strategic Framework linking elements of the Strategic Plan to a reinforced co-missional alignment with *missio Dei*.

2. Increased attention to implementation of consistency between 'Vision and Values' as they are communicated to staff.

3. Appointment of a 'Quality and Standards' Director or Committee to work with internal co-missional culture and identify potential development tracks for departments.

4. The renaming of management and staff agreements to reflect the biblical concept of covenant - 'Staff Covenants'.

5. Intentional connection to broad Church Denominational Leadership aligning the purposes of the Christian organisation to the *missio Dei* / theologically 'living purposes' of major churches/denominations.

6. Work closely with affiliated operations that share your ethos to encourage the deeper pursuit of co-missional outcomes (In media: program content and news).

7. Attention to 'Scenario Planning' with 'wind tunnelling' exercises anticipating change 5, 10 and 20 years out.

8. Reflection on mechanisms to resist 'Mission Drift'.

9. Creative ways to draw people (staff, customers, listeners, readers) into the co-missional 'Purpose' of the organisation.

10. Active attention to the influential capacity of your Christian Organisation to be a positive influence upon other likeminded autonomous Public Christian organisations.

11. Regular review of the organisational structure to ensure it effectively supports fulfilment of the mission. A centralisation of strategy and policy. Responsibilities matched with accountability.

12. Attention to the environment for staff, where for some their workplace is the best nurturing expression of Christian community.

13. That attention be given to the concept of 'sustainable Leadership' in succession planning and pre-requisite professional development for key roles within the organisation.

14. For broadcast media organisations: Attention to the strengthening

of the Australian Christian music industry, with attention to a co-missional alignment.

15. Creating a workplace where people are nurtured and encouraged to do their best work. Do employees love your Christian organisation enough to 'live the brand'?

16. Regular reflection and review of techniques for business/ministry, avoiding potential for coercion and manipulation for fundraising and evangelism, so as not to violate the dignity of people. Dialogue and persuasion are preferred.

17. Increase efforts to connect clients (listeners) to a trusted 'local' church.

18. Professional Development – Individuals and departments.

19. For para-Church operations, the use of the words 'resource range' may be better than the concept of 'product range'.

This is not an exhaustive list of issues and alignments. For the Public Christian organisational leader, a prayerful reflection on your organisation or individual departments, will yield further dimensions where you can identify the need for a different kind of 'fruit'.

Where outcomes lack the 'transcendent' dimension, there will be need for adjustment with a view to new outcomes that counter the enveloping secularisation we are seeing in the wider community.

Endnotes

1   Kassof M. 2017 Psychographic Research, EContent, http://www.kassof.com/psychographic-research/ p.1

2   Pophal L. 2017 Micro-experiences: New opportunities in multichannel marketing, EContent, May-June 2017, p. 6+. Business Collection p.1

3   www.soultime.com introduced this AI feature in 2020.

4   Stakeholders: Board; Executive; Staff; Volunteers; Donors; Advertisers; News Clients; Database – Clients; Guests; Listeners to Vision / Vision 180; UCB Asia Pacific and UCB International; Church Leaders; Content Providers; Governing authorities / regulators; Suppliers; Music Industry; Debtors / Creditors; Social Networks; Allied broadcasters / Publishers / Tour Operators.

5   Macchia S.A. (2013) Becoming A Healthy Team, 5 Traits of Vital Leadership, Leadership Transformations, Lexington, USA. pp.28-30

6   Thomasma N., Van Niejenhuis C., and Kallemeyn J. 2010 Evaluation Essentials for Congregational Leaders, Sustaining Pastoral Excellence, Christian Reformed Church in North America, Michigan, USA. p.14,15

7   Note: Adapted from a process described by Thomasma, Niejenhuis and Kallemeyn 2010, p. 37.

8   Two key parables in the New Testament include the Servants (Luke 12:42-48) and the Shrewd Manager (Luke 16:1-13) illustrate that the Steward's task is to be faithful and accountable to the master, increasing the assets. We are Stewards because God entrusts us with things. Cunningham R.B. 2007 The Purpose of Stewardship, The Leaders Handbook of Management and Administration, Baker Books, Grand Rapids, USA p.453

9   Laniak T.S 2006 Shepherds After My Own Heart, Pastoral Traditions and Leadership in the Bible, Intervarsity Press, Illinois, USA. p.92

Chapter 18: Summary and Conclusion

"But you will receive power when the Holy Spirit comes on you; and you will be my witnesses in Jerusalem, and in all Judea and Samaria, and to the ends of the earth."

Acts 1:8

The thesis of this book project is to understand just how useful (the utility) Christian influence in media is, in expressing the dimension of Divine 'transcendence' to a broader culture described as captive within an 'immanent frame'.

The consequences for decline in religious participation appear to be disguised in modern Australia, but this nation is not alone. As Pippa Norris and Ronald Inglehart have shown us, virtually all advanced industrial societies have progressed towards secular orientations. The modern West has affluence and the experience of high levels of economic and physical security. Cultural values are changing as new generations emerge shaped by their formative experiences and the culture of their elders is gradually being replaced.

A weakening of the influence of religious institutions with statistically lower attendances at formal religious services is synonymous of the lower importance ascribed to religious convictions and aspiration. As attendances diminish, the authority of Church leaders over prescribed ethics and behaviours also loses potency. We might expect religious leaders to lead robust public debate as a defence of religion but being forthright comes into conflict with secular aspirations for progressive change. We are increasingly marginalised and often in retreat when a barrage from opponents attempts to silence the Christian voice in the public sphere.

The authority of Government and the consequences for politics influenced by lobbyists for 'alternative agendas' is likely to continue to marginalise the institutional Church. Evidence is mounting that Christian influence is diminished over issues like marriage and divorce, abortion and euthanasia, sexual orientation, and the robust make-up of traditional family structures.

As Wells[1] argues modernity is 'hostile to all truth claims that are absolute and transcendent in nature' replacing Christian certainties and making them seem implausible. In the modern age where two polarising extremes are becoming prevalent either in adherence to 'transcendent religion' or the rise of an 'exclusive humanist denial', Christian Leaders require more than an intellectual argument. Important to navigating a way forward will be an illuminated path of revealed wisdom and understanding to reorientate the growing 'humanist deception' with the grace to address the resulting pessimism and despair that follows secularism ideals.

For the Public Christian in organisational leadership an affirmed confidence in a personal faith framework is the place to start. What follows are tools to navigate engagement in a 'contest of ideas' with an understanding of the necessary ingredients in the practice of Christian ministry to influence the broader secular public sphere.

We are heartened by the conclusion that the assumption that we live in a secularized world is proven false. We are invigorated by the truth that in a big picture sense, the world today is as 'furiously religious as it ever was' and the presence of 'secularization' has provoked powerful movements of counter-secularization[2].

Progressive minded people think secularization is a good thing, whereas those of religious persuasion often as Christian 'classical' conservatives see the opposite. For Public Christian ministry and business leaders, it may be argued that there is a necessity to take courage, take up instruments of influence, and prepare to engage in a winner takes all 'battle' of ideas.

Responses and strategies are usually founded on one of two positions, either 'rejection' or 'adaptation'. The first calls for 'religious revolution' as has been tried by religious regimes like Islam in endeavours to take over nations using tactics of terror, intimidation and forced behaviours. Under the second response, 'adaptation' becomes a necessity where 'religious sub-cultures' are built to keep out the bad influences and promote those things that are good. Adaptation is akin to 'adjustment' according to rules of the secularized world. Experiments in synthesis usually fail. The ones that succeed are those that have 'beliefs and practices dripping with reactionary supernaturalism'[3].

For Public Christian leaders in media and business, I believe the challenge is not to be victim to the temptation to pursue religious revolution, nor to pursue adaptation to the secularized public sphere, but to pursue a counter-cultural path of presentation of biblical 'transcendence' acknowledging the transforming presence and power of God as revealed in the incarnate Christ and therefore shaping the desires of people towards God.

I believe that re-enchantment is a 'co-missional' project working with both God and His people. A secular public sphere has as a calculated end point like Weber's 'iron cage', a constructed environment where those entrapped in its disenchanted uniformity, experience real difficulty conceiving transcendent or eternal realities. Without re-enchantment of the broader public sphere the self-regulation of elites will likely advance to authoritarian governance as society becomes more subservient to 'charismatic authorities' who will only be able to rule by stringent regulation and oppression.

When the complexities of modernity create contradictions, and the emergence of 'multiple modernity's' result in tensions and conflict, unrest is fuelled. When the flames of unrest are fanned, people grow tired of subservience to the power struggles of the 'rationalist elite'. When we see these tensions emerging, we know that people are open to the alternative, of a new formation of Kingdom. A Kingdom of God future holds appeal for seekers of freedom, as an attractive alternative to secular elitism.

Taking time to reflect on a deepening understanding of the formation of 'social imaginary' is the challenge that lies before Public Christian leaders in media, business and community organisations. Christian leaders have a 'co-missional' role in a future 're-enchantment' of the secularized public sphere.

Identifying what ordinary people 'imagine' about their surroundings as expressed in images, stories and legends can capture the senses that go beyond theory to the deeper issues of social reality. While the secular world is 'thinking', Church leaders and Christian media must aspire to 're-imagining'. The goal of imagination is not to be defeated by past failures, or to 'wallow' in past glories. We can objectively reflect on the structures and systems that have been eclipsed by new anti-structures. Re-imagining the future includes political, social, intellectual, arts, economic, technological and psychological futures that are permeated by conformity to the image of Christ. As the Apostle Paul wrote to the Romans:

> 'Do not conform to the pattern of this world, but be transformed by the renewing of your mind. Then you will be able to test and approve what God's will is – his good, pleasing and perfect will.' (Romans 12:2 NIV).

In these chapters, the importance of influencing culture is elevated to highest levels, recognising the Genesis 'cultural mandate' (Gen 1:26-28).

The consequences of not giving rightful place to the 'transcendent' God of creation are being felt even now. For Public Christian influencers, media as a 'tool for culture formation' must become instinctive. Using all forms of media as a means of 'mass communication' pursues a process of creating, changing and maintaining culture. The content we create as Christians is a pre-requisite for Kingdom 'culture change'.

Transcendence has been reduced to 'a rumour'. The rediscovery of the supernatural will 'above all' be a regaining of openness in our perception of reality. One of the great challenges for modern political policymakers, philosophers, theologians, and the 'gate-keepers' of Christian media content is to deal systematically with the reality of transcendent phenomena, and the legitimacy of people's stories and experiences.

Corr [4] argues reflective analysis does not 'discover or disclose' transcendent reality in people's experience, but what comes to light are 'signals of transcendence' that are part of the common human experience. While a naturalistic interpretation of transcendent experience is always possible, a complete denial of transcendence is a denial of the richness of human experience.

Modernity is not 'evil'. It works for or against the Christian mission according to the influence of leaders. Modernity is 'the *power* to change the structure of systems'.[5] It's influence has power over human beings, whether states, groups or individuals. It exercises power over nature in a practical way in terms of economic production. And power over nature, in the form of capacity for expressed understanding. 'Power' can be defined as a 'capacity to direct energy'.[6] And with a generationally fluid, changing social imaginary comes the opportunity and consequent dangers that await the courageous.

Endnotes

1   Wells D.F. 1994 No Place for Truth: Or Whatever Happened to Evangelical Theology? Eerdmans Publishing, p.127

2   Ibid. Berger 1999 p.3

3   Ibid Berger 1p.3

4   Corr C.A. Peter Berger's Angels and Philosophy of Religion, University of Chicago Press, The Journal of Religion Oct 1972, Volume 52, Issue 4, pp. 426 – 437 (p.435)

5   Ibid Berger 1990 p.211

6   Ibid p.211 Examples: (1) 18th century thermodynamic revolution discovered how to turn heat (undirected energy) into usable work (directed energy). (2) And, military power or internal administrative control increases output per person of goods and services.

Bibliography

Ahern S. 2006 *Making Radio, A Practical Guide to Working in Radio*, 2nd Edition, Allen & Unwin, Crow's Nest, Australia.

Alexander J.C 2007 *On the Interpretation of the Civil Sphere: Understanding and Contention on Contemporary Social Science*, The Sociological Quarterly 48 (2007) 641-659. https://pdfs.semanticscholar.org/a8bd/6b2fbe9c332b9f13344e4371ea7d0731cbeb.pdf [Accessed 4th September 2018)

Anselm St. 1926/2017 *The Works of St Anselm, Proslogium; Monologium; An Appendix in Behalf of the Fool by Gaunilon and Cur Deus Homo*, Translation by Sydney Norton Deane (2017), Global Grey Books, https://www.globalgreyebooks.com/content/books/ebooks/works-of-st-anselm.pdf [Accessed 29th August 2018]

Australian Bureau of Statistics 2016, *ABS Census of Population and Housing*, www.abs.gov.au/ausstats/abs@.nsf/Lookup/by%20Subject/2071.0~2016~Main%20Features~Religion%20Data%20Summary~70 [Accessed 28th July 2018]

Australian Law Reform Commission 2012, *Classification – Content Regulation and Convergent Media (ALRC Report 118)*, https://www.alrc.gov.au/publications/classification-content-regulation-and-convergent-media-alrc-report-118 [Accessed 9th Aug. 2018]

Barbier M. 2005 *Towards a Definition of French Secularism*, (Translated by Elliot G.), https://www.diplomatie.gouv.fr/IMG/pdf/0205-Barbier-GB-2.pdf [Accessed 2nd August 2018]

Barker R. 2017, *Religion and the Census: Australia's Unique Relationship to Faith and Belief*, ABC Religion and Ethics, 5 Jul 2017, http://www.abc.net.au/religion/articles/2017/07/05/4696888.htm [Accessed 3 Aug 2018]

Banks R.J, Ledbetter B.M, Greenhalgh D.C 2016 *Reviewing Leadership, A Christian Evaluation of Current Approaches*, 2nd Edition, Baker Academic, Michigan, USA. https://www.google.com.au/books/edition/Reviewing_Leadership_Engaging_Culture/0XlSDAAAQBAJ?q=governance&gbpv=1#f=false [Accessed 11th May 2018]

Barna Research 2018 *Atheism Doubles Among Generation Z*, https://www.barna.com/research/atheism-doubles-among-generation-z/ [Accessed 2nd Aug 2018]

Batten, D. 2020, *Radicalizing young people*, Creation 42(1): 6, Jan 2020. Creation.com

Beasley-Murray, G.R 1992 *The Kingdom of God in the Teaching of Jesus*, Journal of the Evangelical Theological Society, 35/1. http://www.etsjets.org/files/JETS-PDFs/35/35-1/JETS_35-1_019-030_Beasley-Murray.pdf [accessed 10th May 2018)

Benke W., Benke L.N. 2011 *Church Wake-Up Call, A Ministries Management Approach that is Purpose-Oriented and Inter-Generational in Outreach*, Hayworth Press Inc, Binghamton, NY, USA.

Berger P.L. 1990 *A Rumour of Angels, Modern Society and the Rediscovery of the Supernatural*, Anchor Books Doubleday, New York, USA

Berger P.L. 1999 *The Desecularization of the World, Resurgent Religion and World Politics*, Eerdmans, Michigan, USA.

Berger P.L. 2011 *Dr Peter Berger on Religion & Modernity*, Faith Angle Forum on Religion, Politics and Public Life. YouTube https://www.youtube.com/watch?v=bv3aLp27sO4 [Accessed 29th Sept 2018)

Blackaby H & R. 2011 *Spiritual Leadership, Moving People on to God's Agenda*, B&H Publishing, Tennessee, USA.

Blackaby H, Blackaby R. 2008 *God in the Marketplace*, B&H Publishing, Tennessee, USA.

Blamires H. 1963 *The Christian Mind, How should a Christian Think?* Regent College Publishing, Vancouver British Columbia, Canada.

Bouma G. 2009 *Australian Soul: Religion and Spirituality in the Twenty-first Century*. Cambridge University Press, Melbourne, Australia.

Bouma G. 2018 *Religion in Australia: What are the Implications of 'None' being the New Normal?* ABC Religion and Ethics 28th June 2018, http://www.abc.net.au/religion/articles/2018/06/28/4863516.htm [Accessed 2nd Aug 2018]

Boyer P.S. 2004 *Sexual Morality and Sex Reform*, The Oxford Companion to United States History, Oxford University Press, Published online 2004, http://pserver.chc.qld.edu.au:2054/view/10.1093/acref/9780195082098.001.0001/acref-9780195082098-e-1391?rskey=Z1NHR5&result=2 [Accessed 12th Aug 2018]

Broadcasting Act 1942, (No longer in force) *Federal Register of Legislation*, https://www.legislation.gov.au/Details/C2004C02568

Carson D.A. 2008 *Christ and Culture Revisited*, Eerdmans, Michigan, USA.

Carson D.A., Keller T. 2011 *Gospel-Centred Ministry*, The Gospel Coalition Booklets, Crossway, USA.

Christian Media and Arts Australia, *2016 AGM Annual Report*, Australia. https://mediaarts.org.au/cmaa_theme/documents/Christian%20 Media%20Australia%20AGM%20Report%202016.pdf [Accessed 27 May 2018]

Clark M. 1993 *History of Australia*, Abridged by Michael Cathcart, Melbourne University Press, Australia.

Clarke, F.G. 1992 *Australia: A Concise Political and Social History*, Harcourt Brace Jovanovich Group, Marrickville, Australia.

Corr C.A. *Peter Berger's Angels and Philosophy of Religion*, University of Chicago Press, The Journal of Religion Oct 1972, Volume 52, Issue 4, pp. 426 – 437 https://www.journals.uchicago.edu/doi/pdfplus/10.1086/486313 [Accessed 28th Sept 2018]

Cotter K., Cho J., Rader E. 2017 *Explaining the News Feed Algorithm: An Analysis of the "News Feed FYI" Blog*. Michigan State University, https://www. researchgate.net/publication/316612050_Explaining_the_News_Feed_ Algorithm_An_Analysis_of_the_News_Feed_FYI_Blog [Accessed Sep 15 2018].

Creswell. J.W 2014 *Research Design, Qualitative, Quantitative, and Mixed Methods Approaches*, SAGE, California, USA.

Cunningham R.B. 2007 *The Purpose of Stewardship, The Leaders Handbook of Management and Administration*, Baker Books, Grand Rapids, USA

Daston L. 2001 *The Nature of Nature in Early Modern Europe*, https://pdfs. semanticscholar.org/5d19/a5414d061949fb60c3acf5f2662d14cd7d86. pdf [Accessed 18th Aug 2018]

Davie G. 1999 *Europe, The Exception That Proves the Rule*, Chapter 5. *The Desecularization of the World, Resurgent Religion and World Politics*, Edited by Peter L Berger, Eerdmans, Michigan, USA.

Dart R. 2004 *Being 'Business-Like' in a Nonprofit Organisation: A Grounded and Inductive Typology*, Nonprofit and Voluntary Sector Quarterly, Vol 33, no.2 June 2004, Association for Research on Nonprofit

Organisations and Voluntary Action. http://journals.sagepub.com/doi/pdf/10.1177/0899764004263522. (Accessed 2/05/2017).

Elvin M. 1986 *A Working Definition of 'Modernity'*, Past & Present, No 113 (Nov.1986) pp.209-213, Oxford University Press on behalf of the Past and Present Society. https://www.jstor.org/stable/650986 [Accessed 30th August 2018]

Erickson M.J. 1987 *Christian Theology*, Unabridged, one-volume edition, Baker Book House, Michigan, USA.

Fortunato J.A. Martin S.E. 2016 *The Intersection of Agenda-Setting, the Media Environment, and Election Campaign Laws*, Penn State University Press, https://www.jstor.org/stable/10.5325/jinfopoli.6.2016.0129 [Accessed 29th Aug 2018)

Gangel K.O. 1989 *Feeding and Leading, A Practical Handbook on Administration in Churches and Christian Organisations*, Baker, Grand Rapids USA.

Habermas J.H. 1962 (Trans. Burger T. 1991*) The Structural Transformation of the Public Sphere,* First MIT Press, Massachusetts, USA. https://pages.uoregon.edu/koopman/courses_readings/phil123-net/publicness/habermas_structural_trans_pub_sphere.pdf [Accessed 15th Aug 2018]

Habermas J.H. 1973 (Translated by John Viertel) *Theory and Practice*, Beacon Press, Boston, USA.

Haidt J. 2012 *The Righteous Mind, Why Good People are Divided by Politics and Religion*, Penguin, Random House, New York, USA.

Haidt J. 2012 *Religion, evolution, and the Ecstasy of Self-transcendence, TED Talk* https://www.youtube.com/watch?v=2MYsx6WArKY [Accessed 20th Sept 2018]

Hammond, T.C. 1968 *In Understanding Be Men, A Handbook of Christian Doctrine* (edited and revised by David F Wright), Inter-Varsity Press, Leicester, England.

Hastings R. 2012 *Missional God, Missional Church, Hope for Re-Evangelizing the West*, IVP Academic, Illinois, USA.

Henry C.F.H. 1992 *Reflections On The Kingdom of God,* Journal of The Evangelical Theological Society, 35/1 (March 1992) pp. 39-49 https://pdfs.semanticscholar.org/17ee/8920da89acd3fe8b4c66acb909eba909dc02.pdf [Accessed 28th

May 2018)

Hey S. 2013 *Megachurches: Origins, Ministry and Prospects*, Mosaic Press, Preston, Australia.

Herbert D.E.J 2011 *European Journal of Cultural Studies* 14(6) 626–648

https://mail.google.com/mail/u/0/#inbox/153eb60ab68da087?projector=1

[Accessed: 9 Apr 2016]

Hofstede G, Hofstede G.J, Minkov M. 2010 *Cultures and Organizations, Software of the Mind, Intercultural Cooperation and Its Importance for Survival*, McGraw Hill, New York, USA. http://testrain.info/download/Software%20of%20mind.pdf [Accessed 21st May 2018)

Holy Bible 2005 *New International Version*, Zondervan, Michigan, USA.

Hynd D. 2008 *Public Theology after Christ and Culture: Post Christendom Trajectories*, https://www.csu.edu.au/ data/assets/pdf file/0006/789225/Hynd.pdf [Accessed 29 May 2018]

Johnson N. 2017 *An Integrated Management Framework for Vision Media, with Implementation Plan*, Essay, Christian Heritage College CMC, p.10

Johnson T.L., Rudd J., Neuendorf K., Jian G. 2010 *Worship Styles, Music and Social Identity: A Communication Study*, Journal of Communication and Religion, Jul 2010, https://pdfs.semanticscholar.org/3553/9885ae573a18e8153ee9aeacdc8ed1eb9e1d.pdf [Accessed 10th Oct. 2018]

Kahneman D. 2011 *Thinking, Fast and Slow*, Penguin Books, London, England.

Kassof M. 2017 *Psychographic Research, EContent*, http://www.kassof.com/psychographic-research/ (Accessed 20th May 2017).

Katz & Lazarsfeld (1955) https://www.scribd.com/doc/6446504/Lazarsfeld-Theory [Accessed 17th Sept 2018]

Katz E., Lazarsfeld P. 2007 *Personal Influence*, Free Press, Gazi Üniversitesi, Ankara Turkey http://iletisimdergisi.gazi.edu.tr/arsiv/24.pdf#page=281 [Accessed September 2018]

Kim, S.M. 2009, *Transcendence of God, A Comparative Study of the Old Testament and the Qur'an*, PhD Thesis, University of Pretoria, South Africa, https://repository.up.ac.za/bitstream/handle/2263/28792/Complete.pdf?sequence=8 [Accessed 7th Oct 2018]

Kim, Sung Ho, 2017 'Max Weber', The Stanford Encyclopedia of Philosophy (Winter 2017 Edition), Edward N. Zalta (ed.), https://plato.stanford.edu/archives/win2017/entries/weber [Accessed 11th Aug 2018]

Kinsey Institute, Dr Alfred C Kinsey *A Brief History*, Indiana University website, https://kinseyinstitute.org/about/history/alfred-kinsey.php [Accessed 13th Aug 2018]

Lake M. 2018 *The Bible in Australia: A Cultural History*, New South Publishing, University of New South Wales, Sydney, Australia.

Laniak T.S 2006 *Shepherds After My Own Heart, Pastoral Traditions and Leadership in the Bible*, Intervarsity Press, Illinois, USA.

Lewis C.S. 1950 *The Lion, The Witch and the Wardrobe, A Story for Children*, Macmillan, Project Gutenberg Canada, Ebook #1152 Samizdat, http://www.samizdat.qc.ca/arts/lit/PDFs/LionWitchWardrobe_CSL.pdf

Lewis C.S. 1955 *Surprised By Joy, The Shape of My Early Life*, Project Gutenberg Canada ebook #1275, https://gutenberg.ca/ebooks/lewiscs-surprisedbyjoy/lewiscs-surprisedbyjoy-01-h.html [Accessed 25th Oct 2018]

Lewis D.M., Pierard R.V. (Editors) 2014 *Global Evangelicalism, Theology, History and Culture in Regional Perspective. Essay by Mark A. Noll, Defining Evangelicalism*, IVP Academic, Downers Grove, Illinois, USA.

Liston b. 2012 *The Role of Theological Reflection in Education for Ecclesial Ministry*, Thesis submitted to Regis College, University of Toronto. https://tspace.library.utoronto.ca/bitstream/1807/34903/3/Liston_Brid_201211_DMin_Thesis.pdf [Accessed 21 Apr 2018]

Lindsley A. 2013 *The Priesthood of All Believers,* Institute for Faith, Work & Economics, https://tifwe.org/wp-content/uploads/2013/10/The-Priesthood-of-All-Believers-Lindsley.pdf (Accessed 3/05/2017)

Macchia S.A. (2013) *Becoming A Healthy Team, 5 Traits of Vital Leadership*, Leadership Transformations, Lexington, USA.

Mangalwadi V. 2009 *Truth and Transformation, A Manifesto for Ailing Nations*, YWAM Publishing, Seattle, USA.

Mangalwadi V. 2011 *The Book That Made Your World, How the Bible Created the Soul of Western Civilization*, Thomas Nelson, Nashville, USA.

Martin D. 2005 *On Secularization, Towards a Revised General Theory*, Ashgate

Publishing, Hants, England.

Martin H.S 2011 *Lessons From the Life of Zacchaeus*, Study of Luke 18:31-19:10, Bible Helps Inc. http://biblehelpsinc.org/publication/lessons-from-the-life-of-zacchaeus/ (Accessed 14th May 2017)

Masci D. 2019, *Darwin in America, The Evolution Debate in the United States*, Pew Reseaarch Centre, Religion & Public Life, https://www.pewforum.org/essay/darwin-in-america/ [Accessed 4th May 2020]

Mazzalongo M. 2017 *The Result of Biblical Worship: Transcendence*, Bible Talk, viewed 7 August 2018, https://bibletalk.tv/the-result-of-biblical-worship-transcendence

McCombs M. *The Agenda-Setting Role of the Mass Media in the Shaping of Public Opinion* http://www.infoamerica.org/documentos_pdf/mccombs01.pdf p.1

McCrindle Research 2017 *Faith and Belief in Australia, A National Study on Religion, Spirituality and Worldview Trends*, McCrindle Research Pty Ltd, Balkham Hills, Australia. https://mccrindle.worldsecuresystems.com/blog/2017/05/Faith%20and%20Belief%20in%20Australia%20Report_McCrindle_2017.pdf [Accessed 25th Apr 2018]

McGavran D.A. 1970 *Understanding Church Growth*, Eerdmans, Michigan, USA

McGrath A.E. & McGrath J.C. 2007 *The Dawkins Delusion? Atheist Fundamentalism and the Denial of the Divine*, IVP Books, Illinois, USA. http://svetlost.org/podaci/the_dawkins_delusion.pdf [Accessed 13th Aug 2018]

Middleton J.R. 1994 *The Liberating Image? Interpreting the Imago Dei in Context*, Christian Scholars Review 24.1 (1994) 8-25.

Nietzsche F. 1887 *The Gay Science*, Leipzig https://web.stanford.edu/~jsabol/existentialism/materials/nietzsche-gay-science-hurry.pdf

Norris P., Inglehart R. 2004 *Sacred and Secular: Religion and Politics Worldwide*, Cambridge Studies in Social Theory, Religion and Politics, Cambridge University Press, https://books.google.com.au/books?id=dto-P2YfWJIC&source=gbs_navlinks_s [Accessed 2nd September 2018]

Odiakaose ODOR, H. 2018 *Organisational Culture and Dynamics*, Global Journal of Management and Business Research: Administration and Management. Vol 18, Issue 1, Version 1.0 2018. https://globaljournals.

org/GJMBR_Volume18/3-Organisational-Culture-and-Dynamics.pdf [Accessed 21 Apr 2018)

O'Neill B. 2011 *Media Effects in Context*, 10.1002/9781444340525.ch16.

Pennington J.T. 2015 *A Biblical Theology of Human Flourishing*, Institute for Faith, Work & Economics, http://tifwe.org/wp-content/ uploads/2015/03/Pennington-A-Biblical-Theology-of-Human-Flourishing.pdf [Accessed 7th Oct 2018]

Piggin S., Linder R.D. 2018 *The Fount of Public Prosperity: Evangelical Christians in Australian History 1740-1914*, Monash University Press, Clayton, Australia.

Piggin S., Linder R.D. 2020 *Attending to the National Soul*, Evangelical Christians in Australian History 1914 – 2014.

Piper J. 2013 *Risk is Right, Better to Lose Your Life Than to Waste It*, Crossway, Illinois, USA. https://document.desiringgod.org/risk-is-right-en.pdf?ts=1446648045 [Accessed 20th May 2018]

Pophal L. 2017 *Micro-experiences: New opportunities in multichannel marketing*, EContent, May-June 2017, p. 6+. *Business Collection*, https://go.gale.com/ [Accessed 20 May 2017.]

Powers B.P. 2008 *Church Administration Handbook*, Third Edition Revised and Updated, B&H Publishing, Tennessee, USA.

Robbins S.P., Judge T.A., Millett B., Waters-Marsh T. 2008 *Organisational Behaviour, 5th Edition*, Pearson Education Australia, Prentice Hall, Frenchs Forest, Australia.

Rodin R.S. 2011 *The Steward Leader, Transforming People Organisations and Communities*, Intervarsity Press, Illinois, USA.

Rubin B. 1987 *Modern Dictators: Third World Coup Makers, Strongmen, and Populist Tyrants*, Gloria Centre Global Research in International Affairs, McGraw-Hill, New York, USA http://www.rubincenter.org/wp-content/ uploads/2012/12/Modern-Dictators.pdf [Accessed 21st Oct 2018]

Saler M. 2006 *Modernity and Enchantment: A Historiographic Review*, American Historical Review, USA. http://chnm.gmu.edu/courses/omalley/393/ saler.pdf [Accessed 24th Jun 2018]

Samuel, V. & Sugden C. (Editors) 2009 *Mission as Transformation, A Theology of the Whole Gospel*, Chapter 7, Howard Snyder, 'Models of the Kingdom',

Wipf & Stock, Eugene, OR. USA.

Sanger M. Brief biography, *Margaret Sanger* https://www.biography.com/people/margaret-sanger-9471186 [Accessed 13th Aug 2018]

Scaff L.A. 1991 *Fleeing The Iron Cage: Culture, Politics, and Modernity in the Thought of Max Weber*, University of California Press, USA https://www.google.com.au/books/edition/Fleeing_the_Iron_Cage/Xqg3uNWyVmgC?hl=en&gbpv=1 [Accessed 16th Oct 2018]

Schein E.H 2017 *Organizational Culture and Leadership*, 5th Edition, Wiley & Sons, New Jersey, USA.

Schäfer T., Sedlmeier P., Städtler C., Huron D. 2013 *The Psychological Functions of Music Listening*, Frontiers in Psychology, August 2013, Vol. 4, Article 511, http://biomedsearch.com [Accessed 9th Oct 2018]

Schaeffer F 1984 *The God Who Is There*, The Complete Works of Francis Schaeffer, Vol 1. 1968, Crossway, Illinois, USA.

Schaeffer F. 1984 *The Great Evangelical Disaster*, The Complete Works of Francis Schaeffer Vol.4 1982, Crossway, Illinois, USA.

Schoemaker P.J.H. 1995 *Scenario Planning: A Tool for Strategic Thinking*, MIT Sloan Management Review, Winter Edition, USA http://sloanreview.mit.edu/article/scenario-planning-a-tool-for-strategic-thinking/ (Accessed 1/05/2017)

Schultze Q.J. 1993 *Media and Modernity*, Transformation, Vol 10, No. 4 The Bible, Truth and Modernity (October 1993) pp. 27-29, Sage Publications https://www.jstor.org/stable/43052415 [Accessed 30th August 2018]

Segal M.T. 2013 *Reflections on Latour, Tarnas, and the Misenchantment of the World*, Footnotes 2 Plato, https://footnotes2plato.com/2013/03/10/reflections-on-latour-tarnas-and-the-misenchantment-of-the-world/ [Accessed 28 July 2018)

Schiller F. 1788 *Die Götter Griechenlandes*, https://www.uni-due.de/lyriktheorie/texte/1788_schiller.html [Accessed 5th Aug 2018]

Simpson S., Potter R. 2012 *Restrictions on Freedom of Expression,* Collections Law, Legal Issues for Australian Archives, Galleries, Libraries, and Museums, http://www.collectionslaw.com.au/chapter-25-restrictions-on-freedom-of-expression [Accessed 10 Aug 2018]

Skillen J.W. 2014 *The Good of Politics, a Biblical, Historical, and Contemporary*

Introduction, Baker Academic, Michigan, USA.

Smith J.K.A. 2009 *Desiring the Kingdom, Worship, Worldview and Cultural Formation*, Baker Academic, Michigan, USA.

Smith J.K.A. *How (Not) To Be Secular Reading Charles Taylor*, Eerdmans, Michigan, USA.

Spencer N. 2016 *The Evolution of the West, How Christianity has Shaped our Values*, SPCK, London, UK.

Stark R. 2005 *The Victory of Reason, How Christianity Led to Freedom, Capitalism, and Western Success*, Random House, New York, USA.

Stark R. & Finke R. 2000 *Acts of Faith: Explaining the Human Side of Religion*,

University of California Press, USA, p. 38

Storey D. 2009 *Breaking the Spell of the Immanent Frame: Charles Taylor's A Secular Age*. Published in Rethinking Secularization: Philosophy and the Prophecy of a Secular Age (pp.177-209). www.academia.edu/1816674/ [Accessed 25th Oct 2018]

Sydney Morning Herald, 2018 *Is the ABC really biased?*, Article by Vincent O'Donnell, https://www.smh.com.au/national/is-the-abc-really-biased-20180629-p4zoh5.html [Accessed 9th October 2018]

Tacey D. 2000 *Re-enchantment, The New Australian Spirituality*, Harper Collins, Sydney, Australia.

Tidball D. 1987 *A World Without Windows: Living as a Christian in a Secular World*, Scripture Union, London.

Taylor C. 2007 *A Secular Age*, Belknap Press of Harvard University Press, Cambridge, Massachusetts, USA and London, England.

Thomasma N., Van Niejenhuis C., and Kallemeyn J. 2010 *Evaluation Essentials for Congregational Leaders*, Sustaining *Pastoral Excellence*, Christian Reformed Church in North America, Michigan, USA. https://www.crcna.org/sites/default/files/ Evaluation Essentials.pdf (Accessed 14 May 2017)

Trueman C. 2017 *Did Luther Really Cause Secularism?* The Gospel Coalition US Edition Nov 10th 2017. https://www.thegospelcoalition.org/reviews/rebel-ranks-martin-luther-brad-gregory/ [Accessed 15 Apr 2018].

Villa D., Dorsey J. 2017 *The State of Gen Z 2017: Meet The Throwback Generation*,

The Centre for Generational Kinetics, http://genhq.com/wp-content/uploads/2017/04/The-State-of-Gen-Z-2017-White-Paper-c-2017-The-Center-for-Generational-Kinetics.pdf [Accessed 2nd Aug 2018]

Vision Christian Media 2018 *Our History,* https://vision.org.au/history/ [Accessed 2nd May 2018]

Vision Christian Media 2018 *Staff Handbook,* Version 2 January 2018

Voas D., Doebler S. 2011 *Secularization in Europe: Religious Change between and within Birth Cohorts,* Journal: Religion and Society in Central and Eastern Europe, RASCEE 2011, 4(1) – p.41 [Accessed 23 Oct 2018]

Wells D.F. 1994 *No Place for Truth: Or Whatever Happened to Evangelical Theology?* Eerdmans Publishing, https://books.google.com.au/books?id=ItV2asz-87wC&source=gbs_navlinks_s [Accessed 16th Sept 2018]

Welch R.H. 2011 *Church Administration, Creating Efficiency for Effective Ministry,* B&H Academic, Tennessee, USA.

Whelchel H. 2014 *Four Defining Characteristics of Biblical Flourishing,* Institute for Faith Works and Economics, hppts://tifwe.org [Accessed 17th July 2018])

Williams R. 2015 *Post-God Nation?* Harper Collins, Sydney, Australia.

Willsey, J.K., 2003 *Recovering Transcendence and Immanence,* NARBC Pastors Conference, https://pdfs.semanticscholar.org/617a/c358b6006a081749066f02b89d92a1c46ee8.pdf [Accessed 7th August 2018]

Wilson T.R. 2014 *Reclaiming the Kingdom of God Metaphor for the Twenty-First-Century Church,* DMin Thesis, George Fox University, Oregon USA, http://digitalcommons.georgefox.edu/dmin/87 [Accessed 10th May 2018)

Index

transcendent reality 48, 60, 72, 87, 263

Triune God 230

U

UCB 136, 258

United Christian Broadcasters 136

Utilitarianism 170, 173

V

Vernon Turner 98, 133

Vishal Mangalwadi 72, 81

Vision Christian Media 8, 136, 141, 224, 235, 239, 275

Vision, Mission and Values 132

W

Walter Lippman 181

War of the Worlds 175, 176

Western civilization 54

Western Civilization 47, 85, 187, 270

William James 77

Wind Tunnelling 226

Winter-Spring Theory 169

World Values Survey 163, 173

X

Y

yoga 81, 83

Z

Zacchaeus 238, 251, 252, 271